JCT
INTERMEDIATE FORM
OF CONTRACT
(IFC 84)

– A PRACTICAL GUIDE

by

David Chappell
and
Vincent Powell-Smith

JCT INTERMEDIATE FORM OF CONTRACT (IFC 84)

– A PRACTICAL GUIDE

by
David Chappell
and
Vincent Powell-Smith

Legal Studies & Services (Publishing) Ltd

Published by: **Legal Studies & Services (Publishing) Ltd**
57/61 Mortimer Street
London W1N 7TD

Copyright: **David Chappell and
Ingramlight Properties Ltd 1991**

ISBN   ISBN: 85271 1.85271.179.5

Typeset by: JH Graphics Ltd, Reading, Berkshire
Printed by: Hobbs the Printers, Second Avenue, Millbrook, Southampton

Professor Vincent Powell-Smith, LLM, DLitt, FCIArb, MBAE, is Visiting Professor at Universiti Teknologi Malaysia and at Universiti Sains Malaysia. He was formerly lecturer in law at the University of Aston Management Centre. He acts as a consultant specialising in building contracts and as a practising international arbitrator. A well known conference speaker, he has been Legal Correspondent of *Contract Journal* for the past 18 years and is a regular contributor to *Architects' Journal, Surveyor,* and *International Construction.* A former member of the Council of the Chartered Institute of Arbitrators, for several years he was a member of the Minister's Joint Advisory Committee on Health and Safety in the Construction Industry. He has written a number of highly successful titles on Construction Law topics, many of them published by Legal Studies & Services (Publishing) Ltd. When he is not travelling he divides his time between his homes in Malaysia and Portugal.

Dr David Chappell, BA (HonsArch), MA, PhD, ARIBA, has previously worked as an architect in public and private sector practice, as contracts administrator for a building contractor and as a lecturer in construction, building law and contractual procedures. He is now a senior consultant with James R Knowles. He is a regular contributor to *Architects' Journal* and other professional publications, and has written *Contractual Correspondence for Architects, Contractors' Claims: An Architect's Guide* and *Understanding JCT Contracts* amongst others. He is also joint author with Professor Vincent Powell-Smith of *Building Contract Dictionary, JCT Minor Works Form of Contract: A Practical Guide* and *Concise Encyclopaedia of Architectural Practice* with Ray Cecil, all published by Legal Studies & Services (Publishing) Ltd.

–Preface

Ever since the 1980 edition of the Standard Form of Building Contract (JCT 80) was published by the Joint Contracts Tribunal, there has been a demand for a form of contract which was less complicated than the full standard form, but more comprehensive than the Agreement for Minor Building Works 1980 (MW 80). After much drafting and redrafting, the JCT Intermediate Form of Building Contract (IFC 84) was published in September 1984 to satisfy that demand. It has now been proved in use.

The structure follows that of MW 80, but in detail it owes much to JCT 80. It appears to be shorter than it really is, because it is laid out in two columns. The language is no less complex than that of JCT 80 and, in places, there are ambiguities.

We hope that this book will be useful to architects, quantity surveyors and contractors. It explains not only what the clauses mean but also their implications in practice. Although based on a previous book of ours, it is effectively a new work and has been expanded and largely rewritten to take account of changes in the law and the various amendments to IFC 84.

The book is not a clause-by-clause interpretation. Instead, the form has been dealt with by considering the roles of the parties involved and by devoting separate chapters to important topics such as claims, payment, determination, and arbitration. Legal language has been avoided, and a series of flowcharts, tables, and sample letters has been included to make up a practical working tool.

The copyright in IFC 84, Tender and Agreeement NAM/T, and Employer/Specialist Agreement ESA/1, and in the supporting practice notes, is vested in RIBA Publications Ltd, and we are indebted to them for permission to quote from those publications for the purposes of this book.

David Chappell
Vincent Powell-Smith

–Contents

1–The Purpose and Use of IFC 84

1.1 The Background

The JCT Intermediate Form of Building Contract (IFC 84) was first published in September 1984 and is a member of the growing family of standard contract forms issued by the Joint Contracts Tribunal. IFC 84 has been amended five times since its issue, the latest amendment being dated April 1989. **Table 1.1** sets out the JCT forms currently available.

It is intended that IFC 84 should fill the gap between MW 80, which is suited to smaller projects, and the very complex JCT 80 with its lengthy and complicated provisions for nominated sub-contractors. Its most significant features are as follows:

- The provisions (clause 3.3) enabling the architect to select specialist sub-contractors by "naming" them.
- The provision (clause 3.13) for the architect to issue instructions regarding failure of work and the inspection of similar work.
- The absence of restraint on opening arbitration proceedings during the progress of the works.

In arrangement, the form follows the pattern of MW 80 in setting out the conditions under eight main headings, the clauses being printed in two columns, but the wording follows very closely that of JCT 80 in many places.

IFC 84 is arranged as follows:

ARTICLES OF AGREEMENT

CONDITIONS
1 Intentions of the parties
2 Possession and completion

3 Control of the works
4 Payment
5 Statutory obligations
6 Injury, damage, and insurance
7 Determination
8 Interpretation

APPENDIX

SUPPLEMENTAL CONDITIONS
A Value Added Tax
B Statutory tax deduction scheme
C Contributions, levy, and tax fluctuations (published separately)
D Use of price adjustment formulae (published separately)

The subdivisions within the main conditions are not always logical, and in this book
we have adopted what we believe to be a more realistic arrangement.

1.2   IFC Documentation

In addition to the printed contract form itself, which must be completed and
executed formally by the employer and the contractor, there is also a set of supporting
documentation:
● Fluctuations Clauses and Formula Rules (Supp/IFC 84)
● Tender and Agreement for Named Sub-contractors under IFC 84 (NAM/T)–
  summarised in Appendix A, p 273
● Sub-contract Conditions for Named Sub-contractors under IFC 84 (NAM/SC)–
  summarised in Appendix B, p 277
● Sub-contract Formula Rules for Named Sub-contractors under IFC 84
  (NAM/SC/FR)

The Joint Contracts Tribunal has also published two related practice notes.
● Practice Note IN/1: Introductory notes on the JCT Intermediate Form of
  Building Contract IFC 84
● Practice Note 20: Deciding on the Appropriate Form of JCT Main Contract–
  Revised July 1984
Independently, but in consultation with the JCT, the RIBA and CASEC have
prepared a form of Employer/Specialist Agreement under IFC 84 (ESA/1). This is
summarised in Appendix C (p 289). It is a vital document. The architect is responsible
for arranging for its completion on the employer's behalf. Its effect is to create a direct
contractual relationship between the employer and the named sub-contractor for
limited purposes, and it gives the employer the necessary protection against design
and related failures in a named sub-contractor's work.

Table 1.1
JCT forms of contract in current use

Title	Contract documents	Comments
Standard Form of Building Contract 1980 (JCT 80)	Drawings Bills of quantities (*Variants:* with Approximate quantities; *or* Specification)	Complex and sophisticated: for use on major projects where it is wished to use nominated sub-contractors or suppliers
Intermediate Form of Building Contract (IFC 84)	Drawings and *either* Specification *or* Schedules of work *or* Bills of quantities	Only suitable where contract is not long or complex and any specialist work is of a simple nature. Value ranges from £90,000 to £300,000 (1990 prices). Cannot be used where sectional completion is desired
Agreement for Minor Building Works 1980 (MW80)	Drawings *and/or* Specifications *and/or* Schedules	Normal maximum value of £90,000 (1990) prices. Short contract period, as no provision for full labour and materials fluctuations, and only where simple conditions are appropriate
Fixed Fee Form of Prime Cost Contract	Specifications *with or without* drawings	Little used in practice – prime cost plus fixed fee
Standard Form with Contractor's Design	Employer's requirements Contractor's proposals Contract sum analysis	For use where contractor is to be responsible for all of the design. If the contractor is to be responsible for part of the design. JCT 80 with quantities should be used together with the Contractor's Designed Portion Supplement which modifies the form
Standard Form of Management Contract (JCT 87)	Project drawings Project specification Contract cost plan Schedules	Low risk to management contractor Works carried out by works contractors. Provision for acceleration
Measured Term Contract (MTC 11/89)	Schedule of rates	For use by employers who need regular maintenance and minor works to be carried out by one contractor over a specified period on receipt of individual orders

1.3 The Use of IFC 84

IFC 84 is issued for contracts in the range between JCT 80 with quantities and MW 80. It is suitable for use where the proposed works are:

- simple in content, involving the normally recognised basic trades and skills of the industry;
- without any building service installations of a complex nature; and
- adequately specified, or specified and billed as appropriate before the issue of tenders.

IFC 84 is suitable for use only where the criteria are met. Practice Note 20 contains a little further guidance, from which it may be deduced that IFC 84 is suitable for most such projects, with or without quantities, whose value is between £90,000 and £300,000 (at 1990 prices), with a contract period of not more than 12 months.

Contract value in not, however, the deciding factor, and the practice note points out that IFC 84 may "be suitable for somewhat larger or longer contracts" provided that the three basic criteria are met. Certainly since IFC 84 contains adequate provisions for contractors to recover fluctuations, the contract period is not the decisive factor.

Three things would preclude the use of the form:
- complexity of work;
- the wish or need for nominated sub-contractors and nominated suppliers; or
- the wish to make the contractor responsible for design, wholly or in part.

In summary, IFC 84 is highly suitable for use on projects of medium size with a simple work content. IFC 84 should not be used merely to avoid the complexities of nomination under JCT 80. In their own way the IFC provisions for named sub-contractors are just as complicated!

Table 1.2 sets out the main differences between the Association of Consultation Architects' Form of Building Agreement 1984 (Revised 1990) (ACA 2), JCT 80 and IFC 84.

1.4 Completing the Form

Normally, a formal contract will be executed by the parties, and the printed form IFC 84 will be used for this purpose.

The articles of agreement

Page 1 should be completed with the descriptions and addresses of the employer and the contractor. The date will not be inserted until the form is signed or sealed by the parties.

The first recital must be completed with special care because the description of "the Works" is important in many respects, not least when considering the question of variations, and the appropriate deletions should be made to both the first and second

Table 1.2
ACA 2, JCT 80 and IFC 84 compared

Subject	ACA 2	JCT 80	IFC 84
Cost limits (upper)	None	£300,000 + but can be used for smaller projects with specialist work content or complex	£90,000 to £300,000 – and works must be of simple content and with no specialist service
Contract documents	Drawings Schedule of rates *or* Bills of quantities Specification	Drawings Bills of quantities (Variants with approx quantities or specification)	Drawings Bills of quantities *or* schedules of rates *or* specification
Date for possession	To be given to contractor as specified in time schedule Provision for possession to be given in parts	Must be given on date stated in appendix No power to postpone possession	As JCT 80, but power to defer giving of possession for up to six weeks in return for time and money
Extension of time	Alternative clauses–11.5.1 covers "any act, instruction, default or omission of employer or architect on his behalf"; The other similar to JCT 80. Detailed provisions for notification	Detailed provisions and long list of grounds, not comprehensive and exact scope not clear	Similar listing to JCT 80, but some omission, and deferment of possession an optional ground Notification procedures less detailed
Liquidated damages	Alternative clauses – conventional liquidated damages *or* unliquidated damages. Architect's certificate of delay a precondition to deduction and architect empowered to make deduction Interest to contractor if extension given later	Liquidated damages deductible by employer if architect certifies late completion and employer so requires Provision for adjustment if new completion date fixed later but no provision for interest	Similar to JCT 80

Table 1.2 (continued)

Subject	ACA 2	JCT 80	IFC 84
Variations	Detailed provisions – contractor can be required to submit estimate of cost, time, and loss and/or expense Detailed valuation rules	Detailed provisions with valuation rules	Similar to JCT 80
Payment and retention	Interim payments monthly but conditional on contractor making application vouchered 95% Final account must be submitted by contractor within 60 days of expiry of maintenance period	Interim payments monthly unless otherwise stated Final account	Broadly similar to JCT 80 – 95% of value of work and materials in monthly interim certificates, 97% at practical completion
Fluctuations	Optional fluctuations clause based on ACA Index – 80% only payable	Alternative provisions for contributions, levy, and tax fluctuations, or labour, materials and tax fluctuations, or formula adjustment where there are contract bills	As JCT 80 except no option for labour and materials and tax fluctuations
Loss and/or expense	Detailed provisions entitling contractor to claim for disturbance of regular progress caused by employer's or architect's "acts, omissions, default, or negligence". Notice of claim required if payment to be included in interim certificate and estimates of cost required. Otherwise	A long list of matters and detailed claims procedures; not comprehensive, and many claims must be dealt with at common law	Similar to JCT 80

Table 1.2 (continued)

Subject	ACA 2	JCT 80	IFC 84
	architect adjusts in Final Certificate but contractor loses by interest element		
Selection of sub-contractors	Provision for named sub-contractors and suppliers Architect can be involved in negotiations Contractor fully responsible for performance, including design failure	List of three "selected" Detailed and bureaucratic provisions for nominated sub-contractor and complex supporting documentation Contractor exempted from design responsibility Provision for nominated suppliers	Sub-contractors can be named in contract documents or ps instruction No provision for naming suppliers
Disputes settlement	Alternative methods: • Conventional arbitration • Adjudication followed by arbitration • Litigation If adjudication option chosen, an immediate decision can be given which is binding on both parties unless upturned in arbitration	Conventional arbitration, generally cannot be opened while works still in progress JCT Rules applicable	Similar to JCT 80 but no restraint on arbitration while works in progress Optional provision for legal points to be settled by High Court
Advantages/ disadvantages	Flexible Simple payment scheme Provision for design responsibility by contractor with indemnity cover Useful range of alternative clauses Time periods not always realistic	Comprehensive Widely known Complex nominated sub-contractor provisions Unrealistic fluctuations	Wide testing provisions Not suitable for long or complex contracts

recitals as indicated in the footnotes. Consistency is important, since the contractor is required to carry out and complete the works in accordance with the contract documents identified in the second recital. This is in two mutually exclusive alternatives, as described in **Chapter 3.**

Completion of articles 1 to 4 is routine and self-explanatory.

Attestation

Alternative attestation clauses are provided, as the contract may be executed by hand or as a deed. The employer will have made this decision at pre-tender stage, and there is an important practical difference.

The Limitation Act 1980 specifies a limitation period–the time within which an action may be commenced–of six years where the contract is merely signed by the parties or of 12 years in the case of a contract entered into as a deed. These periods begin to run "when the cause of action accrues", which, in a case of a contractual claim, is the date when the defective work was done (ie, the date of the breach of contract). From the employer's point of view, it it usually sensible to contract as a deed.

In order to contract by deed, it used to be necessary to affix red wafer seals or write "LS" (meaning "in the place of the seal") if the seals were not obtainable. Provisions in the Law of Property (Miscellaneous Provisions) Act 1989 applicable to individuals and the Companies Act 1989 applicable to companies have changed the situation by abolishing the necessity to seal a deed. In the case of companies, it must be stated on the face of the document that it is a deed and it must be signed by two directors or a director and a company secretary. At the time of writing, current copies of the form had not been amended to provide for this legislation. Until it is so amended, signatories should get specific advice before attempting to execute the contract as a deed.

If – as is not generally desirable – any amendments are made to the printed text or any clauses are deleted, these should be initialled by both contracting parties.

The appendix

This should be fully and carefully completed by the architect, consistently with the information which he gave to the contractor at tender stage since his tender is based on the information supplied.

Appendix entries which are inconsistent with the printed conditions generate much income for lawyers! **Figure 1.1** shows an IFC 84 Appendix completed.

Figure 1.1

Appendix

| 2·1 | Date of Possession | *3 September 1991* |
| 2·1 | Date for Completion | *1 September 1992* |

2·4·10 and 2·4·11   Extension of time for inability to secure essential labour or goods or materials
[n] Clause 2·4·10 *(Labour)* applies/~~does not apply~~
[n] Clause 2·4·11 *(Goods or materials)* applies/~~does not apply~~

2·2 and 2·4·14 and 4·11(a)   Deferment of the Date of Possession
[n] Clause 2·2 applies/~~does not apply~~
Where clause 2·2 applies,
Four weeks (period not to exceed 6 weeks)

2·7   Liquidated damages
at the rate of
£ *200-00 (Two Hundred Pounds)*
for every week ~~or part of a week~~

2·10   Defects liability period (if none stated is 6 months from the day named in the certificate of Practical Completion of the Works)
Twelve Months

4·2   Period of interim payments if interval is not one month
One Month

4·9(a) and C7   Supplemental Condition C: Tax etc. fluctuations
[o] Percentage addition *Three* %

4·9(b)   Formulae fluctuations (not applicable unless Bills of Quantities are a Contract Document)
[o] Supplemental Condition D
[n] ~~applies~~/does not apply

D1   Formula Rules (only where Supplemental Condition D applies)
rule 3: Base Month
_____ 19_____
[p] rule 3: Non-Adjustable Element
_____ (not to exceed 10%)
rules 10 and 30(i)
[n] Part I/Part II of Section 2 of the Formula Rules is to apply

6·2·1   Insurance cover for any one occurrence or series of occurences arising out of one event
£ *1,000,000 (One Million Pounds)*

6·2·4   Insurance – liability of Employer
[n] Insurance may be required/is not required
Amount of indemnity for any one occurrence or series of occurrences arising out of one event
[p-1] £ *200,000-00 (Two Hundred Thousand Pounds)*

6·3·1   Insurance of the Works – alternative clauses
[n] Clause 6·3A/~~Clause 6·3B/Clause 6·3C applies~~
(See Footnote [k] to clause 6·3)

6·3A·1   Percentage to cover professional fees
Twelve %

6·3A·3·1   Annual renewal date of insurance as supplied by Contractor
2 May 1991

Figure 1.1 (continued)

6·3D	Insurance for Employer's loss of liquidated damages – clause 2·4·3	[n] Insurance ~~may be required~~/is not required
6·3D·2		Period of time _____
8·3	Base Date	3 August 1991
9·1	Appointor of arbitrator	President or a Vice-President of:
		[n] ~~Royal Institute of British Architects~~
		[n] ~~Royal Institution of Chartered Surveyors~~
		[n] Chartered Institute of Arbitrators
9·6	Reference to Arbitrator under NAM/SC	[n] clause 9·6 applies/~~does not apply~~

[n] Delete as applicable.

[o] In accordance with clause 4·9, if Supplemental
Condition D is not stated to apply then Supplemental
Condition C applies.

[p] Only applicable when the Employer is a Local
Authority.

[p-1] If the indemnity is to be for an aggregate amount
and not for any one occurrence or series of
occurrences the entry should make this clear.

IFC 2/89

2-Contracts Compared

IFC 84 is a very flexible contract, and its content establishes it as a member of the Joint Contracts Tribunal family. Its provisions closely parallel those of JCT 80 in many respects, although the format and layout follow MW 80. Like the latter, it is silent on many important matters: eg, there is no express provision which entitles the architect to access to the contractor's workshops, etc. Such gaps would have to be filled in by the common law.

The revised Practice Note 20 (July 1988), Deciding on the Appropriate Form of JCT Main Contract, contains some broad general guidance. Among other things, it compares the JCT contracts by reference to contract documents and price, and an appendix summarises the main differences in the contract conditions in matters of major significance in building contracts.

Table 2.1 compares IFC 84 with JCT 80 and MW 80, and also with the second edition of the ACA Form of Building Agreement, published in September 1984, as revised in 1990 (ACA 2).

Table 2.1
IFC Clauses compared with those of other common standard contracts

IFC clause	Description	JCT 80 clause	MW 80 clause	ACA 2 clause	Comment (on IFC 84 unless otherwise stated)
1	**Intentions of the parties**				
1.1	Contractor's obligations	2	1.1	1.1	
1.2	Quality and quantity of work	14	–	–	
1.3	Priority of contract documents	2.2.1	–	1.3	The printed conditions, etc, prevail over any specially prepared clauses insofar as there is any conflict
1.4	Instructions as to inconsistencies, errors, or omissions	2.3 2.2.2.2	4.1	1.4 1.5	
1.5	Contract bills and SMM	2.2.2	–	1.4	
1.6	Custody and copies of contract documents	5.1	–	–	
1.7	Further drawings and details	5.4	1.2	2.1	
1.8	Limits to use of documents	5.7	–	–	
1.9	Issue of certificates by architect	5.8	1.2	23.1	
1.10	Unfixed materials or goods: passing of property, etc	16.1	–	6.1	These provisions would not be effective against a retention of title clause in a supplier's contract of sale
1.11	Off-site materials and goods: passing of property, etc	16.2	–	6.1	These provisions would not be effective against a retention of title clause in a supplier's contract of sale
2	**Possession and completion**				
2.1	Possession and completion dates	23.1	2.1 2.4	11.1	
2.2	Deferment of possession	23.1.2			ACA clause 11.8 empowers architect to order acceleration and postponement

Table 2.1 (continued)

IFC clause	Description	JCT 80 clause	MW 80 clause	ACA 2 clause	Comment (on IFC 84 unless otherwise stated)
2.3	Extension of time	25	2.2	11.6	
2.4	Events referred to in 2.3	25.4	2.2	11.5	
2.5 2.6	Further delay or extension of time	25.1	–	11.6	
2.6	Certificate of non-completion	24.1	–	11.2	There is express power to issue further certificates of delay should further extension be made
2.7	Liquidated damages for non-completion	24.2	2.3	11.3	
2.8	Repayment of liquidated damages	24.2	–	11.4	
2.9	Practical completion	17.1	2.4	12.1	In ACA, the concept of "taking over" is similar to "practical completion"
2.10	Defects liability	17.2	2.5	12.2	
3	**Control of works**				
3.1	Assignment	19.1	3.1	9.1	
3.2	Sub-contracting	19.2	3.2	9.2	
3.3.1	Named persons as sub-contractors	–	–	9.4 9.5	The IFC and ACA provisions for named sub-contractors are not really comparable
3.4	Contractor's person-in-charge	10	3.3	5.2	
3.5	Architect's instructions	4.1	3.5	8.1	There is no provision for confirmation of oral instructions
3.6	Variations	13	3.6	8.1	
3.7	Valuation of variations and provisional sum work	13.4 13.5	3.6 3.7	8.2	
3.8	Instructions to expend provisional sums	13.3	3.7	8.1	
3.9	Levels and setting out	7	–	–	
3.10	Clerk of works	12	–	–	

Table 2.1 (continued)

IFC clause	Description	JCT 80 clause	MW 80 clause	ACA 2 clause	Comment (on IFC 84 unless otherwise stated)
3.11	Work not forming part of the contract	29	–	10	
3.12	Instructions as to inspection; tests	8.3	–	8.1	
3.13	Instructions following failure of work, etc	8.4.4	–	–	
3.14	Instruction as to removal of work, etc	8.4	–	8.1	
3.15	Instructions as to postponement	23.2	–	11.8	
4	**Payment**				
4.1	Contract sum	14	–	15	
4.2	Interim payments	30.1	4.2	16.1 16.2	
4.3	Interim payment on practical completion	–	4.3	–	
4.4	Interest in percentage withheld	30.5	4.2	16.4 16.5	MW clause 4.2 is not exactly comparable with similar clauses in other contracts
4.5	Computation of adjusted contract sum	30.6	4.4	19.1	
4.6	Issue of final certificate	30.8	4.4	19.2	
4.7	Effect of final certificate	30.9	–	19.5	
4.8	Effect of certificates other than final	30.10	–	19.5	
4.9	Fluctuations	38, 39 & 40	4.5	18	Under ACA terms, the fluctuations clause is optional. A single index is used and only 80% is payable to the contractor
4.10	Fluctuations; named persons				
4.11	Disturbance of regular progress	26.1	–	7.1	
4.12	Matters referred to in clause 4.11	26.2	–	7.1	

Table 2.1 (continued)

IFC clause	Description	JCT 80 clause	MW 80 clause	ACA 2 clause	Comment (on IFC 84 unless otherwise stated)
5	**Statutory obligations, etc**				
5.1	Statutory obligations, notices, fees, and charges	6	5.1	1.6 1.7	
5.2	Notice of divergence from statutory requirements	6	5.1	1.6	
5.3	Extent of contractor's liability for non-compliance	6	5.1	1.7	
5.4	Emergency compliance	6	–	–	
5.5	Value added tax	15	5.2	16.7	
5.6	Statutory tax deduction scheme	31	5.3	24	See Inland Revenue publication IR/14/15, Construction Industry Tax Deduction Scheme (1980 edn)
5.7	Fair wages	19A	5.4	–	
6	**Injury, damage and insurance**				
6.1	Injury to persons and property and indemnity to employer	20	6.1 6.2	6.3	
6.2	Insurance against injury to persons and property	21	6.1 6.2	6.3	
6.3A	Insurance in joint names of employer and contractor (new buildings)	22A	6.3A	6.4	
6.3B	Sole risk of employer (new buildings)	22B	–	–	
6.3C	Sole risk of employer (existing structure)	22C	6.3B	6.4	
7	**Determination**				
7.1	Determination by employer	27.1	7.1	20.1	
7.2	Contractor becoming bankrupt, etc	27.2	7.1	20.3	

Table 2.1 (continued)

IFC clause	Description	JCT 80 clause	MW 80 clause	ACA 2 clause	Comment (on IFC 84 unless otherwise stated)
7.3	Corruption – determination by employer	27.3	–	–	
7.4	Consequences of determination under clauses 7.1–7.3	27.4	7.1	22.1	
7.5	Determination by contractor	28.1	7.2	20.2	
7.6	Employer becoming bankrupt, etc	28.1	7.2	20.3	
7.7	Consequences of determination under clauses 7.5 or 7.6	28.2	7.2	22.2	
7.8	Determination by employer or contractor	28A	–	21	
7.9	Consequences of determination under clause 7.8	–	–	22.3	
8	**Interpretation**				
8.1	References to clauses, etc	1.1	–	–	
8.2	Articles to be read as a whole	1.2	–	–	
8.3	Definitions	1.3	–	–	
8.4	The architect/supervising officer	Art 3A	–	–	
8.5	Priced specification or priced schedules of work	N/A	–	–	

3–Contract Documents and Insurance

3.1 Contract Documents

3.1.1 Types and uses

IFC 84 is designed to be a very flexible contract to cover a broad range of work and costs. To give effect to this intention, there is a number of possible combinations which can constitute the "contract documents".

What are contract documents? They are those documents which give legal effect to the intentions of the parties. In principle, the contract documents may consist of, and contain, whatever the parties wish. IFC 84 sets out the options in the second recital:

- the contract drawings and the specification, priced by the contractor; *or*
- the contract drawings and the schedule of work, priced by the contractor; *or*
- the contract drawings and the bills of quantities, priced by the contractor; *or*
- the contract drawings and the specification and the sum the contractor requires for carrying out the works.

One of these options, together with the agreement and conditions annexed to the recitals, forms the contract documents. They must all be signed by, or on behalf of, the parties.

The options must be studied carefully in order to arrive at the most suitable combination for a particular project.

The contract drawings and the specification priced by the contractor

This combination is usually appropriate for relatively small works or for works of a simple nature. It must be remembered that, if bills of quantities are not provided, the contractor will have to take off his own quantities in order to arrive at a tender sum. The prices eventually put to the specification will inevitably be somewhat rough and ready unless the specification is a model of clarity. Since the priced specification will be the basis of the valuation of variations (clause 3.7), there could be pitfalls for contractor and employer alike.

The contract drawings and the schedule of work priced by the contractor

Useful for work which is somewhat more complicated than the last example but does not warrant full bills of quantities. Again, the contractor will be obliged to take off his own quantities, and the employer, or the building industry in general, will in effect bear the cost. A schedule of work demands that there is agreement on the order in which the work will be carried out. Even on a relatively simple job, the contractor may be able to devise cheaper and more efficient methods of arriving at the result than those envisaged by the architect. Some form of two-stage tendering procedure is indicated to allow such a contribution by the contractor before the schedule is completed. Whether that is warranted will depend on all the circumstances. A priced schedule is more comprehensible, for the purpose of valuations, than a priced specification, but it requires the utmost clarity of thought to prepare properly.

The contract drawings and the bills of quantities priced by the contractor

If the size of the job justifies it, this must be the most satisfactory all-round combination. It is tried and tested, and each party knows not only the price of the whole job, but also the cost of variations. Monthly valuations are simplified, and there is less likelihood that the contractor will perpetrate some terrible undetected mistake at tender stage.

The contract drawings and the specification and the sum the contractor requires for carrying out the works

This combination requires the contractor to take off his own quantities and supply a total price, which will become the contract sum. He is not required to price the specification but, instead, to supply the employer with a contract sum analysis of the stated sum or a schedule of rates on which the stated sum is based. The first point to note is that the contract does not include either the contract sum analysis or the schedule of rates as a contract document. This appears to be a serious miscalculation, although clearly it is intentional (second recital, alternative B). There seems to be no good reason why either document should not be as important as, say, the priced specification in the first option. It is suggested that, if the employer uses alternative B, the second recital should also be amended to include the pricing documents as contract documents. The contract sum analysis is stated (clause 8.3) to mean an analysis of the contract sum in accordance with the stated requirements of the employer. The definition purposely leaves room for the architect to require the contractor to provide the analysis in any form he requires, presumably including bills of quantities. The schedule of rates is more familiar and may be thought more useful than the schedules of work in another option. It is likely that this option will be used in most cases where bills of quantities are not prepared.

The contract drawings are to be noted by number in the designated place in the first recital. There tends to be some disagreement over the number and type of drawings to be designated contract drawings. They must be sufficiently detailed to show the location and extent of the work; those from which the contractor obtained information to submit his tender; and related to the other contract documents.

Ideally, the contract drawings should include every drawing prepared for the work. In practice, this is not always possible, but if drawings and specification are being used to obtain tenders, the drawings must be detailed enough to allow the contractor to carry out his own taking off. If bills of quantities are provided, small details may be omitted.

The further drawings and details which the architect is to provide under clause 1.7 are not contract documents. If they show different or additional or less work and materials than are shown on the contract documents, the contractor will be entitled to a variation.

All the contract documents must be signed and dated by both parties. That means every separate drawing or separate piece of paper, but not every sheet of the specification or bills of quantities – signing the cover or the last page is sufficient. An endorsement on each document should read: "This is one of the contract documents referred to in the agreement dated . . ." or other words to the same effect.

3.1.2. Importance and priority

The significance of the contract documents has already been discussed briefly. If a dispute arises and it is necessary to discover what was agreed between the parties, the arbitrator or the court will look at the contract documents.

In a number of places throughout the contract, reference is made to work being or not being in accordance with the contract (eg clause 3.14) That means in accordance with what is contained in the contract documents. A problem arises if the documents are in conflict. Clause 1.2 sets out rules which are to be followed depending on which combination of documents have been chosen.

In order to decide on the quality and quantity of work agreed to be carried out for the contract sum, it is necessary to look at the particular documents.

Drawings and specification (or schedules of work)

They must be read together, provided that no quantities are shown. If there is a conflict, the drawings are to be given preference over the specification or schedules of work. If quantities are shown for some items, those quantities will prevail.

Drawings and bills of quantities

The quality and quantity of work shown in the bills of quantities will prevail.

So if the drawings show a total of 60 holding-down straps and the specification states that 50 holding-down straps are required, the contractor may quite correctly price for 50 holding-down straps. If, at a later stage in the contract works, the architect decides that he does need 60 straps as shown on the drawings, the employer will have to pay for the additional 10.

If, on the other hand, the straps are mentioned in the specification without being quantified, the contractor will be deemed to have priced for 60 straps. This clause will be welcomed by contractors, because it clarifies a situation which can be a source of dispute when the architect for a particular project maintains that the contractor should price for everything, whether it is mentioned in the specification or on the drawing. This position, however, still applies in this contract unless quantities are mentioned. In practice, the result is likely to be that the architect will have to take great care when he prepares the specification, or the employer will face large bills for additional work.

Clause 1.3 provides that nothing in the bills of quantities/the specification/the schedules of work (as appropriate) will override or modify the application or interpretation of anything in the articles, conditions, supplemental conditions, or appendix. In effect, it means that nothing in the printed form can be amended by inserting a clause in the bills of quantities, etc which attempts to modify or alter what any printed clause says. This is so even if the insertion is written in ink and signed by both parties. The clause has been upheld by the courts: *English Industrial Estates Corporation* v *George Wimpey & Co Ltd* (1973) 1 Lloyds Rep 511. The way to amend the printed form is to do so on the form itself and have the amendment signed or initialled by the parties. Alternatively, suitably amended or special clauses can be annexed to the form, duly signed by the parties, or clause 1.3 itself can be deleted. Were it not for this clause, the general law would give effect to any amendments which were contained in the bills, etc. This clause is therefore of great significance. Consideration should be given to the possibility of deleting clause 1.3 and allowing the sensible interpretation offered by the general law to take effect.

3.1.3 Errors

Clause 1.4 further stresses the importance of having a thoroughly prepared set of contract documents and of using the same care to include anything which may be issued to the contractor to assist him in carrying out the works.

The architect is obliged to issue instructions (see **section 4.1.4**) to correct any of the following:

- inconsistencies which occur within any one of the contract documents or between the contract documents: this obligation extends to inconsistencies which may occur following the architect's issue of further information under clause 1.7 or levels and setting-out information under clause 3.9;
- errors in description or quantity or omissions of any item in any of the contract documents;
- errors or omissions in the particulars which the employer provides in relation to a person who is named in accordance with clause 3.3.1 (see **section 8.2.2**);
- departures from the method of preparation of the bills of quantities referred to in clause 1.5: this states that the bills of quantities must be prepared in accordance

with the Standard Method of Measurement of Building Works, seventh edition, except where certain items are expressly stated to have been measured in a different way. This is always a fruitful source of claims by the contractor.

None of these errors, inconsistencies, or departures will invalidate the contract, but if an instruction changes the quality or quantity of works as understood from clause 1.2 or changes any clause 3.6.2 obligations or restrictions, a variation will result.

There is a crumb of comfort to be gained from the fact that it is established law that, if something is omitted from the bills or specification which it is quite clear to everybody should be there and is necessary, the contractor will be deemed to have included it in his price: *Williams* v *Fitzmaurice* (1858) 3 H & N 844. There is scope for dispute in applying this principle. The contractor will always maintain that it certainly was not clear to him, or that he assumed that the employer was going to employ someone else to do or supply the thing in question. In the context of a particular contract, however, it should be possible to make a fair decision on any particular item.

An example will clarify the point. Assume that the bills of quantities provide for the contractor to supply damp-proof course of a particular quality and in a given quantity, but the item requiring him to lay it has been inadvertently omitted. He will be deemed to have included the laying in his price because it is clear to everyone that laying is required. On the other hand, if the architect fails to include the supply and fixing of, say, door furniture, the contractor may have a point in claiming that he assumed that the employer wanted to carry out this operation himself. Moreover, he will have had no information at all on which to base any price, and he would be entitled to his extra costs. In practice, the extreme situation should never arise, because the contractor would certainly query the omission of door furniture at tender stage.

3.1.4 Custody and copies

Clause 1.6 makes it quite clear that the contract documents must remain in the custody of the employer. There is a proviso that the contractor must be allowed to inspect them at all reasonable times, but this provision appears to be redundant in the light of the fact that the architect must provide him with a copy of the documents certified on behalf of the employer. It is essential that the copy is the same as the original. Very often, two sets of documents are prepared and all are signed by both parties, but it is not strictly necessary. The employer should check that the copy is the same as the original and sign the certificate himself, since that is the employer's responsibility. The certificate is usually inscribed on each document, including the drawings. Some architects favour a very elaborate pseudo-legal turn of phrase, but it is sufficient to state, "I certify that this is a true copy of the contract document."

The clause imposes a further duty on the architect to supply the contractor with two copies (uncertified) of each of the contract documents.

The further drawings and details which are to be supplied under clause 1.7 are not contract documents. They are intended merely to amplify the information contained in the contract documents. The obligation of the architect is to supply only such drawings and details as are reasonably necessary to enable the contractor to carry out and complete the works in accordance with the conditions: ie among other things, to complete by the stipulated completion date. The contractor has no claim for extension of time or loss and/or expense if the architect fails, unless the contractor has made a specific written application at the proper time in accordance with clause 2.4.7 or clause 4.12.1 (see **section 10.2.4**).

3.1.5 Limits to use

Clause 1.8 contains safeguards for both contractor and architect. It prohibits the use for any purpose other than the contract of any documents (contract documents or others) issued in connection with the contract. It also prohibits the employer, the architect, and the quantity surveyor from using any of the contractor's rates or prices in the contract documents, the contract sum analysis, or the schedule of rates for any purpose other than the contract. None of the contractor's rates or prices must be divulged to third parties.

The prohibition against the use of documents by the contractor simply states expressly what is understood from the general law with regard to the architect's copyright.

The prohibition against divulging the contractor's rates is designed to protect the contractor's most precious possession – his ability to tender competitively and thus secure work. To divulge his rates to a competitor is probably one of the most harmful things which could be done to any contractor. In practice, it is extremely difficult for the contractor to ensure that his prices are not used, for example, by the quantity surveyor to help him estimate some other current job.

There is no requirement for the contractor to return any drawings or details at the end of the contract. There is nothing to prevent the architect from asking for them in order to be sure that they will not be used for any other purpose, but he cannot require the contractor to return his certified copy of the contract documents, which he will need for his own records.

3.2 Insurance

3.2.1 Indemnity

The indemnity and insurance provisions were completely revised by amendment 1 in November 1986.

Under clause 6.1, the contractor assumes liability for, and indemnifies the employer against, any liability arising out of the carrying out of the works in respect of the following:

- personal injury or death of any person, unless and to the extent due to act or neglect of the employer or of any person for whom he is responsible: the persons for whom the employer is responsible will include anyone employed and paid by

him, such as directly employed contractors, the clerk of works, and the architect;
- injury or damage to any kind of property arising from the works, but other than the works themselves, provided and to the extent that it is due to the negligence, breach of statutory duty, omission, or default of the contractor or of any person employed or engaged upon the works or any of their respective employees or agents or any other person who may properly be on the site: the contractor's liability is limited, as compared to his liability to personal injury or death, since he must be at fault for the indemnity to be operative. He has no liability under this clause for any loss or damage which the employer is to insure under clauses 6.3B or 6.3C.

From the point of view of the employer, he is responsible for the injury or death of any person only insofar as the injury or death was caused by his or his agents' act or neglect. He is responsible for all loss or damage to property except to the extent it is caused by the contractor's or sub-contractor's default. In practice, if any claim does arise, it is likely to be the employer who will be sued. In turn, he will join the contractor as a third party in any action and claim an indemnity from him under this clause.

3.2.2 Injury to persons and property

Clause 6.2.1 requires the contractor to take out insurance (unless his existing insurances are adequate) to cover his liabilities under clause 6.1. This requirement is stated to be without prejudice to his liability to indemnify the employer under that clause. Thus the fact that the contractor has taken out or maintains the appropriate insurance cover does not affect his liabilities. If, for some reason, the insurance company refused to pay in the case of an incident, the contractor would be obliged to find the money himself. The contractor must ensure that all sub-contractors maintain similar insurance in respect of their own and the contractor's liability.

The insurance cover must be for a sum not less than whatever is stated in the appendix to the contract for any one occurrence or series of occurrences arising out of one event. The insurance against claims for personal injury or death of an employee or apprentice of the contractor or a sub-contractor must comply with Employer's Liability (Compulsory Insurance) Act 1969.

The employer has the right (clause 6.2.2) to inspect documentary evidence that the contractor and his sub-contractors are maintaining proper insurance cover, and in particular to inspect policies and premium receipts. The clause requires them to be sent to the architect for inspection by the employer. The employer is not to exercise this right unreasonably or vexatiously: he is likely to enforce it at the beginning of the contract and at the time of any required premium renewal. It is always wise to retain the service of an insurance broker in connection with all the insurance provisions of the contract. It is for the employer to appoint him on the architect's advice. He should inspect the relevant documents and confirm in writing that they comply with the contract requirements.

If the contractor fails to insure under clause 6.2.1, the employer has the right (clause 6.2.3) to take out the appropriate insurance himself and deduct the amount of any premium from monies due or to become due to the contractor. Alternatively, the employer may recover the amount from the contractor as a debt. It is essential that the employer exercises that right, and such is the importance of maintaining continuous insurance cover, the architect is probably justified in taking action on the employer's behalf immediately he discovers that the contractor has defaulted. The cover should be effected through and on the advice of the employer's broker. The architect must immediately confirm his actions to the contractor and the employer. The exact circumstances may vary widely, but the letters in **Figures 3.1** and **3.2** are examples.

3.2.3 Things which are the liability of the employer

Clause 6.2.4 provides for insurance against damage caused by the carrying out of the works when there is no negligence or default by any party. The clause is operative only if it is stated in the Appendix that the insurance may be required. The contractor, if so instructed by the architect, must maintain the insurance in the joint names of the employer and the contractor. The amount of cover must be specified in the contract documents. Liability envisaged by this clause covers damage to any property, other than the works and site materials, caused by collapse, subsidence, heave, vibration, weakening or removal of support, or lowering of ground water. Not covered is damage which is caused by the contractor's or sub-contractor's negligence, omission, or default or that of their respective employees or agents; due to errors or omissions in the architect's design; reasonably foreseen to be inevitable; which is the responsibility of the employer to insure under clause 6.3C.1 (if applicable); or due to nuclear risk, war risk, or sonic booms.

The contractor must obtain the employer's approval of the insurers he proposes to use, but not, apparently, to the amount of the premium. One method of sorting this out is for the employer to place the matter in the hands of his broker. He will need that advice in any event. If the employer later indicates to the contractor that he would be prepared to approve the insurer recommended by the broker, the contractor will probably be delighted to place the insurance with whomsoever the employer wishes. The device of the "double letter" (**Figures 3.3.** and **3.4**) is useful in such circumstances, as it leaves the responsibility where it belongs – with the contractor. the two letters are sent at the same time.

The contractor must deposit the policy and premium receipts with the employer. The amounts paid by the contractor in premiums under this clause are to be added to the contract sum. If the contractor fails to insure or to maintain the insurance under this clause, the employer may take out the insurance himself, in which case nothing is added to the contract sum under this clause. Since the employer, or the architect on the employer's behalf, know what insurance is needed and know with which insurer it is desired to place the cover, there may be something to be said for amending this clause to make the employer responsible for insuring under this clause.

There is a general proviso, contained in clause 6.2.5, stating that the contractor shall not be liable to indemnify the employer or to insure against damage to the works, the site, or any property due to nuclear perils and the like. This clause overrides anything contained in clauses 6.1 and 6.2.

Figure 3.1
Architect to contractor if contractor fails to maintain clause 6.2.1 insurance cover

Dear Sir

I refer to my telephone conversation with your Mr [*insert name*] this morning and confirm that you are unable to produce the insurance policy, premium receipts, or documentary evidence that the insurances required by clause 6.2.1 are being maintained.

In view of the importance of the insurance and without prejudice to your liabilities under clause 6.1 of the conditions of contract, [*the employer*] is arranging to exercise his rights under clause 6.2.3 immediately. Any sum or sums payable by him in respect of premiums will be deducted from any monies due or to become due to you or will be recovered from you as a debt.

Yours faithfully

Copy: Employer
        Quantity surveyor

Figure 3.2
Architect to employer if contractor fails to maintain clause 6.2.1 insurance cover

Dear Sir

The contractor is unable to provide evidence to show that he is maintaining the insurances required by clause 6.2.1 of the conditions of contract.

In view of the importance of the insurance, I have taken action on your behalf, under clause 6.2.3, and instructed your broker to provide the necessary cover effective from today. You are entitled to deduct the amount of the premium from your next payment to the contractor, or alternatively, you may wish to recover it as a debt. [*Add if appropriate*] In this instance, simple deduction would appear to be the easiest method of recovery.

A copy of my letter to the contractor, dated [*insert date*] is enclosed for your information.

Yours faithfully

Figure 3.3
Employer to contractor regarding clause 6.2.4 insurance (double letter 1)

Dear Sir

I should be pleased if you would inform me of the name of the insurers with whom you intend to place insurance in accordance with clause 6.2.4 of the conditions of contract. The contract provides that I must give my approval before you proceed to place the insurance.

Yours faithfully

3.2.4 Insurance of the works: alternative clauses

Clause 6.3 provides alternative works insurance clauses to deal with loss and damage to the works and unfixed materials and goods.

Clause 6.3.1 refers to alternative clauses which are:

- Clause 6.3A – As far as new buildings are concerned, this is the most usual provision. The contractor is required to take out All Risks insurance.
- Clause 6.3B – This deals with the situation if the employer wishes to take out insurance for new building work himself.
- Clause 6.3C – This deals with the insurance of works in or extensions to existing buildings. The employer is required to insure the existing structure and contents and the new work.

One or other of these provisions must apply, as stated in the Appendix.

There are two very important definitions: "All Risks insurance" and "site materials". The former states the risks for which insurance is required and the latter refers to all unfixed materials and goods delivered to, placed on or adjacent to the works and intended for incorporation therein. The key point about "All Risks insurance" is that it must provide cover against "any physical loss or damage to work executed and site materials". Cover is not limited to "Specified Perils" (defined in clause 8.3). It includes other risks such as impact, subsidence, theft and vandalism. The distinction between the two types of risk has to be carefully noted because the contract very often limits the risks to "Specified Perils" (for example when an extension of time is being considered).

"Specified Perils" are the same as the old "clause 6.3 perils", ie fire, lightning, explosion, storm, tempest, flood, bursting or overflowing of water tanks, apparatus or pipes, earthquake, aircraft and other aerial devices or articles dropped therefrom, riot and civil commotion, excluding any loss or damage caused by ionising radiations or contamination by radioactivity from any nuclear fuel, radioactive toxic explosive or other hazardous properties of any explosive nuclear assembly or nuclear component thereof, pressure waves caused by aircraft or other aerial devices travelling at sonic or supersonic speeds.

Clause 6.3 is divided into three parts, two of which must be deleted. So, if the contractor is to insure a new building, 6.3B and 6.3C must be deleted. If the employer is to insure a new building, clauses 6.3A and 6.3C must be deleted. Clauses 6.3A and 6.3B must be deleted if the employer is to insure existing structures and new work to them.

3.2.5 A new building where the contractor is required to insure

Clause 6.3A covers this situation. It obliges the contractor to take out and maintain a Joint Names Policy for All Risks insurance. The list of risks is extensive and a footnote advises that some of the risks may not be able to be covered. The matter should be agreed at tender stage and appropriate amendments made to the clause. The insurance must cover:

Figure 3.4
Employer to contractor regarding clause 6.2.4 insurance (double letter 2)

WITHOUT PREJUDICE

Dear Sir

With regard to the insurer whose name you are required to submit to me under clause 6.2.4 of the conditions of contract, if you were to suggest [*insert name of insurers recommended by the broker*] I should be prepared to approve them.

Yours faithfully

- the full reinstatement value of the works; and
- the cost of any professional fees expressed as a percentage. The percentage must be inserted in the Appendix by the employer. Failure to make the insertion would probably result in the cost of professional fees being borne by the employer.

Care must be taken in regard to "full reinstatement value". It should be remembered that the works will increase in value as the contract progresses. The sum insured must reflect the actual cost of reinstatement of the works and any lost or damaged site materials, which will include the cost of removing debris. It should be noted that the term does not cover what is referred to as "consequential loss". An example of this would be where the employer suffered loss because of the increased costs of carrying out work not completed at the time of the damage. The contractor can only recover the actual insured sum. If it proves to be insufficient, he has to bear the excess. The policy must be maintained up to and including practical completion of the works, the date of determination of the contractor's employment under clauses 7.1 to 7.3 or clauses 7.5, 7.6 or 7.8 (whether or not the validity is contested) whichever is the earlier.

The Joint Names Policy is to be taken out with insurers approved by the employer. The policy, premium receipts and any relevant endorsements must be sent to the architect who must deposit them with the employer. If the contractor defaults in taking out or in maintaining the insurance, the employer is entitled to take out the insurance himself. In that situation, the employer may deduct the amounts of any premiums from the sums otherwise due to the contractor (eg certified amounts) or he may recover them as a debt, ie by suing through the courts. It is unlikely that any employer will take the latter course when the former is so readily available.

Contractors usually have general insurance to cover the risk of damage to the works. This type of insurance is acceptable under the terms of the contract if the policy provides "All Risks" cover for no less than full reinstatement value and the appropriate percentage of professional fees and it is in Joint Names and the contractor can send documentary evidence that the insurance is in force. If the contractor defaults, the employer may take out and maintain a policy and deduct the cost as before.

If loss or damage occurs due to one of the risks covered by the policy, the contractor is obliged to notify the architect and the employer under the provisions of clause 6.3A.4. He must do this as soon as he discovers the loss or damage.

Clause 6.3A.4.2 stipulates that the occurrence of loss or damage is to be disregarded in computing amounts payable to the contractor under the contract. This clause covers the position if the architect issues a certificate which includes work which is later damaged. He is not to allow for the damaged work in later certificates. Such work must be treated, for certification purposes as if it was undamaged. Thus, the architect may have to certify, as work properly done, work which has been destroyed by one of the insured risks. There is nothing strange in this. Without this provision, the contractor must restore damaged work after any inspection which the insurer may require has taken place. The effect of this is that the contractor could be under a duty to restore the work before the insurance monies have been paid. Clause 6.3A.4.4 states that the contractor and the sub-contractors must authorise the insurers to pay the insurance monies to the employers. He must pay all the money he receives, less only professional fees, to the contractor in instalments under the architect's certificates.

3.2.6 A new building where the employer insures

This is not very common, but where the employer wishes to insure, clause 6.3B deals with the situation. It is in very similar terms to 6.3A. The employer must take out insurance in joint names for the full reinstatement value of the works together with an appropriate percentage for professional fees. The contractor must give notice as before if there is any loss or damage, but a very important difference to the position under clause 6.3A is that the restoration and repair work is to be treated as a variation. The result of this is that, although the employer is entitled to be paid the full amount of any insurance money, he must stand any further expense himself. The contractor, on the other hand, receives the full cost of repair.

3.2.7 Alterations or extensions to an existing building

Clause 6.3C deals separately with loss or damage to existing structures and contents and with loss or damage to the works carried out to the structures or as extensions. If an existing building is involved, there is no option. The employer must take out and maintain insurance.

Clause 6.3C.1 requires the employer to insure existing structures and contents owned by him or for which he is responsible. The risks to be covered are Specified Perils. If part of an extension is taken into the employer's possession (where a suitable clause has been inserted), the relevant part will form part of the existing structures for insurance purposes from the relevant date. Loss or damage to the works is covered by clause 6.3C.2. It is similar to the position under clause 6.3B against "All Risks". Both sets of insurance must be in joint names and the contractor authorises payment of insurance money directly to the employer. In common with clause 6.3B, if the insurance payment is insufficient to cover the cost of restoration, the employer must stand the amount of shortfall.

Except where the employer is a local authority, the contractor is entitled to demand proof that the insurances have been taken out and maintained. In default, the contractor may take out the appropriate insurance himself and the amount he pays is to be added to the contract sum. The position is the same under clause 6.3B.2. The contractor has an important extra power under clause 6.3C.3. He has right of entry as may be required to make a survey and inventory of the existing structures and contents.

The contractor must notify the employer and the architect in writing upon discovering loss or damage covered under either of the Joint Names policies. If neither party then determines the contractor's employment (see **section 12.1.6**) the contractor must proceed to carry out appropriate restoration work after the insurers have carried out any inspection they may require.

3.2.8 Benefits for sub-contractors

The Joint Names policies required under clauses 6.3A, 6.3B or 6.3C must provide either for recognition of a named sub-contractor as an insured or it must include a waiver of the insurer's rights of subrogation against any named sub-contractor in respect of loss or damage by any of the Specified Perils. This is a very useful provision for named sub-contractors who, if responsible for the loss, may otherwise face a writ from the insurers. The provisions are largely extended to embrace domestic sub-contractors also except in the case of Joint Names policies for existing structures under clause 6.3C.1.

3.2.9 Employer's loss of liquidated damages

Clause 2.3 empowers the architect to make an extension of time if the contractor is delayed, so that the date for completion is exceeded, by loss or damage caused by any one or more of the specified perils (clause 2.4.3). For example, if the works are partly destroyed by fire, it is most unlikely that the contractor would be able to remove the debris, rebuild and then finish the works within the original contract period quite apart from any wait for inspections by insurers and the like. In such circumstances, the empoyer normally has the disadvantage of having the building later than he wished and he has no compensation in the form of liquidated damages because the contractor has received, quite properly, an extension of the contract period.

Clause 6.3D has been introduced to overcome the problem. It is for the employer to state in the Appendix if he may require the contractor to take out insurance to cover loss of liquidated damages due to loss or damage due to Specified Perils. If he does so state, the architect must either inform the contractor, as soon as the contract is executed that no such insurance is required or instruct him to obtain a quotation. The insurance is to be on an "agreed value basis" which is to avoid any dispute arising at a later date regarding the amount of payment due. The sum is to be the amount in the Appendix as liquidated damages. If the quotation is acceptable, the architect must further instruct the contractor to accept it. The amount expended by the contractor must be added to the contract sum and if the contractor defaults in taking out such insurance, the employer has power to take out the insurance himself under the provisions of clause 6.3D.4. It must be remembered that the insurance is only for the period noted in the Appendix. Thus, if insurance is required for liquidated damages for ten weeks and the contract period is extended by eight weeks, the employer will recover all the liquidated damages he would otherwise have been entitled to deduct. However, if the extension of time is for eleven weeks, the insurers will pay only the ten weeks insured.

3.3 Summary

Contract documents

- Contract documents are the only evidence of the contract.
- They may consist of whatever the parties agree.
- Drawings prevail over the specification.
- Any quantities prevail over the drawings.
- Printed conditions prevail over all.
- Errors, inconsistencies, and departures are to be corrected by architect's instructions and a variation allowed if appropriate.
- Items missing from the specification may be deemed to be included if it is obvious to all that they should be there.
- Contract documents must be kept by the employer with a true copy to the contractor.
- No other drawing or detail is a contract document.
- Contract documents and any other documents issued for the contract must not be used for any other purpose.
- Contractor's rates must not be divulged or used for another purpose.

Insurance

- Employer's indemnity covers personal injury and death and damage to property, subject to certain exceptions.
- Contractor must insure to cover the indemnities.
- Employer has the right to insure if contractor fails.
- Special insurance can be taken out to cover instances where there is no default by any party.
- Either party may insure new work against All Risks.
- Only the employer may insure existing structures against Specified Perils and new work thereto against All Risks.
- The employer may require insurance against loss of liquidated damages after loss and damage due to Specified Perils.

4–The Architect's Authority and Duties

4.1. Authority

4.1.1 General

The extent of the architect's authority depends on his agreement with the employer. If the architect is wise he will have entered into a formal written contract, preferably incorporating the terms of the RIBA *Architect's Appointment*. The architect's powers and duties under IFC 84 (see **Table 4.1**) flow directly from his agreement with the employer not from the building contract itself, to which he is not a party. It follows that if the architect fails properly to carry out his duties, the employer, but not the contractor, can take legal action against him under the terms of his contract with the employer. It is possible for the contractor to bring an action against the architect in tort for negligence but he must show that the architect owed a legal duty of care to the contractor and that the architect was in breach of that duty, and that, by reason of the breach, the contractor suffered loss or damage. The chances of the contractor being successful in such a contention have been severely reduced, if not totally extinguished, following *Pacific Associates* v *Baxter* (1989) 13 ConLR 80 where an engineer was found to have no duty of care to the contractor when administering the contract. His duty was to the employer from whom the contractor could seek redress.

Generally, contractors must take action against the employer under the contract, the employer in turn taking action against the architect. If the architect fails to carry out his duties under the contract, this is generally a default for which the employer will be held responsible: *Croudace Ltd* v *London Borough of Lambeth* (1986) 6 ConLR 70.

Traditionally, the architect's role changes when the contract between employer and contractor is signed. Up to that time, he has been acting as agent, in a limited capacity, for the employer. After the signing, he assumes a dual and difficult role. He is still an agent of the employer, but he is also charged with seeing that the terms of the contract are administered fairly – "without fear or favour" is the usual term.

"Without favour" is absolutely right, but "without fear" is obsolete nowadays. It used to be thought that, when the architect carried out his duties under the contract, he was immune from any action against him in negligence by either party. If such a state ever really existed, it was changed in 1974 by the celebrated case of *Sutcliffe* v *Thakrah* (1974) AC 727. There is now no doubt that the architet is open to an action for negligence on every decision he takes, certainly from the employer he is not acting in a "quasi-arbitral" capacity. Notwithstanding that he is still required to act fairly between the parties in his administration of the contract. The situation is totally unrealistic, because there may be instances when the architect has to decide whether he himself is in default and to act accordingly – for example, in cases of claims for extension of time or for loss and/or expense. If he issues instructions late, he is duty bound, if the contractor makes a proper claim under the contract, to award an extension or ascertain a financial claim as the case may be. The employer may well be able to recover that loss from the architect. As a result of the controversial decision of the Court of Appeal in *Pacific Associates Inc* v *Baxter* (1988) 13 ConLR 80, it is presently unlikely that the contractor can maintain a direct action in tort against the architect, eg for negligent undercertification resulting in financial loss to the contractor, but this in no way affects the architect's legal and professional duty to act fairly between the parties in such matters as the issue of certificates and the grant of extensions of time.

It is important to note, that, as far as the contractor is concerned the architect's authority is stated in the contract, and is neither more nor less. Thus if, for example, the architect attempts to issue an instruction not empowered by the contract, the contractor need not carry it out. Indeed, if he does carry out an instruction which is not empowered by the contract, the employer probably has no liability (but see **section 4.1.3**). If the architect's instruction is empowered, the contractor need not worry whether the architect has the employer's consent: the contractor may carry it out and the employer is bound.

Two simple examples should make the position clear. Assume that the architect's contract with the employer is on the terms set out in the *Architect's Appointment*. Part 3.3 provides that the architect is not to make any material alteration, addition, or omission from the approved design without the employer's consent unless it becomes necessary during construction for constructional reasons and he informs the employer without delay – in other words, if an emergency arises. If, as a first example, the architect issues an instruction to vary the quality of the electrical fittings without the employer's consent, he will be in breach of his contract with the employer. The contractor can carry out the work, because the architect is empowered to issue such instructions by IFC 84, and the employer must pay if any extra cost is involved. The employer can recover any costs from the architect.

As a second example, suppose the architect informs the contractor that he may take possession of the site two weeks before the appointed date. The contract gives the

Table 4.1
Architect's powers and duties under IFC 84

Clause	Power/duty	Precondition/comment
1.4	**Duty** Issue instructions as to inconsistencies, errors, or omissions in or between the contract documents, drawings, etc **Duty** Value the correction under clause 3.7 if instruction changes quality or quantity of work	The power to correct errors in description or quantity applies only to items and not to prices
1.6	**Duty** Provide contractor with one copy of contract documents certified on behalf of employer and two further copies of contract documents and specification/schedule of work/bills	
1.7	**Duty** Provide contractor with two copies of further drawings or details necessary for the proper carrying out of the works	
1.8	**Duty** Not to divulge to third parties or use any of the contract rates for prices except for purposes of the contract	
1.10	**Power** Consent in writing to removal of unfixed materials or goods delivered to, or placed on or adjacent to, the works	Contractor's request must be for good reason; consent must not be unreasonably withheld
2.3	**Duty** Make in writing a fair and reasonable extension of time for completion as soon as he is able to estimate length of delay	It must become apparent that the progress of the works is being, or is likely to be, delayed *and* Contractor must forthwith give written notice to the architect of the cause of the delay *and* Architect must form the opinion that completion is likely to be, or has been, delayed beyond the original or extended completion date *and* Reasons for delay must be a relevant event as listed in clause 2.4

Table 4.1 (continued)

Clause	Power/duty	Precondition/comment
2.3	**Power** Make in writing a fair and reasonable extension of time for completion even if contractor has not given notice **Power** Review extensions of time granted	He can do this at any time up to 12 weeks after date of practical completion This is implied, and the power should always be exercised in order to reserve the employer's right to liquidated damages if there has been some default for which the employer is responsible
2.6	**Duty** Issue a certificate of non-completion **Duty** Cancel clause 2.6 certificate in writing and issue further certificate	If contractor fails to complete the works by the date for completion or within extended period If an extension of time is granted subsequent to the issue of the former certificate
2.9	**Duty** Certify the date when practical completion is achieved	When he is of the opinion that this is so
2.10	**Power** Issue instructions that defects etc, be not made good **Duty** Certify discharge of contractor's defects liability	If the employer consents. An appropriate deduction must be made from the contract sum When he is of the opinion that the contractor has discharged his obligations
3.2	**Power** Consent to employment of sub-contractor	Application from contractor Consent must not be unreasonably withheld
3.3.1	**Duty** Issue instructions changing particulars or omitting the work or substituting a provisional sum	Where contractor is unable to sub-contract in accord with particulars and so inform architect
3.3.1	**Power** Issue instruction requiring named sub-contractor work to be carried out by another person	Must be done before contractor notifies architect of his entering into named sub-contract
3.3.2	**Power** Instruct that provisional sum work be carried out by named person	In an instruction as to the expenditure of a provisional sum, the instruction must incorporate a description of the work and relevant tender particulars from NAM/T sections I and II Contractor has right of reasonable objection to named person

Table 4.1 (continued)

Clause	Power/duty	Precondition/comment
3.3.3	**Duty** Issue necessary instructions should employment of named person be determined before completion of sub-contract work	Instruction must: *either* name another person and give description of work and relevant particulars; *or* instruct contractor to make his own arrangements; *or* omit the work
3.5.1	**Duty** Issue written instructions **Power** Require compliance with an instruction by written notice to contractor	If the contractor fails to comply, the employer may employ others
3.5.2	**Duty** Specify in writing the contract clause empowering issue of an instruction	On contractor's written request
3.6	**Power** Issue variation instructions and sanction in writing any unauthorised variation made by the contractor	The variation ordered must fall within the definition in 3.6.1 or 3.6.2. Variations must be valued by the QS if no prior agreement between employer and contractor
3.8	**Duty** Issue instructions on expenditure of provisional sums	
3.9	**Duty** Determine levels required for execution of the works and provide contractor with information necessary to enable him to set out the works **Power** Instruct contractor not to amend setting-out errors	The information must be conveyed by means of accurately dimensioned drawings If the employer consents. An appropriate deduction must be made from contract sum
3.12	**Power** Issue written instruction requiring opening up of work, etc, for inspection or testing	Cost to be added to contract sum unless results show the work, etc, is not in accordance with the contract
3.13.1	**Duty** Issue instructions following failure of work, materials, or goods	Where architect has *either* not received contractor's proposals within seven days of discovery of failure, *or* is not satisfied with contractor's proposed actions, *or* safety considerations or statutory obligations require urgent action

Table 4.1 (continued)

Clause	Power/duty	Precondition/comment
3.13.2	**Power** Withdraw or modify instruction issued under clause 3.13.1	If contractor objects to compliance within 10 days of receipt of 3.13.1 instructions and architect accepts contractor's reasons
3.14	**Power** Issue written instructions requiring removal of work, materials, or goods not in accordance with the contract	
3.15	**Power** Issue instructions as to postponement of any *work*	
4.2	**Duty** Certify interim payments at monthly intervals calculated from date of possession stated in appendix	This is subject to any agreement between employer and contractor as to stage payments. Different intervals may be specified in the appendix. Interim valuations are to be made by the QS whenever architect considers them to be necessary to ascertain amount to be certified. The amounts to be included are 95% of the total value of: work properly executed, including variations and fluctuations adjustment if appropriate, and materials and goods for incorporation which have been reasonably and properly and not prematurely delivered to site (they must be adequately protected against the weather, etc); and 100% of ascertained disturbance claims, fees, insurance payments etc.
4.2.1	**Power** Include the value of off-site goods and materials in interim certificates	
4.3	**Duty** Certify interim payment to the contractor of 97½% of total amount to be paid to contractor	Within 14 days after the certified date of practical completion
4.5	**Power** Instruct contractor to send to QS documentation needed for adjusting the contract sum	

Table 4.1 (continued)

Clause	Power/duty	Precondition/comment
4.6	**Duty** Issue final certificate	This must be done within 28 days of sending the computations of the adjusted contract sum to the contractor *or* of the date of issue of the clause 2.10 defects liability certificate, whichever is the later
4.11	**Duty** Ascertain, or instruct QS to ascertain, the amount of direct loss and/or expense incurred or likely to be incurred by the contractor due to the employer's deferment of site possession under clause 2.2 (if applicable) or to regular progress being materially affected by one or more of the matters specified in clause 4.12 **Power** Require from contractor such information to support claim as is reasonably necessary to ascertain amount of direct loss and/or expense	If the contractor makes written application within a reasonable time of its being apparent *and* the architect is of opinion that the contractor has incurred or is likely to incur direct loss and/or expense not reimburseable by any other payment under the contract *and* supporting information is supplied
6.2.4	**Power** Issue instructions to contractor to take out insurance against employer's liabilities	If it is stated in appendix that the insurance may be required and the employer does so require
6.3D.1	**Duty** Either inform contractor that insurance is not required or instruct him to obtain quotation Instruct contractor whether or not employer wishes quotation to be accepted	If appendix states liquidated damages insurance may be required Instruction must not be unreasonably withheld or delayed
7.4	**Power** Instruct contractor to remove from the works any temporary buildings, plant, tools, etc	When contractor's employment has been validly determined by the employer

architect no authority to vary its terms – indeed, only the parties to the contract can do that. The contractor would take possession at his peril, the employer would have no liability and, if it came to that, the architect could face action from the contractor in tort.

If the architect is on the staff of the employer (for example, in a local authority), the position is much less clear. The contractor may quite rightly assume that he is acting as agent for the employer. In this respect, the contractor need have no regard to whatever standing orders may say, unless they have been specifically drawn to his attention, but may rely on the architect's apparent authority.

4.1.2 Express provisions

Article 3 of IFC 84 provides for the insertion of the name of the architect. The person whose name is entered is then the person to whom the contract refers whenever the word "architect" appears in the conditions. Ideally, the person who is actually to administer the contract should have his name entered. Problems can arise, however, because he may leave the practice, die, or retire. It is generally accepted that the name to be entered will be the name of the practice (ie XYZ & Partners) or of the chief architect in a local authority (eg C Wren). Most employers and contractors accept this convention and the fact that it will be one of the partners or employees of the practice, or one of the staff of the local authority architect who will administer the contract. If the architect is in private practice or local government, he would be wise to ensure that all interested parties, including the employer and the contractor, are informed, at the beginning of the contract, who are the authorised representatives (**Figure 4.1**). He should also inform them whenever there is a change. The situation is particularly delicate when a client has commissioned the architect, as one of the partners in a practice, to carry out his project. He will expect that the partner personally will oversee every detail. The letter will then serve the purpose of assuring him that, although the practice name is on the contract, the partner is personally looking after the job. All letters, instructions, certificates, notices, and letters must be signed by the registered architect duly authorised "for and on behalf of . . ." It is not usually sufficient for a person to sign his name only, even though he is using headed stationery. The letter may be deemed to be written on his own behalf, which is fine if he is a partner but not so good if merely in salaried employment. The common practice of signing in the name of another, perhaps even the architectural practice, and adding initials is acceptable provided the person signing is authorised to do so. The unfortunate habit of using a rubber stamp should be avoided.

If the architect named in article 3 dies, or if his appointment is terminated, the employer has 14 days in which to nominate a successor. It is now clear that the employer must name a successor. Except where the architect is an official of a local authority, the contractor has the right to object to the nomination (**Figure 4.2**). This provision is inserted because the new architect may be someone with whom the contractor has had unsatisfactory dealings in the past. If the employer thinks the contractor's reasons are insufficient, the matter can be decided by arbitration. Clearly, such a situation should be avoided if at all possible, not least because of the delaying effect on the contract.

Figure 4.1
Architect to contractor naming authorised representatives

Dear Sir

This is to inform you formally that the architect's authorised representatives for all the purposes of the contract are:

[*insert name*]: Partner in charge of the contract
[*insert name*]: Project architect

The above are the only people authorised to act in connection with this contract until further notice.

Yours faithfully

for and on behalf of [*insert name in contract, which should be in the firm's name*]

Copy:Employer
     Quantity surveyor
     Consultant
     Clerk of works

An important provision in this article states that no succeeding architect may disregard or overrule any certificate or instruction given by the previous architect. In the absence of such an express provision, no doubt a similar provision would be implied, because it is essential that the contractor's interests be safeguarded in circumstances which are solely under the control of the employer. The successor architect who disagrees with previous decisions would be wise to inform the employer, in writing, of his position, but he cannot alter them (**Figure 4.3**). If the contractor considers that the successor architect is attempting to disregard or overrule a previous decision, he must register his objection immediately (**Figure 4.4**).

Certain actions under the contract are left to the architect's discretion – for example, whether to include the value of off-site goods or materials in his certificates (clause 4.2.1 (c)). Whether he includes off-site goods or not, he will be deemed to have exercised his discretion. In exercising his discretion, he does not have to account for his actions to the contractor, but he may have to account for them to the employer if things go wrong. So the architect should err on the side of caution.

Other clauses call for the contractor to obtain the architect's consent to certain actions – for example, the removal of unfixed materials delivered to, placed on or adjacent to the works, and intended for use therefor (clause 1.10). **Figure 4.5** is a suggested letter. It is stipulated that the architect's consent must not be unreasonably withheld. If the contractor is not satisfied with the architect's decision, he can refer the matter to arbitration. It is thought that the architect has an obligation to state reasons for withholding his consent. If he does not, the contractor may well refer the matter to arbitration anyway. In stating his reasons, the architect should be brief.

Matters reserved for opinion – for example, whether the completion of the works is likely to be delayed (clause 2.3) – are for his opinion alone. He cannot shift the responsibility on to the quantity surveyor, nor must he accept any interference by the employer. His opinion must not be a whim, however, and he would be prudent to make brief notes for his own files in case his opinion comes up for review during arbitration.

4.1.3 The issue of instructions: general

All instructions which the architect issues to the contractor must be in writing. An instruction need not be written on a specially printed form headed "Architect's Instruction", although such forms are useful for collecting all instructions in one place. Even when they are used, a careful look through the files will normally unearth an instruction buried in the middle of a letter. A letter is quite acceptable as an instruction so is a handwritten instruction given on site, provided it is signed and dated. Instructions written on pieces of plywood or roofing tile used to be quite common. One of the authors has seen an instruction written on an internal wall of a building to be reconstructed. Such practices are not to be recommended. Instructions contained in site-meeting minutes are valid if the architect produces the minutes at a subsequent meeting and they are recorded as agreed. However, there would be an appreciable time lapse before such an instruction could be considered effective.

The position with regard to drawings is less certain. A drawing issued with a letter referring to its use on site is certainly an instruction, but a drawing issued with a

Figure 4.2
Contractor to employer, objecting to nomination of a replacement architect

Dear Sir

Under the provisions of article 3 we hereby formally give notice of our objection to the nomination of [*insert name*] of [*insert address*] as architect for the purpose of this contract in succession to [*insert name and address of previous architect*].

The grounds for our objection are [*insert particular reasons for objection*].

A good working relationship between architect and contractor is vital to the successful completion of any project. With this in mind, we look forward to hearing that you have reconsidered the nomination.

Yours faithfully

Figure 4.3
Architect to employer if disagreement with previous architect's decisions

As you are aware, article 3 of the contract prohibits me from disregarding or overruling any certificate or instruction given by the previous architect. This is a necessary provision to safeguard the contractor's position

I have to put on record, however, that had I been the architect at the time I would not have [*insert as appropriate, eg: issued certificate no 5 in the sum of £23,000*] and of course I can take no responsibility for the consequences.

[*Add if appropriate:*]

The matter cannot be allowed to stand as it is and I propose [*insert proposals*]. I should be pleased to receive your instructions.

Yours faithfully

Figure 4.4
Contractor to architect if ignoring a previous decision

Dear Sir

We are in receipt of your letter/certificate/instruction [*delete as appropriate*] of the [*insert date*] in which you [*summarise contents*].

We draw your attention to the letter/certificate/instruction [*delete as appropriate*] of the [*insert date*] which we have received from the previous architect. Article 3 of the contract states that you are not entitled to disregard or overrule any certificate or instruction given by the previous architect. Your letter/certificate/instruction [*delete as appropriate*] appears to so disregard or overrule, presumably by oversight, and we should be pleased if you would withdraw your letter/certificate/instruction [*delete as appropriate*] forthwith.

Yours faithfully

compliments slip may be an instruction or it may be simply sent for comment. The contractor should make sure before carrying out the work shown thereon (**Figure 4.6**). If the architect simply sends a copy of the employer's letter requesting that something be done, under cover of a compliments slip, it is not an instruction but merely an invitation to the contractor to carry out the work at his own cost.

There is no provision for oral instructions. If the architect gives an oral instruction, the contractor can disregard it with impunity. If the architect confirms an oral instruction in writing, the instruction becomes effective only when the contractor receives the written confirmation. If the contractor attempts to confirm the architect's oral instruction himself, this will probably be of no effect, even if the architect does not dissent, provided he does not acknowledge receipt. Oral instructions should be avoided.

The architect's authority to issue instruction is limited to those instructions which the conditions empower him to issue. A list of those instruction is given in **Table 4.2** and they are discussed in more detail later. The flowchart **Figure 4.7** sets out the procedure.

The contractor must comply with the architect's instructions forthwith. (This does not mean immediately, but simply as soon as reasonably can be managed.) The exception is an instruction requiring a variation (addition, alteration, or omission) of any obligation or restriction imposed by the employer in the specification/schedules of work/bills of quantities in regard to access, limitation of working space, limitation of working hours, or the order of execution or completion of work (clause 3.6.2). The contractor need not comply with a clause 3.6.2 instruction if he makes a reasonable objection in writing. Any dispute as to the reasonableness of his objection must be referred to arbitration.

The contractor is entitled to require the architect to specify in writing the clause which empowers his instruction (**Figure 4.8**). He must respond immediately. It is good practice for the architect to specify the empowering clause in the instruction itself. When the contractor receives the architect's response, he may do one of two things. He may carry out the instruction, in which case the clause nominated will be deemed to be the empowering clause (whether it is or not) for all the purposes of the contract. Alternatively he may give the employer a written notice to concur in the appointment of an arbitrator to decide if the clause nominated does indeed empower the issue of the instruction. (The employer may give notice if he wishes, provided he does so before the contractor has complied with the instruction.) Is is thought that the contractor has the right to await the outcome of any arbitration before complying. If he does comply, he should write to preserve his rights (**Figure 4.9**). If the contractor does not carry out the architect's instruction immediately, the architect may send him a written notice requiring him to comply with it (**Figure 4.10**). If he does not comply within seven days of receiving the notice, the architect should advise the employer that he may employ and pay others to do the work detailed in the instruction, including any work which it is necessary to carry out in order to comply with the instructions. Such additional work will usually consist of protective work, erecting scaffolding, cutting out, and reinstating. If the employer decides to take this course of action, the architect will be expected to handle the details. Wherever possible, he should obtain competitive quotations so that he will be able to show, if it becomes

Figure 4.5
Contractor to architect, requesting removal of unfixed materials

Dear Sir

[*State quantity and nature of goods or materials*] are presently stored on site. It is our view that these materials should be stored at [*name the place*] because [*state reason*]. We should be pleased to receive your written consent to the removal from site of these materials in accordance with the provisions of clause 1.10 of the conditions of contract.

Yours faithfully

Figure 4.6
Contractor to architect if drawing issued without an instruction

Dear Sir

We have today received [*insert number*] copies of your drawings numbers [*insert drawing numbers*]. There was no letter or instruction enclosed with them, merely a compliments slip.

The drawings appear to be revised versions of drawings currently in our possession/entirely new to us [*delete as appropriate*] and we should be pleased if you would instruct us whether you are issuing these drawings under the provisions of clause 1.7.

For the avoidance of doubt, please issue future drawings, details and schedules under cover of a letter making it clear that you wish us to treat the drawing as an instruction if indeed that is your intention.

Yours faithfully

Table 4.2
Instructions empowered by IFC 84

Clause	Instruction
1.4	Correcting inconsistencies between contract documents and drawings Correcting errors in the contract documents Correcting errors in particulars of a named person Correcting departures from the method of preparation of the contract bills
2.10	Not to make good defects
3.3.1	In regard to named persons as sub-contractors: a) to change particulars to remove impediment b) to omit work c) to omit work and substitute a provisional sum Naming a person other than the person in the specification/schedules of work/contract bills
3.3.3	As necessary after determination of employment of named person: a) to name another person b) to require the contractor to make his own arrangements c) to omit work
3.5.1	General power to issue instructions empowered by the conditions
3.6	Requiring a variation
3.8	To expend provisional sums
3.9	That setting out errors shall not be amended and an appropriate deduction be made from the contract sum
3.12	Requiring opening up or testing
3.13.1	Requiring opening up or testing at contractor's cost if similar work or materials have failed
3.14	To remove defective work from the site
3.15	Postponing work
6.2.4	Take out insurance against employer's liabilities
6.3C.4.4	To remove and dispose of any debris
6.3D.1	To obtain quotation for insurance against loss of liquidated damages To accept or not to accept the quotation
7.4(b)	To remove temporary buildings etc after determination

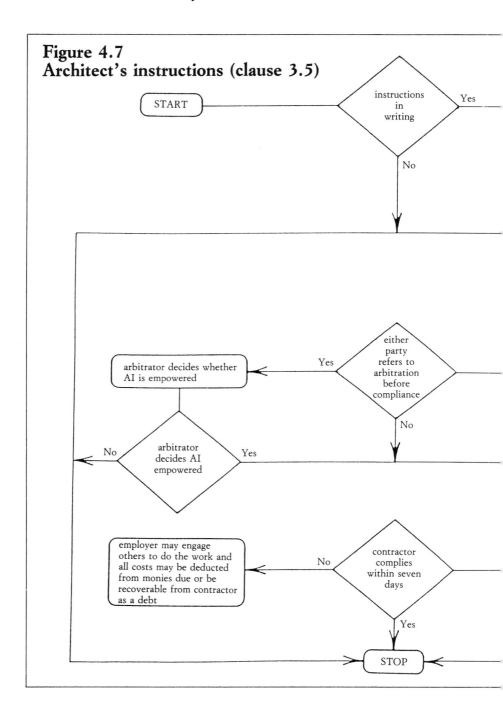

Figure 4.7
Architect's instructions (clause 3.5)

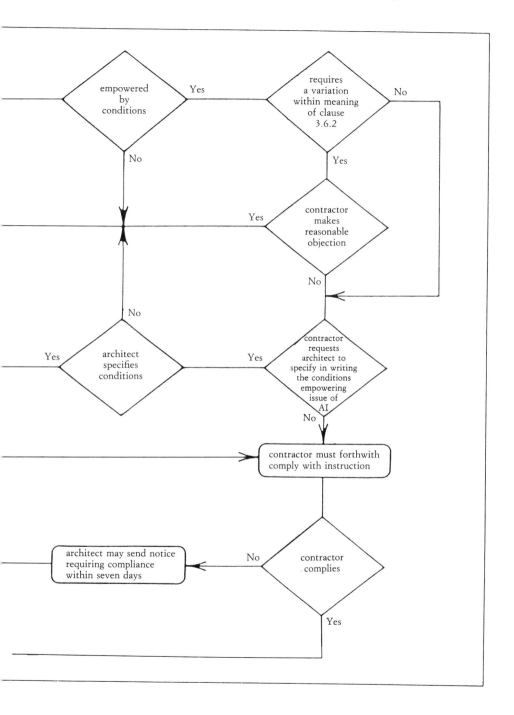

necessary, that he has had the work done at the lowest price it was reasonable to accept in the circumstances. When the work is completed, the employer has the right to deduct all the additional costs which he has incurred from monies due or which will become due to the contractor (ie, from certificates). Alternatively, he can opt to recover the cost as a debt. Generally, it will be easier for the employer to deduct the cost from monies payable on certificates. When deducting such money, the contractor is entitled to a brief statement showing how the figure has been made up. Note that the amount deductible is the additional cost – ie the difference between what the work would have cost had the contractor carried out the instruction and what it did cost in fact. The professionals involved are entitled to charge extra fees, and the employer may include them in his computation of the cost together with any additional incidental expenses caused by the contractor's non-compliance. If the contractor, for his part, considers that the compliance notice is unreasonable, he should respond immediately (**Figure 4.11**). If, despite the letter, the employer persists in employing others to carry out the work a further letter from the contractor is indicated (**Figure 4.12**).

4.1.4 Instructions in detail

The contract empowers the architect to issue instructions in a wide variety of circumstances. In some of these circumstances, he has an obligation to issue an instruction. These are marked by the use of the word "shall", meaning "must". The architect must be aware of the extent of his powers and duties in each case.

Clause 1.4: correcting inconsistencies between contract documents; correcting errors in particulars of a named person; correcting departures from the method of preparation of the contract bills

There are four important points to note:
● The architect has an obligation to issue instructions under this clause.
● His obligation to instruct does not depend on any notice from the contractor, although obviously the contractor will notify the architect for his own benefit.
● No inconsistencies, errors, or departures such as those mentioned will vitiate (invalidate) the contract.
● If the architect's instruction changes the quality or quantity of the work deemed included in the contract sum (clause 1.2), or changes employer's obligations or restrictions, a variation results.

The onus is fairly and squarely on the architect and the quantity surveyor. If they make any errors, the employer will have to pay. It matters not that the errors are discovered only at a late stage in the progress of the works. This clause is admirably clear and leaves scant room for any fudging of the issue.

Clause 2.10: not to make good defects

This clause is discussed in detail in **section 9.3.4.** The important point to remember is that the employer's consent must be obtained before the architect issues the instruction; the contractor has no right of objection.

Figure 4.8
Contractor to architect requiring specification of clause empowering an instruction

Dear Sir

We have today received your instruction number [*insert number*], dated [*insert date*] requiring us to [*insert a summary of the instruction*].

We request you, in accordance with clause 3.5.2 of the conditions of contract, to specify in writing the provision which empowers you to issue this instruction.

Yours faithfully

Figure 4.9
Contractor to architect if complying with instruction pending arbitration

Dear Sir

We refer to your letter of the [*insert date*] purporting to specify the clause empowering the issue of instruction number [*insert number*], dated [*insert date*].

As you will know, we dispute your contention and we have notified the employer that we require the dispute to be referred to arbitration. It is our view that we are not obliged to comply with such instruction until after the arbitrator has decided whether the provision you specified empowers the issue of such instruction.

Notwithstanding the above, we are prepared to comply with your purported instruction without prejudice to the outcome of the arbitration or to any of our rights and remedies under the contract or at common law arising out of or in connection with the purported instruction, such arbitration or any other proceedings whatsoever.

We will proceed as soon as we have the employer's written acceptance of our position as set out in this letter.

Yours faithfully

Copy: Employer

Figure 4.10
Architect to contractor, giving notice requiring compliance with instruction

REGISTERED POST/RECORDED DELIVERY

Dear Sir

Take this as notice under clause 3.5.1 of the conditions of contract that I require you to comply with my instruction number [*insert number*] dated [*insert date*], a further copy of which is enclosed.

If within seven days of receipt of this notice you have not complied, [*the employer*] may employ and pay other persons to execute any work whatsoever which may be necessary to give effect to the instruction. All costs incurred thereby will be deducted from money due, or to become due, to you under the contract or will be recovered from you as a debt.

Yours faithfully

Copy: Employer
      Quantity surveyor

Clause 3.3.1: in regard to named persons as sub-contractors:
(a) change particulars to remove impediment; (b) omit work; (c) omit work and substitute a provisional sum

This clause is discussed in detail in **section 8.2.2**. The architect has an obligation to issue the instruction under this clause, provided that he is satisfied that the particulars specified have prevented the contractor from entering into a sub-contract.

Clause 3.3.3: as necessary after determination of employment of named person:
(a) name another person; (b) require the contractor to make his own arrangements; (c) omit the work

This clause is discussed in detail in **section 8.2.2**. The architect has an obligation to issue an instruction under this clause, subject to receiving a written notice from the contractor stating the circumstances of the determination.

Clause 3.6: requiring a variation

This is a most important clause, giving the architect power to require the contractor to carry out variations or to sanction in writing any variation carried out by the contractor without instruction. The clause states that no such instruction or sanction will vitiate the contract. That is superfluous, because no exercise of a right conferred by the contract can vitiate that same contract. The clause goes into some detail regarding what a variation means. In general, it means what one would assume that it means, namely the alteration or modification of the design or quality or quantity of the works shown on the drawings and described by, or referred to, in the specification or schedules of work or bills of quantities (clause 3.6.1). Difficulties may arise, if bills of quantities are not used, in deciding just what is included and of what quality and, therefore, what is and what is not a variation (see **section 3.1.2**). The clause proceeds to spell out in detail what kinds of situation are included: the alteration of kind or standard of materials to be used in works; the addition, omission, or substitution of any work; the removal from site of any work carried out or materials intended for use except where they are not in accordance with the contract.

This is just a development of the initial statement and requires no further comment. Variation is also said to mean (clause 3.6.2) the imposition by the employer of any obligations or restrictions or the addition, alteration, or omission of any obligations imposed by the employer in the specification or schedules of work or bills of quantities in regard to access to, or use of, any particular parts of the site or the whole site; limitations of working space; limitations of working hours; the order of execution or completion of work. The exercise of the architect's power under this clause is subject to the contractor's right of reasonable objection (**Figure 4.13**).

Clause 3.8: to expend provisional sums

This is mandatory. The architect must instruct the contractor how he wishes to deal with any provisional sums.

Figure 4.11
Contractor to architect on receipt of unreasonable compliance notice

Dear Sir

We have today received your notice dated [*insert date*] which you purport to issue under the provisions of clause 3.5.1 of the conditions of contract.

[*Add either:*]

It is not reasonably practicable to comply as you require within the period you specify because [*insert reasons*]. You may be assured that we have not forgotten our obligations in this matter and we intend to carry out your instruction number [*insert number*], dated [*insert date*] as soon as practicable in the light of the foregoing. We should, therefore, be pleased to hear, by return, that you withdraw your notice requiring compliance. If we do not receive your reply by [*insert date*], we will immediately comply, but take this notice that such immediate compliance will be grounds for substantial claims for extension of time and loss and/or expense and/or a claim for damages at common law.

[*Or:*]

We consider that we have already complied with your instruction number [*insert number*], dated [*insert date*]. Any attempt by the employer to employ other persons and/or to deduct from any money due or to become due to us will be deemed to be a serious breach of contract in respect of which we will take appropriate action. Without prejudice to the foregoing, if you will immediately withdraw your notice requiring compliance, we will be happy to meet you on site to sort out what appears to be a misunderstanding.

Yours faithfully

Copy: Employer

Figure 4.12
Contractor to employer if employer employs others after notice requiring compliance

REGISTERED POST/RECORDED DELIVERY

Dear Sir

We note that you have employed other persons to carry out the contents of architect's instruction number [*insert number*], dated [*insert date*]. You purport to take this action under the provisions of clause 3.5.1 of the conditions of contract.

We wrote to the architect [*copy to you*] on the [*insert date*], explaining why you were not entitled to employ others in this instance and warning that we would take appropriate action if you did.

In our view, you are in serious breach of contract. We formally request you to withdraw your instructions to other persons within seven days from the date of this letter. Failure on your part so to do will result in us taking immediate action to recover damages and possibly to treat the contract as repudiated.

Yours faithfully

Copy: Architect

Figure 4.13
Contractor to architect objecting to compliance with clause 3.6.2 instruction

Dear Sir

We are in receipt of your instruction number [*insert number*], dated [*insert date*] instructing us to [*insert a summary of the instruction*].

Please note that we make reasonable objection to compliance under the provisions of clause 3.5.1 of the conditions of contract. The basis of our objection is [*insert the basis of objection eg, "that closure of the access of Main Road will render the delivery and erection of the long span steel beams difficult if not impossible to achieve*].

Please, therefore, withdraw your instruction or amend it to deal with our objection.

Yours faithfully

Clause 3.9: that setting out errors shall not be amended and an appropriate deduction be made from the contract sum

The architect is responsible for giving the contractor accurately dimensioned drawings and for determining any levels required. The contractor is responsible for setting out the works correctly – ie, in accordance with the information the architect gives him. If he sets out incorrectly, he must amend any errors arising and stand the cost himself. The architect may instruct the contractor not to amend errors arising from inaccurate setting out, but he must obtain the employer's consent before issuing such an instruction, and he must instruct that an appropriate deduction for the errors must be made from the contract sum.

The deduction of an appropriate sum will pose difficulties. Bad setting out could result in, for example, several rooms becoming a metre shorter than intended. The wording of the clause appears wide enough to cover not only the value of work and materials omitted, but also the reduction in value of the rooms to the employer – however that is to be ascertained. **Figure 4.14** is an example of the kind of letter the architect might send to the contractor in these circumstances. If the contractor objects, he should make his position clear (**Figure 4.15**). If the result of bad setting out is to leave the employer with a building substantially larger than he requires, the contractor would not be entitled to any increase for the additional work and materials, but he would face the possibility of a reduction to represent additional costs to the employer (such as increased rates, cleaning charges, and running costs).

What if the setting out is so bad that the building encroaches on a neighbour's land? Presumably the deduction must take all the employer's costs into account, but the situation is likely to arise only if the errors are minor, since if they are anything more, demolition is indicated. The contractor is given no choice in the matter, but, faced with what he considers to be an unreasonable attitude on the part of the employer, he is likely to seek arbitration or litigation.

Clause 3.12: requiring opening up or testing

This clause empowers the architect to instruct the contractor to open up for his inspection any work which has been covered up, or to arrange for any testing of materials whether or not they are already built in. He will instruct the contractor to open up or test because he suspects that work or materials are defective. The architect may have no alternative, but the position is that, if the work or materials are found to be in accordance with the contract, the cost (including the cost of making good) must be added to the contract sum unless provision is made for opening up or testing in the specification or schedules of work or bills of quantities. If the work or materials are found to be not in accordance with the contract, all the costs must be borne by the contractor.

Clause 3.13.1: requiring opening up or testing at contractor's cost if similar work or materials have failed

This clause gives the architect a useful power to check for possible defective work. The exercise of that power will give rise to further responsibilities. Before the

Figure 4.14
Architect to contractor, referring to setting out errors not to be amended

Dear Sirs,

I refer to our meeting on site yesterday and I confirm the position with regard to setting out as follows:

1. At the commencement of this contract, you were provided with all necessary levels and accurately dimensioned drawings to enable you to set out the works.

2. The inspection yesterday revealed that there were errors in the setting out for which you were responsible under the provisions of clause 3.9 of the conditions of contract. The errors are [*insert a description of the errors*] which are clearly not easily amended at this stage in the progress of the works.

3. In accordance with clause 3.9, I enclose my official architect's instruction instructing you not to amend these errors. I have requested the quantity surveyor to carry out the necessary calculations so that an appropriate deduction for such errors may be made. [*If appropriate, add: "You should note that the deduction will include a sum which will reflect the reduction in value of the finished works".*]

Yours faithfully

Copy: Employer

Figure 4.15
Contractor to architect, objecting to amount of deduction after errors in setting out not amended

Dear Sir

We are in receipt of your letter and instruction of the [*insert date*]. We note that you instruct us not to amend the setting out of [*insert details*].

We acknowledge that you are empowered to issue such an instruction, but we strongly object to a deduction of money such as you indicate in your letter. Clause 3.9 refers to a deduction. Nowhere in the contract is it stipulated how such a deduction is to be calculated; only that it is to be "appropriate". In our view, the amount of such a deduction can only be ascertained by agreement. No doubt you will present your proposals for our consideration in due course. If you attempt to deduct any amount whatsoever before we have signified our agreement in writing , we shall take immediate legal action.

Yours faithfully

Copy: Employer

architect may issue an instruction, he must have discovered work or materials which have failed to be in accordance with the contract. After the architect's discovery, the contractor must write to him stating what he intends to do immediately to ensure that there is no similar failure in the work already carried out or materials already supplied. His proposals must be at no cost to the employer. The important point is that only similar failures are under consideration. For example, if it is discovered that, in one section of the work, wall ties have not been provided in sufficient numbers, the architect will be looking to the contractor to satisfy him that wall ties have been properly provided in other parts of the building. Thus, the contractor will not be concerned, on that occasion, with possible failures of damp-proof courses or foundations. It is debatable whether the contractor must also satisfy the architect that, in our example, the other wall ties have been properly bedded if that was not the reason for failure. On balance, he probably has no such duty. In most cases, of course, the contractor's proposals will give the architect the opportunity of checking that other defects are not present – although not necessarily in the case of wall ties.

Since, in the course of a contract, there will be many instances of failures, large and small the architect should make sure that the contractor is aware of those instances when he considers proposals under this clause to be necessary (**Figure 4.16**). But it must be stressed that the onus is on the contractor and the architect has no contractual duty to make the contractor aware. The architect's power to issue an instruction arises after discovery of failure if:

- he has not received the contractor's proposals within seven days of discovering the failure; *or*
- he is not satisfied with the action proposed by the contractor; *or*
- he cannot wait for the contractor's written proposals because of safety considerations or statutory obligations.

The architect may then issue an instruction which requires the contractor to open up for inspection or to arrange for testing any work or materials, whether built in or not. The instruction should state that the work will be at no cost to the employer. The whole process is at the contractor's own cost, whether or not the opening up or testing discovers further failures. (This is in contrast to the provisions of clause 3.12.) The contractor must forthwith comply with the architect's instruction. If he does not, the architect may obtain the employer's consent to applying clause 3.5.1 remedies (see **section 4.1.3**).

Clause 3.13.2 gives the contractor 10 days from receipt of the instruction to decide whether to object to compliance. His right of objection is stated to be without prejudice to his obligation to comply. This means that he must still comply even though objecting. If he decides to object, he must inform the architect in writing, stating his reasons (**Figure 4.17**). The architect has seven days from receipt of his objection to withdraw the instruction, or to modify the instruction to take care of the contractor's objection.

If the architect takes neither action, any dispute regarding whether the nature or extent of the opening up or testing was reasonable in all the circumstances is referred automatically to arbitration. The arbitration is stated to be in accordance with article 5, even if the appendix states that the article is not to apply (see **section 13.5**).

Figure 4.16
Architect to contractor, following failure of work

Dear Sir

When I visited site today, I noted that [*specify work or materials*] failed to be in accordance with the contract.

In accordance with clause 3.13.1 of the conditions of contract, I require you to state in writing, within seven days of the date of this letter, what action you will immediately take at no cost to the employer to establish that there is no similar failure to work already executed/materials or goods already supplied [*omit as appropriate*].

Yours faithfully

The arbitrator is to decide whether the instruction is fair and reasonable. If he decides that it is not, he must decide what amount the employer must pay to the contractor for carrying out the work, including making good. It is clearly envisaged that the arbitrator may find that the instruction is fair in essence but that the architect has gone too far in requiring existing work to be opened up. In such a case, the arbitrator has power to order the employer to pay a contribution. The contractor however, must still comply with the instruction. In the majority of cases, the contractor is unlikely to wish to force arbitration but the wording of the clause makes arbitration inevitable if the architect ignores any objection the contractor makes. The contractor may take advantage of that to try and force concessions when he makes objection. In practice, no matter how automatic arbitration is said to be, it will not take place against the wishes of both parties. It will be seen that, if all parties take the maximum allowable time to act under the various parts of the clause, some 26 days will have elapsed between the discovery of the failure and the date on which arbitration becomes automatic. The procedures and options in this clause are set out in the flowchart, **Figure 4.18.**

Clause 3.14: to remove defective work from the site

This clause empowers the architect to order that defective work or materials be removed from site. Defective work or materials is work or materials not in accordance with the contract. The architect has no power to simply order defective work or materials to be rectified (except under clause 2.10, defects liability). To be effective, the instruction must order removal from site. In most cases, it is to be expected that the contractor will correct defective work or materials without the necessity of an instruction, but that the architect cannot put any sanction into operation until he has instructed removal and the contractor has not complied. So the architect should always send an instruction under this clause whenever such work or materials comes to his attention. For the same reason, the contractor must not hesitate to put the matter on record if he thinks the instruction is not justified (**Figure 4.19**).

Clause 3.15: postponing work

The architect is entitled to issue an instruction to postpone any of the work required by the contract. There is a price to pay and the employer has to pay it, so the architect must take care. If he postpones work, the contractor can claim an extension of time (clause 2.4.5) and loss and/or expense (clause 4.12.5). Under clause 7.5.3, he may determine his employment if the whole or substantially the whole of the works are suspended for a continuous period of one month due to postponement, among other things (see **section 12.2.2**). It has been held that, in certain circumstances, an instruction given on another matter may imply postponement with all its consequences. The situation should not arise if the architect is careful to quote the correct empowering clause in each case and use the wording of the clause as far as appropriate.

Clause 7.4(b): to remove temporary buildings etc, after determination

Although not prefaced by the mandatory "shall", this is an instruction which the architect is obliged to issue at some time after the employer has determined the contractor's employment. For a fuller discussion, see **section 11.1.7.**

Figure 4.17
Contractor to architect, objecting to compliance with clause 3.13.1 instruction

REGISTERED POST/RECORDED DELIVERY

Dear Sir

We are in receipt of your instruction number [*insert number*], dated [*insert date*] instructing us to [*insert nature of the work*] which you purport to issue under clause 3.13.1 of the conditions of contract. We consider such instruction unreasonable because [*state reasons*].

If within 7 days of receipt of this letter you do not in writing withdraw the instruction or modify it to remove our objection, a dispute or difference will exist as to whether the nature or extent of opening up/testing [*delete as appropriate*] in your instruction is reasonable in all the circumstances. Such dispute or difference to be referred to immediate arbitration. In such event, we will comply with our obligations pending the result of such arbitration and award of additional costs and extension of time.

Yours faithfully

Copy: Employer

4.2 Duties

4.2.1 Duties under the contract

In **section 4.1.1**, the architect's duties under the contract were seen to flow directly from his contract with the employer. Many of those duties can be recognised because they are preceded by the word "shall", eg "the architect shall . . .". A full list is contained in **Table 4.1.**

In performing his duties, he is expected to act competently; as an architect, he will be expected to act with the same degree of skill and care as the average competent architect. If he professes greater than average skill, either generally or in some special area, that is the standard by which he will be judged.

Clause 1.1, Contractor's obligations, paradoxically places a potentially heavy duty on the architect. In essence, it states that if approval of workmanship or materials is a matter for his opinion, the quality and standards must be to his reasonable satisfaction. At first sight, this clause appears to give the architect considerable power, and so it does. The catch is contained in clause 4.7, which states that the issue of the final certificate is conclusive evidence that where anything is reserved to his approval, it is to his reasonable satisfaction. Architects commonly specify that various items are to be to their approval, sometimes even going so far as to state generally that "unless otherwise stated, all workmanship and materials are to be to the approval of the architect". The combined effect of clauses 1.1 and 4.7 is that, if the architect reserves anything for his approval, the final certificate confirms that he does approve it. That is the case whether or not he has specifically expressed approval during the course of the work. Therefore, if the architect puts a general-approval clause in the contract documents, he places on himself a duty of approving everything to which it applies. If he misses anything, the final certificate will make it deemed approved. Moreover, if he approves something which is not in accordance with the contract, his approval will override the contract requirements. He cannot say later that it was not in accordance with the contract and therefore unacceptable. The architect should, therefore, severely limit the items to which he reserves the right of approval. **Table 4.3** lists the certificates to be issued by the architect.

4.2.2 General duties

This is not the place to discuss in detail the architect's general duties to his client and to third parties, but one aspect of his general duties affects the contract. He has a duty to his client to be familiar with those parts of the law which affect his work. For example, his client will expect him to have a thorough knowledge of the planning laws. This is not the specialist knowledge expected of a lawyer who deals with nothing but planning appeals, but is the knowledge which the architect requires to advise his client and make successful planning applications on his behalf. Similarly, the architect is expected to have a thorough knowledge of the various forms of contract, so that

Figure 4.18
Failure of work

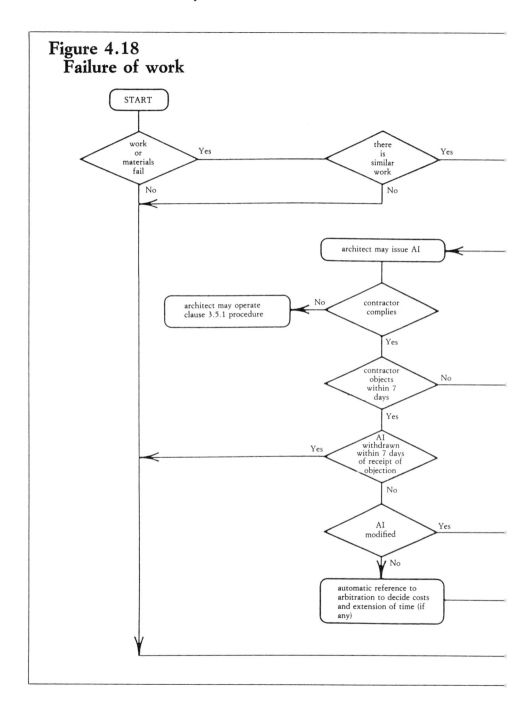

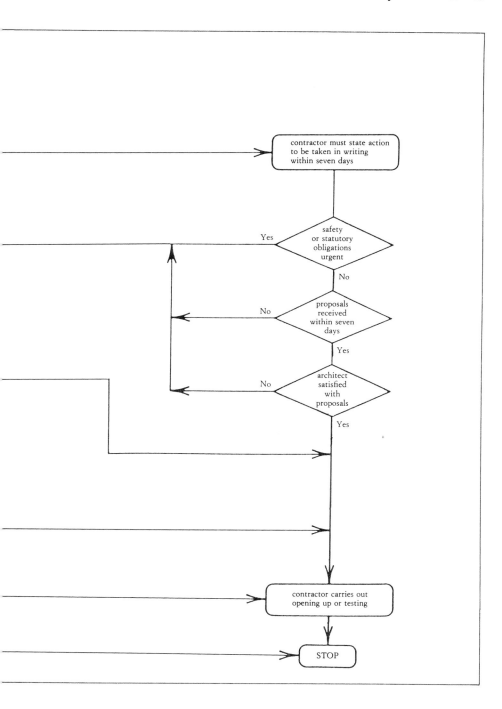

Figure 4.19
Contractor to architect if instruction to remove defective work is not justified

We are in receipt of your instruction number [*insert number*], dated [*insert date*] instructing us to remove [*specify the work noted*] from site.

You purport to issue your instruction under the provisions of clause 3.14 of the conditions of contract. Clause 3.14 expressly restricts the issue of such instruction to work, materials or goods which are not in accordance with the contract.

We formally give notice that the work/material/goods [*delete as appropriate*] noted in your instruction is in accordance with the contract and that, therefore, your instruction is invalid under clause 3.14.

If you withdraw your instruction and rephrase it so as to bring it under the provisions of clause 3.6, we shall be happy to comply.

Yours faithfully

he can advise his client which contract is most appropriate for a particular job. He must be knowledgable about the particular contract which he advises his client to use.

The architect must be aware of the pitfalls in a contract and the correct interpretation of each clause as shown by any applicable case law. If he has never read a contract in his life, much less a legal commentary, then he will be unable to carry out his duty under the contract; he will be unable to act fairly within the meaning of the contract; he will be unable to advise his client when a particularly difficult contractual point arises; and he will make more mistakes than the average competent architect.

If his client is put to unnecessary expense by the architect's inadequate knowledge of contractual provisions, he may well sue to recover any loss which he has suffered as a result of the architect's incompetence.

4.3 Summary

Authority

- His authority depends on what he has agreed with the employer.
- Only the employer can take action against the architect in contract.
- Employer and contractor may be able to take action against the architect in tort.
- The architect has a dual role once the contract is signed.
- He is not a quasi-arbitrator; he is not immune from actions for negligence for his decisions.
- The contractor is entitled to see the architect's authority only in terms of the contract.
- Only the architect named in the contract or his authorised representative can exercise any powers under the contract.
- If one architect takes over a contract from another, he cannot alter decisions of the previous architect with which he disagrees, but he should inform the employer.
- Matters reserved for the architect to decide cannot be delegated to another (eg, the quantity surveyor).
- Instructions must be clear and in writing.
- The architect may issue only those instructions which the contract specifically empowers him to issue.
- The architect must be aware of his specific powers and duties in the case of each instruction which he is empowered to issue.

Duties

- The architect must be as skilled as the average architect.
- He will be judged on any skill which he professes to possess over and above the average
- If items are stated to be to the architect's approval, he has a duty to approve each one.
- He has a duty to know the law as it affects him in the performance of his profession.
- He must know the law as it affects the contract.

Table 4.3
Certificates to be issued by the architect under IFC 84

Clause	Certificate
2.6	Certificate of non-completion
2.9	Certificate of practical completion
2.10	Certificate of making good defects
4.2	Interim certificates
4.3	Interim certificate on practical completion
4.6	Final certificate

5–The Contractor's Obligations

5.1 Express and Implied Obligations

5.1.1 Legal principles

Apart from the express terms of the contract, the general law requires that the contractor will do three things:

- The contractor must carry out his work in a good and workmanlike manner – ie, show the same degree of competence as the average contractor experienced in carrying out that type of work.
- The contractor will supply good and proper materials.
- The contractor must complete the work by the date for completion stated in the contract or, if no date is specified, within a "reasonable time" of his being given possession of the site.

These obligations may be modified by the terms of the contract itself. Under the general law, the contractor is also responsible to the employer for the work done, and goods and materials provided, by his sub-contractors and, in common with most standard form building contracts, under IFC 84 the contractor is responsible to the employer for all the defaults of a sub-contractor, whether named or otherwise. But in the case of named sub-contractors (see **section 8.2.2**), this liability is substantially modified by the very wide terms of clause 3.3.7, which exempts the contractor from responsibility to the employer for design and allied failures in the named sub-contractor's work. This apart, the position under IFC 84 is that the main contractor is liable to the employer for all other sub-contractors' defaults, of fabrication, workmanship, or otherwise.

Statutory obligations are also imposed on contractors by the Supply of Goods and Services Act 1982, although these statutory obligations are included in the express terms of IFC 84.

The contract must be read against this background. It imposes many specific duties on the contractor, some of which alter or affect the common law position. These obligations are scattered throughout the printed form, and only the more important of them are collected in this chapter.

Table 5.1 summarises the contractor's powers and duties under the express terms of the contract.

5.1.2 Execution of the works

Clause 1.1 requires the contractor to "carry out and complete the works in accordance with the contract documents", which are specified in the second recital; this is a basic and absolute obligation. It is not qualified in any way. The contractor must bring the works to a state where they are "practically completed" so that the architect can issue his certificate under clause 2.9. This is what the contractor must do, no matter what difficulties he may encounter, but subject to what is said in clause 7.8 about the determination of his employment under the contract for causes outside the control of either party.

The work must be carried out and completed "in accordance with" the contract documents as defined. It is the architect's responsibility to ensure that the description of the work is adequate, and care should be taken to use precise wording. Generalisations are impossible to enforce. The contract documents must contain all the requirements which the employer wishes to impose, and the use of phrases such as "of good quality" or "of a durable standard" should be avoided.

The contractor must complete all the work shown in, described by, or referred to in the contract documents. His obligation is ended only when the architect issues the certificate of practical completion. Thereafter the contractor must remedy defective work during and immediately after the specified defects liability period (see **section 9.3**).

The proviso to clause 1.1 states that if approval of workmanship or materials is a matter for the architect's opinion then the quality and standard must be to his reasonable satisfaction. The effect of this is discussed in **section 4.2.1**.

The basic contractual obligation is amplified by clause 2.1. Once he is given possession of the site, the contractor must begin and proceed "regularly and diligently" with the works and complete them on or before the specified completion date, as extended. Failure to proceed "regularly and diligently" is one of the grounds which may give rise to determination of his employment under the contract by the employer (see clause 7.1 (b)).

The trouble is that there is no generally accepted definition of "regularly and diligently" in this context, and the judges have not been able to come up with a clear-cut answer. According to one line of authority, merely "going slow" is not a breach of contract as such. It becomes a breach of contract only if there is ultimately a delay in completion. It is a question of fact whether the contractor is going ahead "regularly and diligently", and this is clearly to be judged by the standards to be expected of the average competent and experienced contractor.

Table 5.1
Contractor's powers and duties under IFC 84

Clause	Power/duty	Precondition/comment
1.1	**Duty** Carry out and complete the works in accordance with the contract documents	
1.6	**Power** Inspect the contract documents	At reasonable times: ie, during the employer's normal hours of business
1.8	**Duty** Use the specification/bills/schedules/ drawings/details only for the purpose of the contract	
1.11	**Duty** Use off-site goods and materials which have been paid for by the employer only for the works and not otherwise to remove them or permit their removal	
2.1	**Duty** Begin the works when given permission of the site **Duty** Regularly and diligently proceed with the works and complete them on or before the date for completion specified in the appendix **Power** Consent to the employer using or occupying the site or works before the issue of practical completion certificate **Duty** Notify insurers (6.3A, 6.3B or 6.3C) and obtain confirmation that use or occupation will not prejudice insurance. Notify employer of additional premium and provide him with premium receipts on request.	This is subject to the provisions for extension of time in clause 2.3 If insurers confirm that insurance will not be prejudiced, consent must not be unreasonably withheld If insurers have increased premium as condition of confirmation
2.3	**Duty** Notify the architect in writing forthwith of any cause of delay **Duty** Constantly use his best endeavours to prevent delay and do all that may reasonably be required	If it becomes reasonably apparent that progress of the works is being or is likely to be delayed. The duty is in respect of any cause of delay and is not confined to the events specified in clause 2.4 The second part of this duty does not require the contractor to spend substantial sums of money

Table 5.1 (continued)

Clause	Power/duty	Precondition/comment
	to the architect's satisfaction to proceed with the works **Duty** Provide the architect with sufficient information to enable him properly to exercise his duties as regards extensions of time	This is conditional on a request from the architect, and the information must be "reasonably necessary"
2.4.7	**Duty** Make specific written application to the architect for any necessary instructions, drawings, details, or levels	Failure to do so at the right time vitiates any claim for an extension of time on the ground of late instruction
2.7	**Duty** Pay or allow to the employer liquidated damages at the rate specified in the appendix	If the works are not completed by the specified or extended date for completion *and* If the architect has issued a certificate of non-completion under clause 2.6 *and* If the employer has required liquidated damaged in writing not later than date of final certificate for payment
2.10	**Duty** Make good any defects, shrinkages, or other faults at no cost to the employer	If the defects etc appear and are notified to the contractor by the architect not later than 14 days after expiry of the defects liability period *and* If they are due to materials or workmanship not in accordance with the contract or to frost occuring before practical completion *and* If the architect has not instructed otherwise
3.1	**Power** Assign the contract	If the employer gives consent in writing
3.2	**Power** Sub-contract any part of the works	If the architect consents in writing and subject to clause 3.3 below There are conditions which must be imposed in any ensuing sub-contract
3.3.1	**Duty** Enter into a sub-contract using section III of NAM/T with any	The person must be named in the specification/schedule of work/bills

Table 5.1 (continued)

Clause	Power/duty	Precondition/comment
	named person, not later than 21 days of entering into the main contract **Duty** Immediately inform the architect if unable so to enter into a sub-contract in accordance with the particulars given in the contract documents and specify which particulars have prevented the execution of the sub-contract **Duty** Notify the architect of the date of entering into a sub-contract with a named person	
3.3.2(c)	**Power** Make reasonable objection to entering into sub-contract with a named person	Must be made within 14 days of the architect's issuing a clause 3.8 instruction
3.3.3	**Duty** Advise the architect as soon as is reasonably practicable of any events which are likely to lead to the determination of the named person's employment under a sub-contract **Duty** Notify the architect in writing if the named person's employment is determined before completion of the sub-contract work, stating the circumstances	Whether or not the architect has already been advised of event likely to lead to determination
3.3.6(a)	**Duty** Take such reasonable action as is necessary to recover from the named sub-contractor any additional amount payable as a result of default or failure	Recovery is under clause 27.3.3 of the sub-contract NAM/SC The contractor is not required to commence arbitration proceedings or litigation unless the employer indemnifies him against legal costs
3.3.6(b)	**Duty** Account to the employer for amounts so recovered	
3.3.6(d)	**Duty** Repay to the employer any additional amounts involved	Only to the extent he has failed in his clause 3.3.6 duty
3.4	**Duty** Keep a competent person in charge of the works at all reasonable times	
3.5.1	**Duty** Forthwith carry out all written instructions issued by the architect	Provided the instruction is one which the contract empowers the

Table 5.1 (continued)

Clause	Power/duty	Precondition/comment
		architect to issue. The contractor has a right to make reasonable objection in writing to compliance with an instruction which modifies any obligations or restrictions imposed by the employer in the specification/schedule/bills about site access, limitations of working space/hours, or execution/completion of work in a specific order
3.5.2	**Power** Request the architect to specify in writing which contract clause empowers the issue of an instruction	When he receives an instruction
	Power Serve written request on employer to concur in the appointment of an arbitrator	If dissatisfied with architect's reply and not willing to comply
3.7	**Power** Agree with employer the adjustment to the contract sum in respect of variation instructions and of instructions on the expenditure of a provisional sum	Prior to contractor's complying with the instruction
3.9	**Duty** Set out the works accurately	Architect determines levels and provides contractor with accurately dimensioned drawings to enable this to be done
	Duty Amend at his own cost any errors arising from inaccurate setting out	The architect may instruct otherwise with employer's consent
3.11	**Duty** Permit the execution of work not forming part of the contract to be carried out by the employer or person employed or engaged by him concurrent with the contract works	If contract documents so provide
	Power Consent to the carrying out of such work by others	Where employer requests and contract documents do not so provide Consent must not be unreasonably withheld
3.12	**Duty** Bear cost of opening up and testing and consequential costs of making good	If inspection and test shows that materials, goods, or work are not in accordance with the contract

Table 5.1 (continued)

Clause	Power/duty	Precondition/comment
3.13.1	**Duty** State in writing to the architect the action which the contractor proposes to take immediately to establish that there is no similar failure of work, etc	Where such failure is discovered during the carrying out of the works
	Duty Forthwith comply with any architect's instruction requiring opening up for inspection and testing	Unless within 10 days of receipt of the instruction the contractor objects to compliance, stating his reasons in writing. Then, if within seven days of receipt of the contractor's objection the architect does not withdraw or modify his instructions in writing, the dispute or difference is referred to arbitration
4.5	**Duty** Not later than 6 months after practical completion send to the architect (or to the QS if the architect so instructs) all documents reasonably required for the purposes of the adjustment of the contract sum	
4.11	**Power** Make written application to the architect within a reasonable time	If it becomes apparent that regular progress is being materially affected by one or more of the specified matters or due to deferment of possession of the site by the employer
	Duty Submit to the architect or quantity surveyor such information as is reasonably necessary to enable an ascertainment of direct loss and/or expense to be made	
5.1	**Duty** Comply with, and give all notices required by any statute, statutory instrument, rule, order, regulation, or byelaw	As applicable to the works
	Duty Pay all fees and charges in respect of the works	The amount of such fees, etc, is added to the contract sum unless they are required by the specification/schedules of work/contract bills to be included in the contract sum

Table 5.1 (continued)

Clause	Power/duty	Precondition/comment
5.2	**Duty** Immediately give to the architect a written notice specifying any divergence between the statutory requirements and contract documents, or between such requirements and any architect's instruction	If the contractor finds any divergence
5.4.1	**Duty** Supply such limited materials and execute such limited work as are reasonably necessary to secure immediate compliance with statutory requirements	In an emergency (eg, a dangerous structure notice) and if it is necessary to do this prior to receipt of an instruction from the architect
5.4.2	**Duty** Forthwith inform the architect of such emergency compliance	
6.1.1	**Duty** Indemnify the employer against any expense, liability, loss, claim, or proceedings whatsoever in respect of personal injury to or death of any person	The claim must arise out of, or in the course of, or be caused by, the carrying out of the works and not be due to any act or neglect of the employer or any person for whom he is responsible
6.1.2	**Duty** Similarly indemnify the employer against property damage	If the claim arises out of or in the course of or is caused by reason of the carrying out of the works *and* Is due to any negligence, omission or default of the contractor, his servants or agents or that of any sub-contract, his servants or agents or any other person properly on the works except the employer, his men, local authority or statutory undertaking
6.2.1	**Duty** Maintain, and cause any sub-contractor to maintain, necessary insurances in respect of injury to persons or property	The obligation to maintain insurance is without prejudice to the contractor's liability to indemnify the employer
6.2.2	**Duty** Produce and cause any sub-contractor to produce, for the architect's inspection documentary evidence of insurance cover	When reasonably required to do so by the architect, who may (but not unreasonably or vexatiously) require production of the policy (policies) and premium receipts

Table 5.1 (continued)

Clause	Power/duty	Precondition/comment
6.2.4	**Duty** Maintain in joint names of employer and contractor for such amounts of indemnity as are specified in the contract documents for insurance against damage to property, other than the works, caused by collapse, subsidence etc	If stated in appendix that such insurance may be required and architect so instructs
6.3A.1 6.3A.2	**Duty** Take out and maintain all risks insurance in joint names against loss or damage to the works and unfixed goods **Duty** Deposit the policy (policies) and premium receipt with the employer	New buildings: the obligation continues until the date of issue of the certificates of practical completion. Clause 6.3A.3 enables this cover to be by means of the contractor's "all risks" policy
6.3A.4 6.3A.4.4	**Duty** Give written notice to architect and employer **Duty** with due diligence, restore work damaged, replace or repair any unfixed goods or materials which have been destroyed or damaged, remove and dispose of debris, and proceed with the carrying out and completion of the works **Duty** Authorise insurers to pay insurance monies to employer	Upon discovery of any loss or damage caused by risks covered by joint names policy After inspection by the insured in respect of any claim Acting also on behalf of sub-contractors to clause 6.3.3
6.3B	**Power** Require the employer to produce for inspection the insurance policy and last premium receipt **Power** Insure in joint names all work executed, etc, against all risks and have premium added to contract sum	Only where the employer is not a local authority If the employer defaults in taking out or maintaining the policy
6.3B.3.1 6.3B.3.3	**Duty** Forthwith notify the architect *and* the employer of the extent, nature, and location of any loss or damage affecting the works or any unfixed materials or goods **Duty** With due diligence, restore work damaged, replace or repair any unfixed goods or materials which have been destroyed or damaged,	The contractor must do this on discovering the loss or damage. Clause 6.3B covers new buildings where the employer insures against all risks in joint names After any inspection by the insurers in respect of the claim

Table 5.1 (continued)

Clause	Power/duty	Precondition/comment
	remove and dispose of debris, and proceed with the carrying out and completion of the works	
6.3B3.4	**Duty** Authorise insurers to pay insurance monies to employer	Acting also on behalf of sub-contractors recognised by clause 6.3.3
6.3C.3	**Power** Request employer to produce receipt showing that he has an effective policy under clauses 6.3C.1 and 6.3C.2	In existing structures unless employer is local authority
	Power Insure existing structures in joint names and for that purpose enter on the premises to make a survey and inventory	If employer fails to produce premium receipt when requested
6.3C.4	**Duty** Forthwith give written notice to the architect and the employer of the extent, nature, and location of any loss or damage	Upon discovering the loss or damage caused by risks covered by joint names policy
6.3C.4.2	**Duty** Authorise insurers to pay insurance monies to employer	Acting also on behalf of sub-contractors recognised by clause 6.3.3
6.3C.4.3	**Power** Serve notice determining his employment	If just and equitable so to do and be within 28 days of occurence of loss or damage
6.3C.4.4	**Duty** With all due diligence, reinstate and make good loss or damage and proceed with the carrying out and completion of the work	7 days notice must be given during which period either party may request arbitration If no notice of determination is served or if the arbitrator decides against the notice of determination
6.3D.1	**Power** Require information from the employer, via the architect	To obtain quotation under this clause
6.3D.1	**Duty** Send quotation to the architect	If appendix states that liquidated damages insurance may be required and the architect has so instructed If so instructed by the architect
	Forthwith take out and maintain the relevant policy, and send to architect for deposit with employer with premium receipts	

Table 5.1 (continued)

Clause	Power/duty	Precondition/comment
7.4	**Duty** Give up possession of the site of the works	In the event of determination by the employer under clauses 7.1, 7.2, or 7.3
	Duty Remove from the works any temporary buildings, plant, tools, equipment, goods, and materials belonging to, or hired by, the contractor	As and when so instructed in writing by the architect
7.5	**Power** Serve a default notice on the employer by registered post or recorded delivery, specifying the default alleged	If the employer: Does not pay an amount properly due to the contractor on any interim or final certificate: *or* interferes with or obstructs the issue of any certificate *or* the carrying out of the whole or substantially the whole of the uncompleted works (other than remedial works [defects liability]) is suspended for a continuous period of one month by reason of – Architect's instructions under 1.4 (Inconsistencies); 3.6 (Variations); 3.14 (Postponement) unless caused by contractor's neglect or default or that of those for whom he is responsible – Contractor not having received in due time necessary instructions etc from the architect for which he made specific written application at the right time – Delay in execution of work by employer himself or by others engaged or employed by him or failure to execute such work, or delay or failure in supply of materials or goods which the employer undertook so to supply – Failure by employer to give in due time ingress to or egress from the site if so agreed
	Power Determine his employment under the contract by written notice	If the employer continues his default for 14 days after receipt of

Table 5.1 (continued)

Clause	Power/duty	Precondition/comment
	served on the employer by registered post or recorded delivery	the default notice or thereafter repeats the same default The notice must not be given unreasonably or vexatiously
7.6	**Power** Determine his employment under the contract by written notice served on the employer by registered post or recorded delivery	If the employer becomes bankrupt or is insolvent, etc, or has a receiver appointed
7.8	**Power** Forthwith determine his employment under the contract by written notice served on the employer by registered post or recorded delivery	If the carrying out of the whole or substantially the whole of the uncompleted works (except work required under 2.1 defects liability) is suspended by reason of *force majeure* or loss or damage to the works occasioned by specified perils (unless caused by the negligence of the contractor or those for whom he is vicariously responsible); or civil commotion
7.9	**Duty** Remove from site with all reasonable dispatch all his temporary buildings, etc, and give facilities to his sub-contractors to do the same	
9.1	**Power** Give written notice to the employer	If contractor requires dispute to be settled by arbitration
9.7	**Power** Forthwith appoint another arbitrator jointly with employer	If arbitrator ceases to act

If the architect required the contractor to provide a programme, even though this is not a contract document, it is a standard against which the contractor's progress can be measured. The architect may require a contract programme by means of a clause in the bills, etc, and the contractor is entitled to submit a programme showing completion date earlier than the contract completion date, and may complete the works earlier than the contract date if he wishes, whether or not the works are programmed. However, there is no obligation on the architect to provide information, etc so as to enable the contractor to meet the earlier date: *Glenlion Construction Co Ltd* v *The Guinness Trust* (1987) 11 Con LR 126 is decisive of this question.

5.1.3 Workmanship and materials

The contract is strangely silent about the standards of workmanship and materials or even the skill and care to be expected of the contractor in the performance of his obligations. These matters must be deduced from the other contract documents and under the general law.

Certainly, he is expected to show a reasonable degree of competence and to employ skilled tradesmen and others, although the architect has no power to direct how he should carry out his work or to require him to replace employees whom he believes to be unsatisfactory.

The quality and quantity of work must be adequately defined in the contract documents, as is made plain by clause 1.2, the provisions of which are important in defining the contractor's obligations. In general, it may be said that any extra cost which results from faulty description in the contract documents falls on the employer. For example, if there is an inconsistency in the contract documents or an error of description, the architect must issue the appropriate instruction under clause 1.4.

Clause 1.2 should be studied carefully. Unlike JCT 80, IFC 84 makes no provision in the contract that the contractor is to provide materials, goods, and workmanship "so far as procurable", which would be a valuable protection to him.

The other contractual references to materials and goods are in clauses 1.10 and 1.11, which are concerned solely with the transfer of ownership in materials and goods. The statement in those provisions that "such materials and goods shall become the property of the employer" is misleading, as this is not necessarily the case. If the contractor is not the legal owner of the goods, he cannot pass title to the employer. In practice, this means that the architect needs to take great care before including the value of unfixed goods or materials or off-site items in any interim certificate unless the contractor provides him with proof of ownership (eg, a copy of his sale contract from the supplier). Many architects do not seem to appreciate the legal position.

5.1.4 Statutory obligations

Clause 5.1 places on the contractor an obligation to comply with all statutory obligations and to pay all fees and charges in respect of the works which are legally recoverable from him (eg, fees under the building regulations). Clause 5.2 also imposes on him an obligation to give the architect immediate written notice if he discovers any divergence between the contract documents or an architect's instructions and the statutory requirements.

Contractually, clause 5.3 exempts the contractor from liability to the employer if the works do not comply with statutory requirements provided he has carried the work out in accordance with the contract documents or any architect's instruction where, for example, he does not spot the divergence. The wording in clause 5.2 is "if the contractor finds any divergence . . .", and, unless he does so, he is under no obligation to notify the architect. This is clear and settled law: *London Borough of Merton v Stanley Hugh Leach* (1985) 32 BLR 51. However, whatever the position may be as between contractor and employer under the contract, the exempting provision cannot exempt the contractor from his duty to comply with the building regulations and other statutory obligations, liability under which may be absolute. But the wording is sufficiently wide to protect the contractor from any action by the employer, which leaves the architect in the firing line if the fault is his.

So far as fees and charges in connection with the works are concerned, these are to be added to the contract sum so that the contractor is reimbursed, although clause 5.1 establishes that the contract documents can require such fees and charges to be included in the tender sum. The reference to "rates and taxes" is interesting and is designed to cover those (comparatively rare) occasions when site huts and so on are rateable.

5.1.5 Person-in-charge

Clause 3.4 requires the contractor to keep on the works "a competent person-in-charge". He must do this at all reasonable times – ie, during normal working hours. This person is intended to be the contractor's full-time representative on site, but his appointment and replacement are not subject to the architect's approval.

"Competent" can only mean what it says – ie, having sufficient skill and knowledge – and the person-in-charge is the contractor's agent for the purpose of accepting the architect's written instructions, which are then *deemed* to have been issued to the contractor. If the person-in-charge is intended to be subject to approval by the architect this is a matter which can be dealt with in the contract documents.

5.1.6 Levels and setting out

Although it is the architect's duty to determine any levels which may be required for the execution of the works and to provide the contractor with accurately dimensioned drawings to enable him to set out, clause 3.9 obliges the contractor accurately to set out the work in accordance with the architect's instructions. He is made responsible for his own setting-out errors and must amend them at his own cost. Disputes may arise in this regard and **Figures 5.1** and **5.2** may be used by the contractor as appropriate. The sensible interpretation of the last sentence of clause 3.9 is that the architect may, with the employer's consent, instruct the contractor not to amend setting-out errors and make an appropriate adjustment to the contract sum, although exactly how this is to be assessed is not stated.

Figure 5.1
Contractor to architect if insufficient information on setting out drawings

Dear Sir,

[*Heading*]

We are preparing to commence work on site on [*insert date*]. Our first task will be to set out the works. An examination of the drawings you have supplied to us reveals that there is insufficient information for us to set out the works accurately. We enclose a copy of your drawing number [*insert number*] on which we have indicated in red the positions where we need dimensions/levels [*delete as appropriate*].

We need this information by [*insert date*] in order to avoid delay and disruption to the works.

Yours faithfully

Figure 5.2
Contractor to architect, requesting confirmation that setting out is correct

Dear Sir

[*Heading*]

We refer to our letter of the [*insert date*] in which we informed you that the information on your drawings was insufficient to enable us to set out the works accurately. You responded by telephone, asking us to set out the works to the best of our ability based on the information provided. We have carried out your instructions and we should be pleased to receive your confirmation that the setting out is correct. If we do not receive such confimation, in writing, by return of post, we shall be obliged to notify you of delay to the works and disruption for which we will seek appropriate financial recompense.

Yours faithfully

5.2 Other Obligations

5.2.1 Access to the works and premises

Unlike JCT 80, IFC 84 does not expressly provide that the architect or his representatives should have access to the works at all reasonable times. It is unnecessary for that right to be referred to expressly, because it is implied under the general law. But IFC 84 does contain a gap, because the architect also needs access to the workshops or other places of the contractor where work is being prepared for the contract. Where appropriate a special provision to this effect should be made in the contract documents, following the wording of JCT 80, clause 9, because it is probable that the general law would not give the architect that right of access.

5.2.2 Drawings, details and information

Clause 1.7 requires the architect to provide the contractor from time to time with further drawings, details, and information enabling him to carry out and complete the works, and failure to do this is a breach of contract for which the employer would in principle be liable in damages. But the contractor is also under contractual duty to make a written request for particular details or instructions. This is to be deduced from clause 2.4.7, which states that the contractor must have made a *specific* written application to the architect for any necessary instructions, drawings, details, or levels, "on a date which having regard to the date for completion stated in the appendix or any extended time then fixed was neither unreasonably distant from nor unreasonably close to the date on which it was necessary for him to receive the same".

This wording is very unfortunate, but it means that if the contractor does not apply at the right time he loses any right to an extension of time. The date of the contractor's written application must have regard to the date for completion. This is to be calculated in relation to the actual completion date and not to any earlier date by which the contractor hoped to complete. This view is based on recent case law. **Figure 5.3** is a suitable letter to the architect from the contractor.

Factors to be borne in mind include the state the works have reached and whether the contractor can act on the information; the nature of the instruction or information; any other of the contractor's activities which may depend on the supply of information (eg, pre-ordering of materials); and the time it may reasonably take for the architect to prepare the information.

5.2.3 Compliance with architect's instructions

The architect's authority to issue instructions is limited to those instructions which the contract empowers him to issue. Under clause 3.5.1, the contractor has an obligation to obey all written instructions given by the architect which are authorised by the contract (see **Figure 4.3**). The contractor can require the architect to state in writing the contract clause under which the instruction is given (clause 3.5.2): see **Figure 5.4**. He also has a right to object to instructions falling within clause 3.6.2,

Figure 5.3
Contractor to the architect requesting information

Dear Sir

We hereby apply for the following information required by us for the carrying out and completion of the works:
[*Description of Information*]   *Date required*

Joinery details of entrance screen
Colour schedule for internal paintwork
[*Etc*]

Alternative:
We hereby apply for the supply of [*state information required with supporting details showing why and when it is required*]

Yours faithfully

which is concerned with alterations or obligations or restrictions imposed by the employer in the contract documents. **Figure 5.5** is a suitable letter from the contractor.

The contractor must make "reasonable objection in writing", but no guidance is given as to what is a reasonable objection. It is clearly not a reasonable objection that it is difficult for the contractor to comply, because he is expected to overcome those difficulties, and questions of time and cost are dealt with under the contract. In fact, it seems that the instruction must make continued execution of the work almost impossible: eg, by preventing deliveries to site by further restricting access.

The general sanction for non-compliance by the contractor is set out in the second part of clause 3.5.1. Under that provision, where the architect has served the contractor with a written notice requiring compliance and the contractor has not complied within seven days, the employer may engage others to carry out the work and deduct the cost from monies due to the contractor. **Figure 5.6** shows the sort of letter that might be used.

It is essential that, if the contractor does not comply with an instruction, the architect ensures that the remedy provided by the clause is put into operation. If he does not, there is case law that suggests that the employer may then be taken to have waived his rights under the clause and, of course, the architect's notice of compliance may be regarded as becoming stale.

More effective sanctions are provided by clause 3.13.1 (instructions following failure of work, etc) which is a most useful provision (see **Figure 4.18**). It covers failure of work, materials, or goods discovered during the carrying out of the works. If the contractor discovers a failure of work or of materials or goods while the works are being carried out, he must notify the architect in writing immediately. "Upon such discovery (the contractor) shall state in writing to the architect the action which the contractor will *immediately* take at no cost to the employer to establish that there is no similar failure in work already executed or materials or goods already supplied", is what the clause says. This obligation extends to failures through the fault of any sub-contractor, named or otherwise. The clause goes on to deal with the architect's powers and empowers him to issue instructions requiring opening up of work, etc, in three cases:

- where he has not received the contractor's written statement within seven days of discovery of the failure; or
- if he is dissatisfied with the contractor's proposed action; or
- if he is unable to wait for the contractor's written proposals because of considerations of safety or statutory obligation (eg, service of a dangerous structure notice or a prohibition notice under the Health and Safety at Work etc Act 1974).

The architect's default powers are to issue appropriate instructions in writing, requiring the contractor, at his own cost, "to open up for inspection any work covered up or to arrange for or carry out any test of any materials or goods . . . or any executed work to establish that there is no similar failure and to make good in consequence thereof". The contractor is bound to comply *forthwith* with such instructions and, while clause 3.13.2 gives him the right to object, this is said to be "without prejudice to his obligation" to comply. In other words, even if the contractor disagrees with the architect, he must carry out the instruction.

Figure 5.4
Contractor to architect, requiring him to specify the clause empowering an instruction

Dear Sir

[*Heading*]

We have received today your instruction number [*insert number*], dated [*insert date*] requiring us to [*insert substance of instruction*].

We request you, in accordance with clause 3.5.2 of the conditions of contract, to specify in writing the provision which empowers the issue of the above instruction.

Yours faithfully

Figure 5.5
Contractor to architect, objecting to instruction varying obligations or restrictions

Dear Sir

[Heading]

Thank you for your instruction number [insert number], dated [insert date] which we received today. Your instruction required a variation within the meaning of clause 3.6.2.

We have reasonable objection to complying with your instruction in that [insert grounds of objection].

Our objection is submitted under the provisions of clause 3.5.1 and we should be pleased if you would withdraw or revise your instruction in the light of our comments.

[Add, if appropriate:]

Please let us have your reply by [insert date] in order to avoid the possibility of delay or disruption due to [insert as appropriate].

Yours faithfully

Figure 5.6
Architect to contractor if contractor fails to comply with notice

REGISTERED POST/RECORDED DELIVERY

Dear Sir

[Heading]

I refer to the notice issued to you on the [insert date] in accordance with clause 3.5.1 requiring compliance with my instruction number [insert number] dated [insert date].

During a site inspection this morning, I noted that you have not complied with my instruction. The employer is taking immediate steps to employ others to carry out the work. All costs in connection with such employment will de deducted from money due or to become due to you under the contract or will be recovered from you as a debt.

Yours faithfully

Copies: Employer
        Quantity surveyor

Within 10 days of *receipt* of the architect's instruction under clause 3.13.1, the contractor may object to compliance, stating his reasons in writing. The architect must then consider the objections immediately and decide whether to withdraw or modify the instruction to meet the contractor's objection. If he does not do so within seven days of receipt of the contractor's objection (and reasons), "then any dispute or difference as to whether the nature or extent of the opening up for inspection or testing instructed . . . was reasonable in all the circumstances" is referred to immediate arbitration. The arbitrator is given wide powers to deal with questions of both time and cost (see also **section 4.1.4**).

Figure 5.7 is a letter which the contractor might send to the architect after opening up work for inspection.

5.2.4 Other rights and obligations

Table 5.1 summarises the contractor's powers and duties generally. Other matters referred to in that table are dealt with in the appropriate chapters.

5.3 Summary

The contractor must:
- Carry out and complete the works in accordance with the contract documents.
- Proceed regularly and diligently with the works so as to complete in due time.
- Use workmanship and materials of an adequate standard.
- Comply with relevant statutory obligations.
- Obey architect's instructions as authorised by the contract.
- Appoint and keep on site a competent person-in-charge.

Figure 5.7
Contractor to architect, after work opened up for inspection

Dear Sir

[*Heading*]

We confirm that you inspected [*describe work*] opened up for your inspection in accordance with your instructions under clause 3.12 on [*insert date*] and found the materials, goods and work to be in accordance with the contract.

The cost of opening up and making good, therefore, is to be added to the contract sum and we will let you have details of our costs within the next few days. We will shortly send you details, particulars and estimate of the expected delay in completion of the works beyond the completion date and an application for reimbursement under the appropriate clause of the contract.

Yours faithfully

6–The Employer's Powers, Duties and Rights

6.1 Express and Implied Powers and Duties

Like those of the contractor, some of the employer's powers and duties arise from the express provisions of IFC 84 itself. These are set out in **Table 6.1**.

Others are imposed by the general law by way of implied terms. These are provisions which the law writes into every building contract and apply so far as they are not excluded or modified by the express terms of the contract itself. In practice, there are two important implied terms which are not affected by the contractual provisions.

6.1.1 Co-operation or non-interference

Under the general law, it is an implied term in every building contract that the employer will do all that it is reasonably necessary on his part to bring about completion of the contract. Conversely, it is implied that the employer will not so act as to prevent the contractor from completing in the time and in the manner envisaged by the agreement. Breach of either of these implied terms which results in loss to the contractor will give rise to a claim for damages at common law.

Equally, if the employer – either personally or through the agency of the architect or that of anyone else for whom he is responsible in law – hinders or prevents the contractor from completing in due time, not only is he in breach of contract, but conduct of this sort will also prevent him from enforcing the liquidated damages provision if any delay results.

The various cases put the duty in different ways, but in essence the position may be summarised as follows:
- The employer and his agents must do all things necessary to enable the contractor to carry out and complete the works expeditiously and in accordance with the contract.

- Neither the employer nor his agents will in any way hinder or prevent the contractor from carrying out and completing the works expeditiously and in accordance with the contract.

The scope of these implied obligations is very broad, and in recent years more and more claims for breach of them have been before arbitrators or the courts. The employer must not, for example, attempt to dictate to the architect how to exercise his discretion, nor must he attempt to give direct orders to the contractor. So important is the architect's independent role under the contract that, for example, it has been recently held that the architect is entitled to determine his engagement if the employer interferes with the granting of extensions of time under the contract. Similarly, he must see that the site is available for the contractor and that access to it is unimpeded by those for whom he is responsible. This is especially important in works to existing structures or tenanted buildings.

Some potential acts of hindrance or prevention by the employer are covered by express clauses in the contract, but there are a number of grey areas.

6.2 Rights

6.2.1 General

Although the contract is between the employer and the contractor – who are the only parties to it – an analysis of the contract clauses shows that the employer has few express rights of any substance.

The employer's major right is, of course, to have the completed works handed over to him in due time, properly completed in accordance with the contract documents. But his other rights are of importance as the contract proceeds.

6.2.2 Deferment of possession of the site

Clause 2.2 confers on the employer a right which he would not otherwise possess, namely the right to defer giving possession of the site to the contractor for a period up to six weeks (assuming that the appendix states that this provision is to apply). This is an important right in practice because, under the general law, failure to give the contractor sufficient possession to enable him to proceed with the works is a serious breach of contract.

This power will be especially helpful in renovation works, for example, although the normal intention must be that it is to be exercised sparingly, since if one has reached the contract stage, it is to be assumed that sufficient possession will be given to the contractor on the due date. Certainly, in the absence of such a provision, there would be no power to defer or postpone giving possession, and it would be necessary for the employer and the contractor to reach a separate agreement.

Table 6.1
Employer's power and duties under IFC 84

Clause	Power/duty	Precondition/comment
1.6	**Duty** Be custodian of the contract documents	Contract documents must be available for contractor's inspection at all reasonable times
1.8	**Duty** Not to divulge or use any of the contractor's rates and prices	Except for the purposes of the contract
2.1	**Duty** Give possession of the site to the contractor on the date for possession **Power** Defer giving possession of the site to the contractor for a limited period **Power** Use or occupy the site or the works before issue of practical completion certificate **Duty** Notify insurers under clause 6.3A or 6.3B or 6.3C.2 to .4 and obtain confirmation that use or occupation will not prejudice insurance	Where clause 2.2 is stated in the appendix to apply Deferment is for a period not to exceed stated period; usual maximum period is six weeks With contractor's written consent
2.7	**Power** Deduct liquidated damages for late completion	Architect must have issued a certificate of non-completion *and* employer must have required liquidated damages by writing to the contractor not later than the date of the final certificate
2.8	**Duty** Pay or repay liquidated damages to the contractor	Where the architect cancels his certificate of delay and grants a further extension of time after issuing it
2.10	**Power** Consent to contractor being paid to remedy defects or not make good defects	
3.1	**Power** Assign the contract	Only if the contractor consents in writing
3.3.1 & 3.3.4	**Power** Have a named person's work carried out by his employees or direct contractors under clause 3.11	Where contractor has been unable to sub-contract with the named person *and* the architect has

Table 6.1 (continued)

Clause	Power/duty	Precondition/comment
		instructed omission of the work or has so omitted it and substituted a provisional sum. Such instructions are valued as a variation and give rise to a contractor's claim for both extension of time and loss and/or expense
3.3.6	**Power** Indemnify the contractor against legal costs	If the employer requires the contractor to commence legal or arbitral proceedings against a defaulting named person
3.5	**Power** Employ and pay other persons to execute work	If the contractor does not comply within seven days of the receipt of a written notice from the architect requiring compliance with an instruction
3.7	**Power** Agree with the contractor the amount of an adjustment to the contract sum	In respect of variation or provisional sum instructions, and before the contractor complies therewith
3.9	**Power** Consent to the architect instructing the contractor that setting out errors be not amended	An appropriate deduction is to be made to the contract sum
3.10	**Power** Appoint a clerk of works to act as an inspector under the directions of the architect	
3.11	**Power** Require work not forming part of the contract to be carried out by himself or by persons employed or engaged by him	Where the contract documents so provide, *or* with the contractor's consent
3.13	**Duty** Pay the contractor any amount awarded by the arbitrator in respect of compliance with architect's instructions following failure of work, etc	If the contractor has objected in writing to compliance with reasons, and the architect has not withdrawn or modified his instruction, and the matter has been pursued to arbitration
4.2	**Duty** Pay to the contractor the amount certified within 14 days of the date of the certificate	If the architect issues an interim certificate under clause 4.2

Table 6.1 (continued)

Clause	Power/duty	Precondition/comment
4.3	**Duty** Pay to the contractor the amount certified within 14 days of the date of the certificate	If the architect issues an interim certificate under clause 4.3. On practical completion, a further interim payment to bring the amount to 97½% is made
4.4	**Power** To have recourse to the percentage retained from time to time for payment of any amount to which he is entitled under the contract provisions to deduct from sums due, or to become due, to the contractor	Where the employer is not a local authority
4.6	**Duty** Pay to the contractor the amount certified within 28 days after the date of the final certificate	Subject to any amounts properly deductible
5.5	**Duty** Pay to the contractor any VAT properly chargeable	
6.2.2	**Power** Require documentary evidence of insurance	Where a provisional sum is included in the contract documents and the contractor has made default in insuring or in continuing to insure
6.2.3	**Power** Insure and deduct premium amounts from monies due to contractor or recover them as a debt	If the contractor fails to insure against personal injury or death or injury to property
6.2.4	**Power** Approve insurers **Power** Insure against damage to property other than the works	For instance against damage to property other than the works – employer's liability If the contractor fails to insure
6.3.3	**Duty** Ensure that joint names policies referred to in clause 6.3A.1 or 6.3A.3 or 6.3B.1 or 6.3C.1 and 6.3C2: *either* ● provide for recognition of each named person or sub-contrator as insured; *or* ● include insurers' waiver of rights of subrogation	If clause 6.3B or 6.3C applies In respect of specified perils

Table 6.1 (continued)

Clause	Power/duty	Precondition/comment
6.3A.2	**Power** Approve insurers Insure against all risks and deduct sums from monies due or recover them as a debt	In regard to insurance against all risks to be taken out by the contractor If contractor fails to insure
6.3A.3.1	**Power** Inspect documentary evidence or the policy	If the contractor maintains a policy independently of his obligations under the contract and it is in joint names
6.3A.4.4	**Duty** Pay insurance money to contractor	Less only a percentage to cover professional fees if any
6.3B.1	**Duty** Maintain insurance against all risks Produce premium receipts to the contractor on request	In joint names Unless the employer is a local authority
6.3C.1	**Duty** Maintain insurance against specified perils for existing structures	In joint names
6.3C.2	**Duty** Maintain insurance against all risks for the works of alteration or extension	In joint names
6.3C.3	**Duty** Produce insurance receipts	If the contractor so requests unless employer is a local authority
6.3C.4.3	**Power** Determine the contractor's employment	Within 28 days of clause 6.3C.4 loss or damage It must be just and equitable to do so; and 7 days notice must be given during which time either party may request arbitration
6.3D.1	**Power** Require the contractor to accept the quotation in respect of liquidated damages insurance	Architect must so instruct
7.1	**Power** Serve written notice on the contractor by registered post or recorded delivery specifying a default	If the contractor without reasonable cause wholly suspends the carrying out of the works before completion *or* fails to proceed regularly and diligently with the works; *or* refuses or persistently neglects to comply with a written notice from the

Table 6.1 (continued)

Clause	Power/duty	Precondition/comment
	Power Determine the contractor's employment by written notice served by registered post or recorded delivery	architect requiring him to remove defective work or improper materials or goods and by such refusal or neglect the works are materially affected; *or* fails to comply with clauses 3.2 (sub-contracting) or 3.3 (named persons). The notice must not be given unreasonably or vexatiously. It can be served only if the contractor continues his default for 14 days after receipt of the preliminary notice or if at any time thereafter he repeats that default
7.2	**Power** Reinstate the contractor's employment in agreement with the contract and his trustees (in bankruptcy), liquidator, etc	Where the contractor has become insolvent, etc, his employment is determined automatically
7.3	**Power** Determine the contractor's employment under this or any other contract	Where the employer is a local authority and the contractor is guilty of corrupt practices. No procedure is prescribed, but determination should be effected by written notice
7.4	**Duty** Pay to the contractor any amount due to him after completion of the works by others	
7.7	**Duty** Pay to the contractor the total value of work at the date of determination; sums ascertained as direct loss and/or expense under clause 4.10; the cost of materials or goods properly ordered for the works for which the contractor has paid or is legally bound to pay; the reasonable cost of removal from site of all temporary buildings, plant, tools, equipment, etc; and any direct loss and/or damage caused to the contractor by the determination	Where the contractor has determined his own employment for the employer's default or insolvency under clauses 7.5 or 7.6 Amounts previously paid are taken into account Direct loss and/or damage will include the contractor's loss of profit
7.8	**Power** Forthwith determine the contractor's employment by written	Where the carrying out of the whole or substantially the whole of the

Table 6.1 (continued)

Clause	Power/duty	Precondition/comment
	notice served by registered post or recorded delivery	uncompleted works is suspended for three months by reason of *force majeure*, or loss or damage caused by clause 6.3 perils (eg, fire), *or* civil commotion The notice must not be given unreasonably or vexatiously
7.9	**Duty** Pay to the contractor the total value of work at the date of determination; any sum ascertained as direct loss and/or expense under clause 4.10; the cost of materials or goods properly ordered for the works for which the contractor has paid or is legally bound to pay; the reasonable cost of removal from site of all temporary buildings, plant, tools, equipment, etc	Amounts previously paid are taken into account
9.1	**Power** Give written notice to the contractor	If the employer requires a dispute to be referred to arbitration
9.7	**Power** Together with the contractor, forthwith appoint another arbitrator	If the arbitrator ceases to act

6.2.3 Deduction/repayment of liquidated damages

If the contractor is late in completing the works, then – provided the architect has issued a certificate of non-completion under clause 2.6 – the employer is entitled to recover liquidated damages at the rate specified in the appendix. This is usually done by deduction from sums due to the contractor (eg, under interim certificates), but if (unusually) no sums are due to the contractor, then the employer must sue for them as a debt.

There is a further precondition to deduction or recovery. Clause 2.7 makes it plain that payment of liquidated damages is not obligatory. The mere fact of late completion and the issue of the clause 2.6 certificate is not sufficient. The employer must give notice to the contractor, before the issue of the final certificate, of his intention to exercise his discretion to claim or deduct liquidated damages, because he is required to indicate to the contractor whether he wants them allowed or to be paid.

Figure 6.1 is a suitable letter from the employer to the contractor requiring liquidated damages. Since liquidated damages have been held by the Court of Appeal to be exhaustive of the employer's rights for the breach of late completion, it is clear that the employer cannot recover ordinary unliquidated damages for late completion if he has not exercised his right to deduct or has failed to give the requisite notice to the contractor.

If for some reason the liquidated damages clause fails – for example, if the employer causes delay to completion for which no extension of time is grantable or grantable under the contract or for some technical reason – the employer can then recover general damages by way of arbitration or litigation, subject to proof of actual loss. It may be that the amount so recoverable will be held to be limited to the amount of the failed liquidated damages clause.

The employer must repay any liquidated damages which he has recovered should the architect cancel a clause 2.6 certificate and grant a further extension of time. Undoubtedly, contractors will argue that any damages so repaid should attract interest, and many ingenious arguments are likely to be advanced to support the contention, notably with reference to a decision of the High Court of Northern Ireland. Specialist practitioners are generally agreed that, even if correct on its facts, that decision is not good law generally – and it certainly has no application to IFC 84. If interest was payable , this would be stated in clause 2.7. Should the contractor advance such an argument, **Figure 6.2** is the sort of reply which the employer might send.

The architect has nothing to do with the deduction or enforcement of liquidated damages.

If the architect purports to deduct liquidated damages, **Figure 6.3** is the sort of letter a contractor might send. **Figure 6.4** is a letter from a contractor to an employer who has wrongfully deducted liquidated damages.

Figure 6.1
Employer to contractor, regarding deduction of liquidated damages

REGISTERED POST/RECORDED DELIVERY

Dear Sir

[*Heading*]

The architect having issued his certificate of non-completion under clause 2.6 of the above contract, certifying that you have failed to complete the works by [*insert date as certified*], in accordance with clause 2.7 of the contract, I hereby require that you pay or allow liquidated damages at the rate of £[*insert amount*] for every week or part of a week during which the works remain uncompleted/have remained uncompleted [*omit as appropriate*].

Yours faithfully

Figure 6.2
Employer to contractor if contractor claims interest on liquidated damages repaid

Dear Sir

[*Heading*]

Thank you for your letter of [*insert date*] (addressed to the architect, Mr/Messrs [*insert name*]) in which you claim that you are entitled to interest on the liquidated damages repaid/which will be repaid [*omit as appropriate*] to you as a result of the architect's cancelling the current/original [*omit as appropriate*] clause 2.6 certificate.

I/we formally deny that you are entitled to the interest claimed or to any interest at all. The contract makes no provision for the payment of interest in these circumstances, and interest is not recoverable under the general law.

Yours faithfully

6.2.4 Employment of direct contractors

Clause 3.11 is an important provision, since under it the employer has the right – if the contract documents so provide – to carry out himself or have carried out by others "work not forming part of this contract". The contractor is obliged to permit this work to be executed while the contract works are in progress, provided that reference is made to it in the contract documents. If no such reference is made, the employer can still have such work carried out with consent of the contractor, which must not be unreasonably withheld.

This is an important right which the employer certainly would not have at common law, since, as explained in **Chapter 9,** the contractor is in principle entitled to exclusive possession of the site during the currency of the contract. But the limitations of the provision must be noted.

● It applies only to work "not forming part of this contract" and cannot be used to take away from the contractor work which is his.

This is subject to the limited provision in clauses 3.3.1 and 3.3.4 in relation to the work of named sub-contractors where the contractor has, for good reason, been unable to enter into a sub-contract with the person named and the architect has either instructed its omission or omitted the work from the contract documents and substituted a provisional sum. In either event, the contractor is entitled to extension of both time and money.

The fundamental principle is that a clause of this sort cannot in general be used to omit contract work to give to others, because the contractor has agreed to do a certain quantity of work and has a right to do it. But a provision in terms of clause 3.11 – sometimes called an "Epstein clause" – does enable the employer to carry out work himself while the contract is in progress – eg, through his own direct works department – or to have similar work carried out by others.

The words "not forming part of this contract" mean exactly what they say. It is not work which the employer can require the contractor to do, and it is important to get ths matter clear because of the implications in time and cost. Under clauses 2.4.8 and 4.12.2, the contractor is entitled to both extension of time for any consequent delay and also to a loss and/or expense claim. Statutory undertakers – water boards, gas boards, and the like – may fall under this clause if they are in a direct contract with the employer, but not where they are carrying out work "in pursuance of (their) statutory obligations".

The employer's power directly to employ and pay others to execute the work (clause 3.5) where the contractor has failed to comply with your notice requiring compliance with an instruction does not fall under clause 3.11.

The use of clause 3.11 may be one method of avoiding some of the difficulties thrown up by clause 3.3 with regard to named sub-contractors, since by careful forethought, specialist work can be made the subject of direct employment by the employer; in that case, the employer is solely responsible for the acts or defaults of such sub-contractors and has no action against the contractor, whether for insurance purposes or otherwise.

Figure 6.3
Contractor to architect who wrongfully deducts liquidated damages

Dear Sir

[*Heading*]

We have received a copy of your certificate number [*insert number*] in which you purport to deduct the sum of £x as liquidated and ascertained damages.

This deduction is improper because under the terms of clause 2.7 it is for the employer to deduct liquidated damages and as architect you have no power to do so. In any event, you have not issued a certificate of non-completion under clause 2.6 and so any purported deduction by the employer would also be wrongful. Will you please issue an amended certificate in proper form.

Yours faithfully

Figure 6.4
Contractor to employer where liquidated damages wrongfully deducted

Dear Sir

[*Heading*]

Thank you for your cheque in the sum of £[*insert amount*] in respect of the payment due to us under certificate number [*insert number*]. Your cheque falls short of the sum certified as due to us by £[*insert amount*] and we note that this deduction is purportedly made in respect of liquidated and ascertained damages of £[*insert amount*] for [*insert number*] weeks.

We are advised that this deduction is a breach of contract on your part because [*state reasons, eg the architect has not certified that there is a delay in completion*] and we look forward to receiving your cheque for £[*insert amount*] being the balance due to us.

Failing receipt of that sum within seven days from today's date we shall instruct our solicitors to commence proceedings against you for the recovery of this amount together with interest and costs. We also reserve the right to determine our employment under clause 7.5 of the Contract.

Yours faithfully

6.2.5 Rights as to insurance

The complex insurance clauses of IFC 84 were discussed in **Chapter 3,** but the employer's rights relating to insurance should be noted.

Clause 6.2.3 gives the employer a default power to insure or maintain policies in force where the contractor (or any sub-contractor of his) fails to do so and to recoup himself out of the monies due or to become due to the contractor. A provisional sum for the insurance must have been included in the contract documents if he is to rely on this provision.

Clause 6.3C – Special power of determination (see **section 12.1.6**): the power to determine the contractor's employment can be exercised only if it is just and equitable so to do – a matter which the arbitrator may have some difficulty in deciding.

The employer's other contractual rights are summarised in **Table 6.1,** where they are described as ''powers''. They are discussed in the appropriate chapters.

6.3 Duties

6.3.1 General

The essence of a duty is that it must be carried out. It is not permissive but mandatory, and breach of a duty imposed by the contract will render the employer liable in damages to the contractor for any proven loss.

Not every breach of a contractual duty will entitle the contractor to treat the contract as being at an end: only breach of a provision which goes to the root or basis of the contract will do that. But a breach of any contractual duty will always, in theory, entitle the contractor to at least nominal damages, although in many cases any loss will be difficult if not impossible to quantify.

6.3.2 Payment

From the contractor's point of view, the most fundamental duty of the employer is to make payment in accordance with the terms of the contract. However, while steady payment of certificates is essential from the contractor's point of view, the general law does not regard failure to pay, or to pay on time, as a major breach of contract. Repeated failure by the employer to pay the amounts certified by the architect might, however, constitute a repudiatory breach of contract: *D. R. Bradley (Cable Jointing) Ltd* v *Jefco Mechanical Services* (1988) 6 – CLD – 07 – 1.

IFC 84 is quite specific about payment (see **Chapter 11**). The basic provisions are contained in clauses 4.2 and 4.3 (interim payments) and clause 4.6 (final payment), although the contractor's remedies for non-payment of an interim certificate are limited. He can, of course, sue on the certificate once payment is due, but he is not entitled to interest on the overdue sum. He certainly has no right to suspend work, although, in an extreme case and after going through the specified procedure, he has the right to determine his employment under clause 7.5.1 as there set out (see **Chapter 12).**

Once the architect has issued his interim certificate (clauses 4.2 and 4.3), the employer is given a period of grace before he need honour the certificate. He must make payment within 14 days of the date of the certificate, which means payment before the expiry of that period. If the certificate is sent to the employer by post, then effectively he has 13 days for paying the amount due – assuming, of course, that the certificate is delivered the next day.

Payment by cheque is probably good payment, although some contractors have been known to argue to the contrary under other forms of contract. It is not permitted for the employer to say, for example, that his computer arrangements do not fit in with the scheme of certificates. If this is so, then the payment period should have been amended before the contract was let.

For the final payment (clause 4.6), the period of grace is 21 days, since the last sentence refers to the certified amount being a debt payable "as from the twenty-first day after the date of the final certificate". By the terms of the contract, the employer is entitled to deduct from both interim and final certificates certain specific and ascertained sums – notably, liquidated and ascertained damages under clause 4.7.

The contract also contains other express provisions empowering deductions. These are clause 3.5.1 – costs incurred in employing others to give effect to an architect's instruction; clause 6.2.3 – insurance premiums paid on contractor's default; clause 6.3A.2 – insurance premiums similarly paid; clause 7.4 – payments on determination of employment; supplemental condition B – VAT payments as specified therein.

Despite the clear provisions of the contract, contractors sometimes find it difficult to secure payment. A common situation is that the employer pays less than the amount certified by deducting sums to which he is not entitled. **Figure 6.5** is a pro forma for use by the contractor in such circumstances.

6.3.3 Retention

The employer has certain rights in the retention percentage. The retention monies are a trust fund except where the employer is a local authority, as is manifest by the wording of clause 4.4 which reads as follows. "Where the employer is not a local authority the employer's interest in the [*retention percentage*] shall be fiduciary as trustee for the contractor (but without obligation to invest) and the contractor's beneficial interest therein shall be subject only to the right of the employer to have recourse thereto from time to time for payment of any amount which he is entitled under the provisions of this contract to deduct from any sum due or to become due to the contractor".

The deductions which the employer may make from the percentage retained are those referred to in **section 6.3.2**. Since the retention money is trust money, it is not the employer's property – hence the need to confer on him the contractual right to deduct from it. This apart, the employer has no legal or other interest in the retention

Figure 6.5
Contractor to employer where payment not made in full

REGISTERED POST/RECORDED DELIVERY

Dear Sir

[*Heading*]

We have received your cheque for £[*insert amount*] which is £[*insert amount*] less than the sum certified as due to us by the architect in certificate number [*insert number*]. In your accompanying letter you state that you are withholding the balance because [*state reasons given by employer*].

The contract does not permit you to make this deduction and your action in doing so amounts to a breach of contract. If we do not receive the sum of £[*insert amount*], being the balance due to us, within seven days from the date of this letter, we must regretfully invoke our contractual rights and will instruct our solicitors to institute proceedings against you.

Yours faithfully

and the court can order him – on the contractor's application – to set the percentage withheld aside in a separate bank account. Although there is no express contractual provision requiring the employer to put the monies aside in a separate bank account, it is suggested that he can be required to do so and **Figure 6.6** may be utilised: see *Rayack Construction Ltd* v *Lampeter Meat Co Ltd* (1979) 12 BLR 30. Nothing is said about whether the contractor is entitled to interest on the percentage withheld, and it has been convincingly argued about a similarly worded clause that he is entitled to interest since the employer is in the position of a trustee of the money.

6.3.4 Other duties

These are summarised in **Table 6.1** and are commented on as necessary in appropriate chapters.

6.4 Summary

The employer is under a duty in common law to do all that is reasonably necessary to bring about completion of the contract. Under the contract, the employer has a right to:
- defer giving possession of the site to the contractor for a maximum period of 6 weeks;
- recover liquidated damages for late completion;
- employ direct contractors to carry out works "not forming part of the contract";
- insure in default of the contractor so doing.

The employer must as a duty:
- pay the contractor in accordance with the contract terms;
- observe all the contract provisions.

Figure 6.6
Contractor to the employer requesting that retention money be placed in separate bank account – private employer only

Dear Sir

[*Heading*]

As you are aware, clause 4.4 of the Contract provides that the retention money is trust money to which we are beneficially entitled.

We formally request you to place all retention money in the next and future interim certificates in a separate bank account set up for that purpose, and designated as a trust account. Please inform us of the name and address of the bank, the designation of the account and its number.

Yours faithfully

7–The Clerk of Works

7.1 Appointment

The appointment of a clerk of works is a matter for the employer acting on the advice of the architect. One should certainly be appointed where the nature of the work demands constant or frequent inspections, and it is normal practice for the clerk of works to be appointed directly by the employer. Some organisations have their own clerks of works on their permanent staff. A few firms of architects employ clerks of works directly, but in light of the case law it is inadvisable for the clerk of works to be the employee of the architect.

Whether a clerk of works is necessary on a full-time or part-time basis or at all is a matter about which the architect must decide and advise the employer at tender stage. Where the architect's contract with the employer incorporates the *Architect's Appointment*, clause 3.10 of that document makes it clear that the architect is not required to make frequent or constant inspections. If that service is needed, then clause 3.11 states that a clerk of works will be employed. He is best appointed as soon as the contract is made.

7.2 Duties

The duties of the clerk of works are set out in the contract, clause 3.10: "The Employer shall be entitled to appoint a clerk of works whose duty shall be to act solely as an inspector on behalf of the Employer under the directions of the Architect". The contract makes no other reference to him. He is not given any power to issue even directions (as in JCT 80). His only function is to inspect, ie to examine closely for faults or errors. He is the architect's eyes and ears on site, but the contract makes it clear that he carries out his functions as inspector on behalf of the employer and not on that of the architect.

Since he may only inspect, the subject of any directions from the architect must, presumably, be how and where he should inspect, and to what he should pay particular attention. Although it is traditional for the architect to give directions to the clerk of works in a fairly informal manner, he should always be given written confirmation of any directions which are other than routine. It is generally accepted, by architects, contractors and clerks of works alike, that the clerk of works will do more than simply inspect. For example, the architect will often ask him to take measurements or levels on his behalf, and the contractor may rely on him to solve minor problems on site. It must be understood, however, that the contract recognises none of this.

If the clerk of works issues any instructions or directions to the contractor, these should be ignored. If a contractor complies with an instruction given by the clerk of works and is involved in extra cost, he cannot claim reimbursement. Problems between contractors and clerks of works are not uncommon as some clerks of works appear unaware of the limited nature of their duties and rights. The clerk of works may, of course, make some quite useful suggestions to both architect and contractor. He may provide a valuable service by spotting mistakes on drawings, and a competent and experienced clerk of works can generally assist in the smooth running of the contract.

From the outset, however, it is essential that everyone fully understands the clerk of works' role and this is a matter best dealt with at the first site meeting and clearly recorded in the minutes. The Institute of Clerks of Works consider that the contractual provisions are inadequate and sometimes clause 3.10 is amended on the architect's advice. The provision should be left exactly as it stands or else made much more comprehensive – and any amendment should only be undertaken after obtaining specialist legal advice.

Irregularities do occur. It is, for example, a common practice, for the clerk of works to make marks in chalk or wax crayon to indicate defects. It has been known for a clerk of works to deliberately deface unsatisfactory materials and goods to ensure that they are not incorporated or, if already incorporated, to ensure that they are replaced. The clerk of works is not entitled to take this kind of action. If he does, the employer could find himself facing a large bill from the contractor. The clerk of works would probably argue that he cannot possibly do harm to something that is already defective. He should remember that defective materials are not, by definition, the property of the employer and that a contractor may, and usually does, find another use for them elsewhere.

It is also bad practice for the clerk of works to get into the habit of putting specific marks on work or materials. For the same reason, he should not issue what are usually termed "snagging lists". The clerk of works is on site for the benefit of the employer whose inspector he is. Naturally, he must point out major defects and draw attention to bad materials and so on. Similarly, he must draw the contractor's attention to the host of minor defects which are often present. But being more specific has two dangers. One danger from the employer's point of view is that the contractor may consider that, if he rectifies everything on a clerk of works' list, he has fulfilled his contractual obligations. That is not what the contract says but dispute, however misguided, may follow. The second is that by acting in this way the clerk of works is doing the job which properly belongs to the person in charge.

Figures 7.1 and 7.2 may be used by a contractor as a basis for dealing with two common problem situations.

7.3 Responsibility

The clerk of works has a responsibility to carry out his duties in a competent manner. He is expected to show the same degree of skill as would be shown by the average clerk of works. If he holds himself out as being specially qualified in some branch of the industry, greater skill will be expected of him in that respect.

In spite of the reliance placed on the clerk of works by both employer and architect, until fairly recently the legal position was not clear and there was very little case law authority as to whether the appointment of a clerk of works reduced the architect's responsibility as to supervision. It is now settled that where the clerk of works is employed by the employer, the employer is vicariously responsible for his actions. This is so even though the clerk of works is acting under the directions of the architect. This has an important practical consequence should the work be supervised negligently and a claim is made by the employer against the architect. Although the employment of a clerk of works does not reduce the architect's liability to use reasonable skill and care to ensure conformity with design, if the clerk of works is also guilty of negligent supervision, this will amount to contributory negligence for which the employer is responsible and thus reduce the extent of the negligent architect's financial liability to the employer: *Kensington & Chelsea & Westminster Area Health Authority* v *Wettern Composites* (1984) 1 Con LR 114.

7.4. Summary

- The clerk of works should be appointed by the employer.
- He will be necessary if frequent or constant inspections are required.
- He should be appointed immediately after the successful tender has been accepted.
- He should be thoroughly briefed by the architect.
- He is purely an inspector and cannot give instructions or directions to the contractor.
- He is not entitled to deface or put any mark on the contractor's work or materials.
- He must carry out his duties competently.
- The employer is vicariously responsible for any negligence by him.

Figure 7.1
Contractor to architect where clerk of works issues instructions or directions to contractor

Dear Sir,

[Heading]

The clerk of works has directed us to [specify] or The clerk of works has issued what he describes as an instruction requiring us to [specify], a copy of which is enclosed. As you are aware, such a direction or instruction has no contractual effect and we are not acting upon it. We accept that as inspector the clerk of works is bound to point out to us any defects in workmanship or materials, but we are only contractually obliged to act on instructions issued by you.

We are, however, anxious to avoid any misunderstandings, and in this spirit we suggest that you ask the clerk of works to issue no further directions or instructions. Instead, perhaps you can instruct him to refer any alleged difficulties to you by telephone so that, in your discretion, a proper architect's instruction can be issued.

Yours faithfully

Figure 7.2
Contractor to architect if clerk of works defaces work or materials

Dear Sir,

[*Heading*]

We regret to inform you that the clerk of works has today defaced [*specify*] on the basis that he considers the materials used defective. He has told us that he did so in order to bring the matter to our attention and to ensure that the materials are removed forthwith.

We object to this practice on two grounds:

1. The work or materials so marked may not be defective and we will be involved in extra work and the employer in extra costs in such circumstances.

2. The defaced work or materials, if indeed they are defective, have not been paid for and will be our property if they are removed. Defacement by the clerk of works prevents our re-using such materials if, indeed, they are defective.

We shall be glad if you will instruct the clerk of works to desist from this sort of action. If the practice continues, we will seek reimbursement from the employer for the costs involved.

Yours faithfully

8–Sub-Contractors and Suppliers

8.1 General

This chapter deals with the contract provisions for sub-contractors, suppliers, statutory authorities, and persons engaged by the employer to carry out work not forming part of the contract.

There are no provisions in IFC 84 for nominating sub-contractors or suppliers. Provision is made for the employer to name persons to carry out work priced in the contract documents or included as a provisional sum (see **section 8.2**). There are no similar provisions for suppliers.

8.2 Sub-contractors

8.2.1 Assignment and sub-contracting

IFC 84 contains the usual restriction (clause 3.1) on the assignment of the contract by either party without the written consent of the other. Without this express term, it would be possible for either party to assign the *benefits* of the contract to another. For example, the contractor might wish to assign to a third party the benefit of receiving payments under interim certificates, in return for which the third party would give the contractor financial advances to enable him to carry out the work; this is a well known procedure. Or the employer might wish to sell the building before the issue of the final certificate or even when the structure was only partly completed. Even without the express term, it is a matter of general law that the *burden* of a contract cannot be assigned without the consent of the other party. For example, the contractor cannot transfer to another the burden of carrying out the work and the employer cannot pass to another his obligation to pay the contract sum.

There are very real difficulties for both parties in this clause, since the party withholding consent is not required to be reasonable in doing so. The architect should warn the employer and seek his instructions on amending the clause if he is likely to want to assign his benefit before the time for issuing the final certificate.

In contrast, if the contractor wishes to sublet any part of the works, the architect must not withhold his consent unreasonably. The contractor does not have to inform the architect of the name of the sub-contractor but the architect would probably be reasonable in withholding his consent if the contractor did not do so (clause 3.2). A suitable letter for the contractor to write is **Figure 8.1.** In view of recent case law (*Scott Lithgow* v *Secretary of State for Defence* (1989) 45 BLR 1), the architect should make his consent conditional upon the contractor acknowledging liability for his sub-contractors (**Figure 8.2**). There is a proviso (clause 3.2.1) that the sub-contract must provide for the employment of any sub-contractor to determine immediately on the determination of the contractor's employment for whatever reason. This is a perfectly sensible provision to prevent the situation arising in which the contractor's employment is determined and the sub-contractor is able to sue the contractor because he is prevented from carrying out the sub-contract. It must be remembered that the provisions of a contract cannot bind anyone who is not a party to it. Therefore, this clause places the onus on the contractor to ensure that an appropriate term is included in the sub-contract.

The employer has no contractual relationship with the sub-contractor, and the contractor must bear liability for any defects in the sub-contractor's work. The employer will look to the contractor for redress in such circumstances. The contractor must, in turn, look to the sub-contractor. Any dispute, difficulty, or difference arising between contractor and sub-contractor is a matter solely for the parties involved. The architect should be aware of being drawn into such disputes. Clause 3.2.2 sets out certain provisions which the contractor must ensure are included in any sub-contract. It would not be unreasonable if the architect made his consent to sub-letting subject to the contractor's providing documentary evidence that these provisions are to be included, because contractors commonly sub-contract on their own terms. They relate to the ownership of unfixed materials on site. The intention is to prevent the sub-contractor from reclaiming goods delivered to site which have already been paid for by the employer under the architect's certificate. Subsection (a) of the clause requires the contractor's consent to the sub-contractor's removing such materials from site, and this subsection is made subject to main contract clause 1.10 which requires the architect's consent (see **section 4.2.1**). Effectively, therefore, the sub-contractor requires the architect's consent through the contractor, before unfixed materials can be moved. The consents must not be withheld unreasonably.

Subsection (b) provides that the materials will become the property of the employer if he pays the contractor under a certificate which includes the value of such materials. The sub-contractor is not to deny that the materials are the employer's property. Note

Figure 8.1
Contractor to architect, requesting permission to sub-let

Dear Sir,

We propose to sub-let portions of the Works as indicated below because [*state reasons which may be, for example, because you do not have the required skills within your organisation*]. We should be pleased to receive your consent in accordance with clause 3.2.

Portion to be sub-let   *Name of proposed sub-contractor*

(Complete as appropriate)

Yours faithfully

that this provision takes no account of the fact that the contractor may not have paid the sub-contractor. If the contractor does pay the sub-contractor before he has been paid himself, subsection (c) provides that the materials become the property of the contractor. Subsection (d) makes it clear that the other parts of this clause are not to have the effect of preventing the employer from acquiring ownership of materials in accordance with clause 1.11.

A similar set of provisions is now included in JCT 80. They were prompted by a recent case in which the employer paid for sub-contractor materials, but, before the contractor paid the sub-contractor, the contractor went into liquidation. The goods were held to be the property of the sub-contractor, and the employer had to pay for them again. Whether the current provisions are effective in preventing a recurrence of this problem, time will tell. It may be expected that sub-contractors will increase their prices to cover the risk that they now appear to take.

However, it must be emphasised that these provisions will not necessarily protect the employer. For example, if the sub-contractor's materials have been supplied to him on terms of sale including a retention-of-title clause, this would not be defeated by clause 3.2.2 or any corresponding provision in the sub-contract.

8.2.2 Named persons as sub-contractors

These provisions (clause 3.3) are to be found only in IFC 84. They are also quite complicated and, in places, unclear. It is important to remember that they are not the same as the provisions for nominating sub-contractors under JCT 80. A named person may be involved in one of two ways. One is if work is included in the contract documents to be priced by the contractor and carried out by a named person. In this case, the person is named in the contract documents, and the contractor does not have a choice (eg, one of three). The second is if work is included in an architect's instruction regarding the expenditure of a provisional sum and a person is named to carry it out.

The consequences are slightly different. The flowchart, **Figure 8.3,** outlines the procedures. In the first instance, the contractor has 21 days from entering into the main contract to enter into a sub-contract with the named person. That is 21 days from the date of the employer's acceptance of his tender, not 21 days from signing the contract documents. It is a very short period. The sub-contract must consist of section III of the form of tender and agreement NAM/T (This incorporates sub-contract conditions NAM/SC). Section I of the form should have been completed by the architect, section II by the named person.

These documents are clearly intended by the 1st Recital to be part of the documents given to the contractor when inviting his tender and to be made part of the contract documents (2nd Recital). It is obviously envisaged that all such sub-contract tenders will be invited before the main contract is let. It is certainly not a soft option for architects who are short of the time necessary to produce full drawings and specifications.

The clause provides that if the contractor is "unable to enter into a sub-contract in accordance with the particulars given in the contract documents", he must

Figure 8.2
Architect to contractor, consenting to use of sub-contractors

Dear Sirs,

Thank you for your letter of the [*insert date*] requesting my consent to sub-letting of the following portions of the Works.

If you will give me your written confirmation that, notwithstanding the sub-letting of any portion of the Works, you will remain wholly responsible for the carrying out and completion of the Works in every respect in accordance with the contract, I will give my consent to such sub-letting.

Yours faithfully

immediately inform the architect, specifying which particulars have caused the problem. "Particulars" is the form of tender and agreement NAM/T together with the numbered documents referred to therein. If the architect is satisfied that the particulars specified have indeed prevented the execution of the sub-contract (and he can be sure only if the contractor sends him a letter from the sub-contractor stating as much), he has three courses: alter the particulars to remove the sub-contractor's objection, which creates a variation (3.3.1(a)); or omit the work altogether, which also creates a variation (3.3.1(b)); or omit the work from the contract documents, substituting a provisional sum for which he must then issue an instruction under clause 3.3.2 (3.3.1(c)).

This clause might appear to give the architect the power to vary the terms of the contract, which clearly only the employer can do with the consent of the contractor. It must therefore be assumed that his power is limited under clause 3.3.1(a) to the varying of other than contract terms. If he omits the work altogether, the employer may get someone else to do the work and pay direct, subject to the provisions of clause 3.11 (see **section 8.4**).

The contractor must notify the architect of the date when he has entered into a sub-contract, assuming that all goes well (see **Figure 8.4**). Before he does so, the architect may issue an instruction similar to clause 3.3.1(c).

Clause 3.3.2 deals with the procedure if a named person arises through a provisional sum. This can occur in three ways: if the architect issues an instruction (clause 3.3.1(c)) after the particulars are said to be preventing execution of the sub-contract; or if he issues a similar instruction (clause 3.3.1) omitting the work from the contract documents and substituting a provisional sum before the sub-contract is signed; or if there is a provisional sum in the contract documents (clause 3.8). This clause allows the architect to issue an instruction regarding the expenditure of a provisional sum and to require that the work is to be done by a named person. The named person is to be employed by the contractor as a sub-contractor (clause 3.3.2(a)).

The instruction must describe the work to be done and include all the details of sections I and II of the completed form of tender and agreement NAM/T for the work (clause 3.3.2(b)).

Clearly, there is a difference between a person being named in the contract documents, when the contractor has the opportunity to see who it is before he tenders for the whole contract, and being named in an architect's instruction, when the job is in progress and the contractor is committed. For that reason, the contractor has 14 days from the date of the issue of the instruction in which to make an objection (see **Figure 8.5**). The objection must be reasonable, the contract does not say what is to happen if the contractor does make a reasonable objection. Presumably, the architect must name another person and so on, if the contractor continues to object, until the contractor stops objecting. Under such circumstances, the naming of a person is not a quick process. The architect has to complete section I of the form of tender and agreement NAM/T and send a copy to each of the persons he wishes to tender. Each tenderer must complete section II and return it. Assuming that the architect has an inexhaustible supply of suitable tenderers, the problem is the delay to the contract. He has no power to award an extension of time. Clause 2.4.5 refers

Figure 8.3
Named persons as sub-contractors

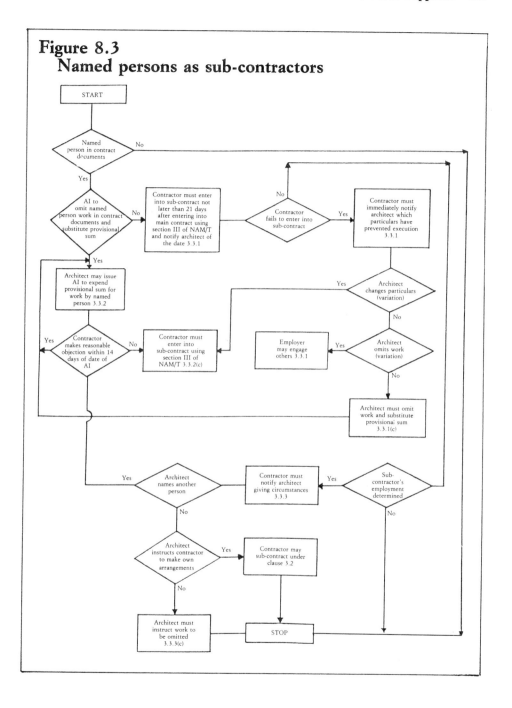

to compliance with architect's instructions "to the extent provided therein, under clause 3.3". Clause 3.3 does not provide for an extension of time for delay caused by the contractor's making reasonable objection. The architect may postpone the work under clause 3.15 and grant an extension under clause 2.4.5. The contractor will then claim loss and/or expense under clause 4.12.5.

When the contractor's objections are sorted out, or if he does not make any objection, he must enter into a sub-contract with the named person, using section III of the form of tender and agreement NAM/T. If the contractor is unable to enter into a sub-contract because of the "particulars", the contract is again silent regarding the next move. What is certain is that the employer has the responsibility of naming a person who will enter into a sub-contract on the basis of the particulars. The best way to settle this situation is by negotiation. The architect should attempt to come to some agreement about the particulars with all parties. If that fails, he should name another person. The provisions apparently work reasonably well in practice despite any lack of clarity in the drafting.

The employer can always arrange to amend this clause, as any other, at tender stage, but he should do so with expert legal advice. It is essential that the employer enters into the RIBA/CASEC Form of Agreement between the employer and a specialist to be named as a sub-contractor under the JCT Intermediate Form of Building Contract. This will enable the employer to take direct action against the named person if he defaults, in particular if he fails in any of the following:

- any design of the sub-contract works which he has undertaken to do;
- the selection of the kinds of materials for the sub-contract works which he has undertaken to do;
- the satisfaction of the sub-contract works which he has undertaken to fulfil.

Clause 3.3.7 of IFC 84 expressly removes the contractor's liability for the above items "whether or not" the named person is responsible to the employer for them. Moreover, the named person is not to be liable for them through the contractor. The only way the employer can obtain any contractual redress is if he has entered into the RIBA/CASEC form. He could sue the sub-contractor for negligence, but in the current legal climate, he is unlikely to meet with success: *Murphy* v *Brentwood District Council* (1990) CILL 604. Even with ESA/1 in place, the employer will be unable to recover directly from the sub-contractor if loss is caused by the carrying out of the sub-contract works: *Greater Nottingham Co-operative Society* v *Cementation Piling and Foundation Ltd* (1988) 17 Con LR 43.

No other sub-contractor is to be responsible for them through the contractor, and in that case, there is no way in which the employer can obtain redress, since there is no privity of contract between the employer and the contractor's domestic sub-contractor under clause 3.2. In the case of some domestic sub-contractors it may be sensible for the employer to enter into a form of warranty to establish a contractual route for redress.

The phrase in this clause is that neither the contractor nor the named person, or any other sub-contractor, is responsible under the contract "for anything to which the above terms relate". The precise meaning of the phrase may be a fruitful source of dispute. The clause, however, does not affect the contractor's normal obligations

Figure 8.4
Contractor to architect if contractor enters into sub-contract with named person

Dear Sir

In accordance with clause 3.3.1 of the conditions of contract, we hereby inform you that we entered into a sub-contract with [*insert name*] on the [*insert date*].

Yours faithfully

Figure 8.5
Contractor to architect making objection to named person

We are in receipt of your instruction number [*insert number*], dated [*insert date*] instructing us to enter into a sub-contract with [*insert name*].

We have reasonable objection, under clause 3.3.2(c), to entering into such sub-contract. The reason for our objection is [*explain*].

Yours faithfully

or those of any sub-contractor in the supply of goods and materials and workmanship. There are extensive provisions to deal with the determination of the named person's employment under the sub-contract and its consequences. The contractor must advise the architect of any events which are likely to lead to determination under the sub-contract. He must do this "as soon as is reasonably practicable"; in other words, he must let the architect know as soon as he finds out (**Figure 8.6**). What the architect does then is not stated. Presumably, he will endeavour to find a solution short of determination.

If determination takes place, whether or not the architect has been advised of the likelihood, the contractor must write to him, giving the circumstances. The architect must then issue such an instruction as may be necessary, which must be one of the following:

- name another person to do the work or the balance of the work, incorporating a description and particulars of the named person in sections I and II of Form of Tender and Agreement NAM/T, subject to the contractor's reasonable objection within 14 days as in clause 3.3.2(c) (clause 3.3.3(a));
- instruct the contractor to make his own arrangements to do the work, either himself or by sub-contract under clause 3.2 (clause 3.3.3(b));
- omit the work still to be finished (clause 3.3.3(c)).

If the architect omits the work, the employer may, under clause 3.11, arrange to have the work done by others and pay direct.

The contract points out a difference in consequence, depending on whether the work was originally included in the contract documents or is the result of an instruction regarding the expenditure of a provisional sum:

- if work originally included in the contract documents: a clause 3.3.3(a) instruction ranks as a clause 2.3 event (extension of time) but not as a clause 4.11 matter (disturbance of progress). The contract sum must be increased or reduced to take account of the price of the second as compared with the first named person. Amounts included in the second price for repair of the first named person's defective work must be excluded from the contract sum. Thus, the contractor is not to be held financially responsible for the determination, but he is held responsible for any defects at that time existing. A clause 3.3.3(b) or (c) instruction ranks as a clause 2.3 event (extension of time) *and* as a clause 4.11 matter (disturbance of progress). It also ranks as a variation;
- if the result of an instruction regarding the expenditure of a provisional sum: a clause 3.3.3(a), (b), or (c) instruction ranks as a clause 2.3 event (extension of time) and as a clause 4.10 matter (disturbance of progress). It also ranks for payment as a further instruction under the provisional sum.

There is an important proviso that, if the instruction was issued as a result of some default of the contractor, none of the above *benefits* apply to the contractor. This is so whether the work was originally included in the contract documents or is the result of an instruction regarding the expenditure of a provisional sum. It is only fair to stress that the above is intended to clarify what is regarded as an unhappily worded clause. A strict reading of clause 3.3.5, for example, makes the employer liable to pay the contractor for the sub-contract work if the contractor is in default and a clause 3.3.3(c) instruction omitting the work is issued. That cannot be what was intended.

Figure 8.6
Contractor to architect if determination of named person's employment possible

Dear Sir

In accordance with clause 3.3.3 of the conditions of contract, we have to advise you that the following events are likely to lead to the determination of [*insert name*]'s employment:

[*Describe events*]

We should be pleased to receive your instructions as a matter of urgency.

Yours faithfully

The contractor must take whatever action is necessary, within reason, to recover from the named sub-contractor any additional amount that the employer has had to pay to the contractor due to the issue of the instructions 3.3.3(a), (b) or (c) and the consequences thereof; and any liquidated damages which the employer would have been able to recover from the contractor had it not been for the instructions. There is no time limit set for the contractor to take action. Presumably, he will take the action after practical completion; otherwise, how is he to know the amount of liquidated damages which would have been recoverable by the employer? (clause 3.3.6)

The contractor is required to take the action only where he has determined the employment of the sub-contractor under NAM/SC clauses 27.1 or 27.2. There is a proviso that he cannot be required to commence any arbitration or other proceedings unless the employer agrees to pay any legal costs he incurs. It is difficult to see what action the contractor can take (unless he is holding some of the named sub-contractor's money) if the employer decides against paying his legal costs. The contractor is to account – ie, presumably prepares an account – for any amounts he recovers. Insofar as the contractor fails to take action, he is liable to the employer for the additional amount, including the amount equal to liquidated damages, payable by, or due to, the employer. Whether or not the employer agrees to fund legal proceedings, it is difficult to understand, assuming that insufficient are retained to allow set-off, how the architect can demonstrate, even to his own satisfaction, that the contractor has failed to take action provided the contractor has written some sternly worded letters to the named person (see **Figure 8.7**). We do not consider that, taken as a whole, the provisions for named persons are satisfactory. A shorter and much simpler approach, such as can be found in some other forms of contract, would be preferred.

8.3 Statutory Authorities

Certain crucial parts of most, if not all, contracts are carried out by local authorities or statutory undertakers such as the gas and electricity boards. Where they carry out the work solely as a result of their statutory rights or obligations, they are not to be considered named persons (clause 3.3.8). The implication is that, where they carry out work which is not a result of their statutory rights or duties, but as a matter of contract, they may be named persons. They may also, in such instances, be considered as sub-contractors to the contractor in the traditional way (clause 3.2) or persons employed by the employer to carry out work outside the contract (clause 3.11; see section 8.4) depending upon the circumstances of their engagement. In carrying out their statutory duties, the authorities have no contractual liability, although in some cases they have tortious liability. When they are carrying out work outside their statutory duties, they are exactly like anyone else who enters into a contract. If an authority delays the completion of the works by carrying out (or failing to carry out) work in pursuance of its statutory duty, the contactor will be entitled to an extension of time (clause 2.4.13), but not for delay caused by other work which the authority carries out or fails to carry out.

Figure 8.7
Contractor to sub-contractor to recover amounts under clause 3.3.6(b) of the main contract conditions

Dear Sirs

In accordance with clause 27.3.3 of the conditions of sub-contract we require you to pay us the sum of [*insert amount*] which we are required under clause 3.3.6(b) of the main contract to recover from you.

If we do not receive the above mentioned sum by [*insert date*], we may take arbitration or other proceedings against you.

Yours faithfully

The contractor must comply with all statutory requirements: for example, the Planning Acts and dependent regulations. He is responsible for giving any notices required and for paying any fees or charges in connection with the works (clause 5.1), for which he is entitled to be reimbursed by having the amounts added to the contract sum, unless they are already included in the contract documents. Thus, if the appropriate contract document is a specification and it states that the contractor must allow for paying all statutory fees and charges, he will be deemed to have included the amount in his price.

The contractor is not liable to the employer if the works do not comply with statutory requirements if this is because he has carried them out in accordance with the contract documents or any of the architect's instructions (clause 5.3). This provision will not, of course affect the liability the contractor may have to the appropriate statutory undertaking or to the local authority. There is a proviso that, if the contractor finds any divergence between the statutory requirements and the contract documents or architect's instructions, he must specify the divergence to the architect in writing (clause 5.2). It may be small comfort, because, if he does not find a divergence which exists he is not liable. It is the architect's duty to provide correct information: *London Borough of Merton* v *Stanley Hugh Leach Ltd* (1985) 32 BLR 51. If an emergency arises, the contractor must comply with statutory requirements without waiting for the architect's instructions. He must carry out and supply just enough work and materials as are necessary to comply as an immediate measure, and inform the architect forthwith, not necessarily in writing. If he satisfies these requirements, he is entitled to be paid as though he has carried out the architect's instructions requiring a variation, provided that the emergency arose because of a divergence between the statutory requirements and the contract documents and/or any of the architect's instructions, drawings, or documents issued under clauses 1.3, 3.5, or 3.9 (clause 5.4).

Thus, if the emergency arises through the contractor's default or inefficiency, he is not entitled to payment except insofar as the architect may be prepared to accept that there would have been some additional cost irrespective of the contractor's default.

8.4 Work not Forming Part of the Contract

The employer has the right to enter into contracts with persons other than the contractor to carry out work on the site (clause 3.11). Such persons are commonly firms or individuals over whom the employer wants complete control. They may be his own employees as, for example, when the employer is a local authority. Or the employer's reason for wanting to employ such persons in a direct way (ie, not through the contractor) is that they have a special relationship with him: they may be artists, sculptors, graphic designers, landscapers, etc. In principle, the contractor should be responsible for all the work to be done. It promotes efficiency on site and removes areas of possible dispute. If the work is to be considered not to form part of the contract, it

Figure 8.8
Contractor to employer objecting to work done by employer's directly employed contractors

Dear Sir

We understand that you wish to arrange for [*insert brief description of the work*] to be carried out by other persons under the terms of clause 3.11.

We consider that it is reasonable for us not to give our consent because [*give reasons briefly*].

Yours faithfully

Copy: Architect

must be the subject of a separate contract between the employer and the person to provide the work, and it must be paid for by the employer directly to the person employed and not through the contractor.

Work carried out by statutory authorities not in pursuance of their statutory duties may fall into this category.

The contract provides for two situations. The first is where the contract documents provide for such work by informing the contractor what is to be carried out, when, and (possibly but not necessarily) by whom. The documents should require the contractor to allow the work to be carried out as stated and give details of any items of attendance which may be required. The contractor should then make provision for the work in his programme. The second situation is where the contract documents do not provide for such work.

In the first situation, the contractor must allow the work to be carried out and provide whatever attendance is specified and priced for. In the second, the employer must first obtain the contractor's consent to his proposals before arranging to have the work carried out. The contractor must not withhold his consent unreasonably. It would be reasonable to withhold consent if the proposed work would constitute a severe disturbance to the contractor's progress (**Figure 8.8**). It would be unreasonable if the work was to be done without affecting the contractor's activities in any way. Between these two extremes lie many situations which are not easy to resolve.

Whether the work not forming part of the contract is provided for in the contract documents or is simply the subject of the contractor's consent does not affect the employer's responsibility under the contract. For the purposes of the insurance clause 6, persons directly employed by the employer are deemed to be persons "for whom the employer is responsible". They are not to be deemed sub-contractors. The result is that the employer may have uninsured liabilities. The employer should, therefore, obtain the necessary cover through his insurance broker. The broker should be given a copy of the insurance clauses and be requested to arrange cover for the employer, and those for whom the employer is responsible, in respect of any act or neglect of those persons. The directly employed persons may already have adequate insurance cover, but it is a matter best left in the hands of a broker with experience in this kind of insurance.

The contractor is entitled to be awarded extensions of time if completion is delayed by the carrying out (or failure to carry out) of work not forming part of the contract (clause 2.4.8). It is a very easy claim to make, and a contractor running late on the contract would do well to give his consent, if required, to any work by the employer's directly-employed persons. They can then be made to appear responsible for any delays thereafter. The architect must, therefore, be especially vigilant when examining such claims; a network analysis is invaluable.

The employer's responsibility to supply those materials which he has agreed to supply, or his failure to do so, is closely linked to the problem of work outside the contract (clause 2.4.9). In both cases, the contractor is not involved with the external contracts, and it may be thought that the employer is assuming needless responsibility. Suppose that the employer wishes to supply all the paint for a contract himself, perhaps because he thinks he can obtain it at a cheap rate. In order to avoid any claims from the contractor, he must supply paint of the correct colours, in the correct quantities, of the correct types (undercoat, etc), and at the time it is required. Moreover, any unsatisfactory paint may provoke a claim.

The wording of the clauses relating to extensions of time, discussed above, is precisely repeated as matters for which the contractor may make a claim for loss and/or expense (clauses 4.12.3 and 4.12.4). The employer is extremely vulnerable, and the architect must exercise great care in deciding whether the claim is valid.

Potentially the most damaging result of the employer's directly employing persons to carry out work outside the contract, or of his arranging to supply materials himself, is that the contractor may aquire grounds to determine his employment (clause 7.5.3(c)). The matter is dealt with in section 12.2.2. Although the contractor's potential remedies of extensions of time, loss and/or expense and determination of his employment may appear severe, they are in truth merely a reflection of the problems caused to the contractor by introducing other contractors or suppliers on the site over whom the contractor has no control.

If the employer expresses his intention of employing his own men or of supplying any materials, the architect has a duty to advise him of the pitfalls. Most of them can be avoided by ensuring that all work is done, and all materials are supplied, through the contractor. In view of the possibility of named persons as sub-contractors in this contract, in our opinion the employer would be unwise to arrange for work to be carried out which does not form part of the contract.

8.5 Summary

Assignment and sub-contracting
- neither party may assign without the other's consent;
- the contractor may sub-let with the architect's consent;
- the sub-contractor's employment determines on the determination of the contractor's employment;
- the contractor must consent to the sub-contractor's removing unfixed materials from site;
- unfixed materials become the employer's property when he pays the contractor;
- unfixed materials become the contractor's property if he pays the sub-contractor before being paid himself.

Named persons
- named persons may arise by inclusion in the contract documents or by an instruction regarding a provisional sum;
- sections I, II, and III of tender and agreement NAM/T must be completed by the architect, the named person, and the contractor;
- the work may be omitted and carried out by the employer's own men;

- the named person in the contract documents may be replaced by a named person in an architect's instruction;
- the contractor may object to any named person in an instruction;
- the employer should enter into the RIBA/CASEC form of agreement with the named person;
- design, selection, and satisfaction are not the liability of the contractor, nor are they the liability of the named person or any sub-contractor through the contractor;
- on determination of a named person's employment, the architect may name another person, request the contractor to make his own arrangements, or omit the work;
- under certain circumstances, extension of time and loss and/or expense may be awarded to the contractor after determination;
- the contractor must take action to recover the employer's losses after determination of the named person's employment;
- if the contractor fails to take appropriate action, he is liable for the losses.

Statutory authorities

- in pursuance of their statutory duties, statutory authorities are not liable in contract but may give grounds for extension of time;
- not in pursuance of their statutory duties, they are liable in contract and may be sub-contractors, named persons, or persons for whom the employer is responsible;
- the contractor must comply with statutory requirements;
- the contractor is not liable to the employer if he works to contract documents or instructions, provided that he notifies any divergence he finds;
- the contractor may carry out and be paid for emergency work without instruction;
- the contractor must notify the architect forthwith if there is an emergency.

Work not forming part of the contract

- the employer may carry out his own work on site;
- the contractor's consent is required if the work is not mentioned in the contract documents;
- there are insurance implications;
- the employer is vulnerable to claims for extension of time and loss and/or expense;
- there are grounds for determination if work is delayed for a month by work not forming part of the contract.

9-Possession, Practical Completion and Defects Liability

9.1 Possession

9.1.1 General

Possession is the next best thing to ownership, If the owner of a motorcar lends it to a friend, the friend has a better claim to the car than anyone else except the owner. The builder in possession of a site can, in general terms, exclude everyone from the site except (and often including) the owner. In practice, there are exceptions to this general rule, laid down by the building contract and by various statutory regulations.

A contractor carrying out building works is said to have a licence from the owner to occupy the site for the length of time necessary to complete the work. The owner has no general power to revoke such a licence during the contract period, but it may be brought to an end if the contractor's employment or the contract itself is lawfully brought to an end.

If there were no express term in the contract giving the contractor possession of the site, a term would be implied that the contractor must have possession in sufficient time to allow him to complete by the contract completion date.

There is no express term in IFC 84 allowing access to anyone other than the contractor. So a term must be implied to allow access to the works at all reasonable times for the architect, clerk of works, and all properly appointed sub-contractors. (Curiously, the sub-contract form NAM/T does provide for the contractor, the architect, and all persons duly authorised by them to have right of access to work being prepared in the sub-contract works [NAM/T clause 23]).

9.1.2 Date for possession

The date for possession is to be entered in the appendix. Clause 2.1 states that, on that date, possession must be given to the contractor, and that, subject to any extension of time which may be awarded, the contractor must proceed regularly and diligently with the works and complete them on or before the date for completion in the appendix.

If the employer fails to give sufficient possession on the due date, it is normally a serious breach of contract; the contractor will have a claim for damages at common law, and the time for completion will become "at large". That is to say, the contractor's obligation will be to complete the work within a reasonable time, and no date can be established from which liquidated and ascertained damages begin to run: *Peak Construction (Liverpool) Ltd* v *McKinney Foundations Ltd* (1970) 1 BLR 111. The problem is partially overcome in IFC 84 by the inclusion of an optional clause (2.2), which permits the employer to defer giving possession for a time which must not exceed a period to be inserted in the appendix. From the employer's point of view the clause should always be included for his protection. The contract recommends that the period of deferment should not exceed six weeks. The period is somewhat arbitrary because, at the time of tender – of signing the contract even – presumably the employer fully intends to give possession on the date stated in the appendix. If he knew, at that time that the date was going to be deferred, the date in the contract could be adjusted accordingly. It is perfectly possible to amend the contract so that the permitted deferment is, say, 12 weeks, but to introduce so large an element of uncertainty into the contract would almost certainly result in increased tender prices. Possession is usually delayed for a very short time (because demolition contractors have not finished their work, or because planning or building-regulation permission is delayed, or for some other similar cause). Otherwise, the delay is caused by some major problem which lasts for a considerable period, and in such circumstances it would be unfair to rely on a clause permitting deferment. The best-laid plans can go wrong, so although the architect may, in consultation with the employer, decide to insert a period shorter than six weeks, he should not omit an insertion altogether.

There is no prescribed form of notice for deferment, but it must come from the employer. The architect would normally draft him a suitable letter, which need not give any reason (**Figure 9.1**).

If possession is deferred, the contractor will be able to claim loss and/or expense (clause 4.11(a)) and an extension of time (clause 2.4.14). The power to defer possession must not be executed under the provisions of the contract. Loss and/or expense (clause 4.12.5) and extension of time (clause 2.4.5) can also be claimed for postponement. If the whole, or substantially the whole, of the works is suspended for one month by postponement, the contractor may determine his employment (clause 7.5.3). If there is postponement, the contractor has possession of the site, but the architect has suspended work. That is not to say that the contractor may not use some or all of the time the work is suspended to work specifically connected with his occupation of the site (for example, repairing or improving site office accommodation, sorting materials, attending to security).

Figure 9.1
Employer to contractor, deferring possession of the site

Dear Sir,

[*If length of deferment is known*]

In accordance with clause 2.2 of the condition of contract, take this as notice that I defer giving possession of the site for [*specify period*]. You may take possession of the site on [*insert date*].

[*If length of deferment is not known*]

In accordance with clause 2.2 of the conditions of contract, take this as notice that I defer giving possession of the site for a period not exceeding [*insert the period named in the appendix*]. I will write to you again as soon as I have a definite date for you to take possession.

Yours faithfully

Copy: Architect
      Quantity surveyor
      Consultants
      Clerk of works

The contractor normally gives up possession of the site at practical completion or on determination of this employment. He is, however, granted a restricted licence to enter the site for the purposes of remedying defects (see **section 9.3**).

9.2 Practical Completion

9.2.1 Definition

Clause 2.9 states that the architect must issue a certificate forthwith when, in his opinion, practical completion of the works is achieved. The consequences of the certificate are considerable (see **section 9.2.2**). Despite that, the contract does not define the meaning of "practical completion" (although it take the trouble to define "person" [clause 8.3]). It is not the same as "substantial completion", nor does it mean "almost complete". There is conflicting case law, but the point that emerges seems to be that the architect is not to certify practical completion if any defects are apparent or if anything other than very trifling items remain outstanding (*H W Nevill (Sunblest) Ltd* v *Wm Press & Sons Ltd* (1981) 20 BLR 78). Within these guidelines, he is free to exercise his discretion. A practical test to apply is whether the employer would be seriously inconvenienced if he occupies the building while outstanding items are being finished. If he would be inconvenienced, the architect is probably justified in withholding the certificate. When issuing a certificate, it is good practice to exclude any such outstanding items: *Tozer Kemsley & Milbourne (Holdings) Ltd* v *J Jarvis & Sons Ltd and Others* (1983) 4 ConLR 24.

But there is no obligation on the architect to tell the contractor what items remain to be completed before the issue of the certificate. The temptation to issue lists of outstanding items should be resisted. The contractor knows what is required of him by the contract. The issue of lists at this stage is confusing and often leads to disputes. The onus of inspecting the work and preparing work lists for the contractor lies with the person-in-charge.

The contractor is not bound to notify the architect when practical completion has been achieved, but it is wise to do so, probably some weeks in advance (**Figure 9.2**). Some architects are in the habit of arranging so-called "handover meetings" at which representatives of the employer and sometimes his maintenance organisation are present. This can be a prudent move by the architect on the principle that many eyes are better than one. He will also have any consultants on hand to inspect their own particular portions of the work. However, the decision to issue a certificate is solely the architect's. He cannot move the responsibility on to the employer simply because he is present. The exception to that is if the employer insists that the building is ready, even though the architect makes clear his dissatisfaction to the employer. The employer may agree with the contractor to take possession of the building despite the architect's protests. This often happens if an employer is anxious to get into a building, but the position is that the architect is not obliged to issue his certificate. There is no contractual requirement for him to do so. The architect will usually write

Figure 9.2
Contractor to architect, notifying imminence of practical completion

Dear Sir,

We anticipate that the works will be complete on [*insert date*]. Please confirm that you intend to carry out your inspection on that day. We are arranging for Mr [*insert name*] to be on site to give immediate attention to any queries which may arise. We look forward to receiving your certificate of practical completion following your inspection.

Yours faithfully

to the employer and make the position clear (**Figure 9.3**). If the employer later discovers that outstanding items cause him trouble, or if the contractor does not complete as quickly and efficiently as he promised, the employer will have himself to blame. The architect will have carried out his duties properly with due regard for the employer's interests. The architect's duty to issue a certificate of practical completion will remain, but not until, in his opinion, the works have achieved that state.

9.2.2 Consequences

Clause 2.9 states that "Practical Completion of the Works shall be deemed for all the purposes of this contract to have taken place on the day named in" the certificate. The "purposes of this contract" are to found in a number of clauses throughout the contract. They are as follows:

- the contractor's liability for insurance under clause 6.3A ends;
- liability for liquidated damages under clauses 2.7 ends;
- liability for frost damage ends (clause 2.10);
- the employer's right to deduct full retention ends. Half the retention percentage becomes due for release within 14 days (clause 4.3);
- the 6 months period begins during which the contractor must send all documents reasonably required for adjustment of the contract sum to the architect (clause 4.5);
- the period of final review of extensions of time begins (clause 2.3);
- the defects liability period begins (clause 2.10).

All these "purposes", with the possible exception of the review of extensions of time, are positively beneficial to the contractor and are ample reason for him to be anxious to secure a certificate of practical completion at as early a date as possible.

9.3 Defects Liability Period

9.3.1 Definition

Clause 2.10 refers to defects liability. Reference is also made to the defects liability period, which is to be "named in the Appendix". The period is for the benefit of all parties but principally for that of the contractor. The idea is to allow a specific period of time for defects to appear, list the defects, and give the contractor the opportunity to remedy them. Any defect is a breach of contract on the part of the contractor, who has agreed to carry out the work in accordance with the contract documents. If there were no defects liability period, the employer's only remedy for defects would be to take action at common law. So the insertion of the period provides a valuable method of identifying defective work and having it corrected. Without it, the contractor would have no right or duty to return.

Figure 9.3
Architect to employer if employer wishes to take possession of building before practical completion achieved

Dear Sir,

I refer to our meeting on site with the contractor on [*insert date*].

I confirm that, in my opinion, practical completion has not been achieved, so it is my duty under the provisions of the contract to withhold my certificate. I note, however, that you have agreed with the contractor to take possession of the building for reasons of your own. Although I think that you are unwise, as I explained on site, I respect your decision and I will continue to inspect until I feel able to issue my certificate. At that date, the defects liability period will commence.

Yours faithfully

The contractor's liability for defects does not end at the end of the defects liability period; what does end is his right to correct them (and even that right is limited, as will be seen). Afterwards, the employer is free to take legal action for damages if further defects appear, although, in practice, the employer will normally be satisfied if the defects are corrected.

Contractors commonly refer to the defects liability period as the "maintenance period". This is misleading and wrong. Maintenance implies a far greater responsibility than simply making good defects – for example, touching up scuffed paintwork and attention to general wear and tear. Even in other standard form contracts where the term is used (ie ACA 2) it is usually restricted to making good defects by the actual wording of the clause.

9.3.2 Defects, shrinkages, or other faults

The contractor is required to make good "defects, shrinkages, or other faults". At first sight, this might appear to be all-embracing. In fact "other faults" is to be interpreted *ejusden generis*. That is to say that they must be faults which are similar to defects or shrinkages. A defect occurs when something is not in accordance with the contract. If an item occurs when something is not in accordance with the contract, it is not defective for the purposes of this clause. It might be less than adequate in some way, but that could be due to a fault in design, and, therefore, the architect's responsibility. Shrinkages are a source of dispute on many contracts. They become the contractor's liability only if they are due to material or workmanship not in accordance with the contract.

For example, shrinkage most commonly occurs in timber, caused by a reduction in moisture content after the building is heated. It is the architect's job to specify a suitable moisture content for the situation. If shrinkage occurs during the defects liability period, it can only be because the timber was supplied with too high a moisture content, or because the architect's assumption about the appropriate moisture content was incorrect. Only the first explanation is the contractor's liability. In practice, it is often very difficult to decide which explanation applies, and the architect will naturally be drawn to the conclusion that specification is correct. If the contractor objects (**Figure 9.4**), the only way to be sure is to have samples cut out and tested in the laboratory, a very expensive procedure. All too often, the culprit is the occupier of the building, who is running the central heating above the recommended temperatures. In such a case, the architect's assumptions were, in effect, wrong, and the contractor is not responsible for making good.

9.3.3 Frost

The contractor's liability to make good frost damage is limited to damage caused by frost which occurred before practical completion – in other words, when the contractor was in control of the building works and could have taken appropriate measures to prevent the damage by introducing heating or stopping vulnerable work.

Figure 9.4
Contractor to architect, objecting to some items on the schedule of defects

Dear Sir,

Thank you for your instruction number [*insert number*], dated [*insert date*] scheduling the defects you required to be made good now that the defects liability period has ended.

We have carried out a preliminary inspection and we are making arrangements to make good most of the items on our schedule. However, we do not consider that the following items are our responsibility for the reasons stated:

[*List, giving reasons*]

Naturally, we shall be happy to carry out such items of work if you will let us have your written agreement to pay us daywork rates for so doing.

Yours faithfully

Any damage caused by frost after practical completion is at the employer's own expense. The difference is usually easy to spot on site. Frost damage occurring after practical completion is often due to faulty detailing or maintenance.

9.3.4 Procedure

The defects liability period starts on the date given in the certificate of practical completion as that on which practical completion was achieved. The architect is to fill in the length of period required in the appendix. If he does not fill in any period, the length will be six months. The period should agree with the employer, who will ask for the architect's advice. Although six months is a common defects liability period, there are really no good reasons why the period should not be extended to nine or, better, 12 months. Specialist work such as heating often has a 12-month period to fully test the system through all the seasons of the year. It is probable that a contractor asked to tender for a contract including a 12-month general defects liability period would increase his tender figure slightly, but lengthening the period does not increase his actual liability, but only as we have seen his right to return to make good defects. The increase in tender price probably reflects the confusion with "maintenance period" and the fact that the final certificate would be delayed somewhat. In fact, only 2½% of the contract sum should be outstanding after practical completion (clause 4.3).

The equivalent clause (17.1) in JCT 80 refers to defects, etc, which "shall appear within" the period. In IFC 84, the clause simply refers to defects, etc, "which appear". Although the time limit is the need of the period, the wording of the clause seems to give the architect the power to notify the contractor of all the defects which appear, including those which are present at the date of practical completion. Some commentators maintain that the JCT 80 clause gives the architect that power anyway, but it is by no means certain. IFC 84 removes any uncertainty.

The architect is to notify defects to the contractor not later than 14 days after the expiry of the period. This is normally done as soon as possible after the end of the period. The architect should have inspected just before the period expired. There is no set form for notifying the contractor, but it is advisable for the architect to send him a letter (**Figure 9.5**) enclosing a schedule of defects. The architect's power to require defects to be made good is not confined to the issue of the schedule. The wording of the clause makes it clear that he can notify the contractor at any time within the period.

The requirement is for the contractor to make good the defects which are notified to him. No particular time limit is set, but he must carry out his obligation within a reasonable time. What is a reasonable time will depend on the circumstances, including the number of defects, their type, and any special arrangement to be made with the employer for access.

Ideally, the contractor should return to site within a week or so after receiving the architect's list and bring sufficient labour to make good the defects within, say, a month. If the architect decides to exercise his right to require defects to be made good during the currency of the period, he should confine such requests to really urgent matters to be fair to all parties.

Defects liability period

- the defects liability period is for the benefit of the contractor;
- the end of the period does not mark the end of the contractor's liability for defects;
- defects can only be workmanship or materials not in accordance with the contract, or damage caused by frost occuring before practical completion;
- the length must be entered in the appendix;
- all defects apparent during the period or on practical completion are covered;
- defects must be notified to the contractor during the period and not later than 14 days after the end;
- defects are to be made good at the contractor's own cost; *or*
- if the employer agrees, may instruct the contractor not to make good defects and deduct an appropriate sum from the contract sum;
- after the contractor has made good, the architect must issue a certificate to that effect.

10–Claims

10.1. General

This chapter covers claims by the contractor for both extra time and extra money, although there is not necessarily any link between the two. The subject of claims is an emotive one, but the architect has a duty under the contract to deal with claims, and in doing so he must hold the balance fairly between the employer and the contractor. Although employed by the employer, in ascertaining and settling monetary claims and in granting extensions of time, the architect has an independent role.

Two points should be noted. The first is that the architect's powers under the contract are limited. He can settle only claims which he is authorised to deal with under the express terms of the contract. This means that he cannot deal with common-law claims or make *ex gratia* settlements. To do that, he would need the express authority of the employer. **Table 10.1** summarises the contract clauses which give rise to claims which the architect is empowered to settle and those which are the employer's province.

The second point is that if the architect rejects a valid claim under the contract, case law establishes that this is a breach of contract for which the employer is responsible at common law. Recent case law establishes that in principle the contractor has no right to sue the architect if he fails properly to administer the claims provisions but this in no way negates the architect's professional and contractual duty to act fairly and impartially as between the employer and contractor. These observations apply to claims for extra money under the contract provisions or claims for "direct loss and/or expense", as the contract puts it.

There is an important point to note about extensions of time: failure by the architect properly to exercise his duties as to the granting of extensions of time may result in the contract completion date becoming unenforceable, in the sense that the contractor will no longer be bound by the contract period, but will merely be required to complete "within a reasonable time". The important consequence of this is that the employer would forfeit any right to recover liquidated damages, which would leave him with the difficult and unenviable task of proving his actual loss at common law. In such circumstances the architect might well be held to be negligent.

10.2 Extension of Time

10.2.1 Legal principles

Under the general law, the contractor is bound to complete the works by the agreed date, unless he is prevented from so doing by the employer's fault of breaches of contract – and the employer's liability extends to the architect's wrongful acts or defaults within the scope of his authority. Unless there is an extension of time clause in a contract, neither the architect not the employer has any power to extend the contract period.

Clause 2.3 deals with the architect's power to grant extensions of time and lays down the procedure which must be followed. It is closely linked with clause 2.7 – which provides for liquidated damages – and case law establishes that clauses in this form will be interpreted very strictly by the courts. In practice, this means that if delay is caused by something not covered by the clause – or if the architect fails to exercise his duties under it properly and at the right time – the employer will lose his right to liquidated damages.

10.2.2 Liquidated damages

Clause 2.7 provides for the contractor to "pay or allow" the employer liquidated damages at the rate specified in the appendix should he fail to complete on time. The amount of liquidated damages should have been calculated carefully at pre-tender stage. The figure must represent a genuine pre-estimate of the loss likely to be suffered by the employer should the contractor fail to complete on time, or a lesser sum. If the sum arrived at is a genuine re-estimate of the likely loss, then that is the sum which will be recoverable, even if the sum agreed is greater than the actual loss or in the event there is no loss. But liquidated damages are exhaustive of the employer's remedy for the breach of late completion. The calculation is sometimes difficult. In the case of profit-earning assets, there is no problem, and all the architect needs to do is analyse the likely losses and additional costs. The following should be considered:

- loss of profit on a new building: eg, rental income, retail profit;
- additional supervision and administrative costs;
- any other financial results of the contract's being late: eg, staff costs;
- on-costs under later direct contracts: eg, a contract for fitting out;
- interest payable during the delay.

Table 10.1
IFC 84 clauses which may give rise to claims (*see key on page 176*)

Clause	Event	Type	Usually dealt with by
1.4	Inconsistencies, etc	C	A
1.6	Architect fails to provide documents	CL	E
1.8	Divulging or improper use of rates	CL	E
2.2	Deferment of possession Deferment exceeding time stated in appendix	C CL	A E
2.3	Financial claims	CL	E
2.7	Improper deduction of liquidated damages	CL	E
2.8	Failure to repay liquidated damages	CL	E
2.9	Failure to issue certificate of practical completion	CL	E
2.10	Including items which are not defects Failure to issue certificate of making good defects	CL CL	E E
3.1	Assignment without consent	CL	E
3.2	Architect unreasonably withholding consent to sub-letting	CL	E
3.3.1	Failure to issue instruction	CL	E
3.3.3(b)	Contractor instructed to make own arrangements after determination	C	A
3.3.7	Failure of sub-contract design, selection of materials, or satisfaction of performance specification	CL	E
3.5.1	Instructions issued orally or by employer	CL	E
3.6	Valuation of variations not carried out in accordance with the contract	CL	E
3.9	Failure to determine levels, etc	CL	E
3.10	Clerk of works exceeding duties	CL	E
3.11	Employer's work Employer's work without getting through procedure	C CL	A E
3.12	Opening up and testing	C	A

Table 10.1 (continued)

Clause	Event	Type	Usually dealt with by
3.13.2	Unreasonable instructions following failure of work	C	Arb
3.14	Wrongly phrased instructions	CL	E
3.15	Postponement of work	C	A
4.2	Certificate not issued or not issued at the proper time	CL	E
4.3	Failure to certify	CL	E
4.4	Retention money, interest	CL	E
4.5	QS's failure to send computations to the contractor forthwith	CL	E
4.6	Failure to issue final certificate, or certificate not in proper form	CL	E
4.9, 4.10	Fluctuations	C	A
4.11	Disturbance of regular progress	C	A
5.1	Statutory fees and charges	C	A
5.2	Divergence between statutory requirements and contract documents	C	A
5.4	Emergency compliance	C	A
5.5	Recovery of VAT	C	A
6.3A.4	Failure to pay insurance monies	CL	E
6.3B.2	Employer's failure to insure (unless a local authority)	C	A
6.3C.3	Employer's failure to insure (unless a local authority)	C	A
7.1	Invalid determination	CL	E
7.8.1	Invalid determination	CL	E

Key
C–Contractual; CL–Common Law; E–Employer; A–Architect; Arb–Arbitrator

These points are not exhaustive, and clearly much depends on the type of project. For example, in the public sector, late completion may require the temporary occupation of a more expensive building, and invariably there will be extra administrative costs and almost inevitably some financial penalties for late completion.

There are three possible bases for formulating liquidated damages in such cases:
1 The notional rental value of the property can be taken and based on this some notional return on its capitalised value. We do not recommend this option, nor its variant of fixing a sum commensurate with an average commercial project of comparable value.
2 The sources of likely loss can be used as a basis – for instance, subsidies, capitalised interest on money advanced, and the spin-off effect on departmental costs. This method normally produces a nominal figure which does not encourage the tardy contractor to make up lost time. If the figure is unrealistic and the contractor has two contracts runnning late, he will be tempted to throw his resources into the contract which has the more realistic provision for liquidated damages.
3 The best method is to use formula calculation that gives an approximation of all individual costs. The best known is that put forward by the society of Chief Quantity Surveyors in Local Government. This suggests three main headings under which a calculation should be made:
- assume that 80% of the total capital cost of the scheme (including fees) will have been advanced at anticipated completion and that interest is being paid at the current rate. If that interest rate is 12%, capitalised interest is 80% × 12% ÷ 52 = 0.185 of the contract sum per week;
- assess administrative costs (eg, staff salaries) as 2.75% of the contract sum per year. This gives 0.053% per week
- exceptional costs (eg, temporary accommodation) are assessed realistically.

The result of the first two parts of the formula reduces to 0.237% of the contract sum per week. This may be an underestimate of the likely losses, but it works reasonably in practice.

The main point is that the figure should not be plucked out of the air. A genuine attempt to calculate the likely loss must be made and the resultant figure is used. In commercial projects, the likely loss may produce a figure out of all proportion to the value of the contract. The solution then is to reduce the figure to an acceptable level.

Figure 10.1 is a possible format for a general calculation for liquidated damages.

There are two pre-conditions for the deduction of liquidated damages under clause 2.7.

The first is the issue of a certificate of non-completion by the architect, which states that the contractor has failed to complete the works by the original or extended date for completion. This certificate is a factual statement and more than one certificate can be issued. Should an extension of time be granted by the architect after issuing a certificate of non-completion, the contract provides that he must issue a written cancellation of it and issue a further certificate as necessary.

Figures 10.2 and **10.3** are pro-forma examples.

The second is that the employer must require the contractor to pay or allow liquidated damages. He must do this by writing to the contractor to that effect no later than the date of the final certificate for payment (see clause 4.6).

Figure 10.1
Calculation of liquidated and ascertained damages (typical format)

Contract ....
Client ....
Architect ....

	costs/week
1 SUPERVISORY STAFF (current rates)	
Architect:	
Estimated hrs/wk . . . × time charge of £ . . ./hr	£
Quantity surveyor	
Estimated hrs/wk . . . × time charge of £ . . ./hr	£
Consultants [as above for each one]	£
Clerk of works	
Weekly salary (= yearly ÷ 52)	£
Total (1)	£

2 ADDITIONAL COSTS (current rates)	
Rent and/or rates and/or charges for present premises	£
Rent and/or rates and/or charges for alternative premises	£
Charges for equipment	£
Movement of equipment	£
Additional and/or continuing and/or substitute staff	£
Movement of staff (include travel expenses)	£
Any site charges which are the responsibility of the client	£
Extra payments to directly employed trades	£
Insurance	£
Additional administration costs	£
Total (2)	£

3 INTEREST

Interest payable on estimated capital expended up to the contract completion date, but from which no benefit is derived. Estimated expenditure taken as 80% of contract sum and fees.

Contract sum	£
Architect's fees (90%)*	£
Quantity surveyor's fees (90%)**	£
Consultants' fees (90%)**	£
Salary of clerk of works	£
(£/wk × contract period)	£

Interest charges at current rate of £ . . . %: interest therefore

$$= \frac{80\% \text{ capital expended} \times \text{interest}}{52}$$

Total (3)	£

Figure 10.1 (continued)

		costs/week
4 INFLATION		
Current rate of inflation . . . %/year		
Total (1) × . . . % × contract period (in years)		£
Total (2) × . . . % × contract period (in years)		£
	Total (4)	£
5 TOTAL LIQUIDATED AND ASCERTAINED DAMAGES/WEEK		
	Total (1)	£
	Total (2)	£
	Total (3)	£
	Total (4)	£
	Final total	£

---

* It is essential that all costs are additional: ie they would not be incurred if the contract were completed on the contract completion date.
The headings given are examples only; every job is different

**Professional fees are taken as 90% of total because some professional work remains to be done after practical completion.

If the architect cancels his certificate of non-completion because he has extended time, any liquidated damages deducted by the employer in the meanwhile must be repaid by him to the contractor. For example, the architect has issued a certificate of non-completion and the employer has deducted four week's liquidated damages at £750 a week, making a total of £3,000. The architect then issues a variation instruction, and assesses the resultant delay at three weeks, cancelling his first certificate and issuing a new one once the extended date is passed. The employer must then repay 3 × £750 = £2,250 to the contractor. The employer repays this sum net; the contractor has no right to interest on the money, either under the contract or under the general law (clause 2.8).

10.2.3 Procedure

Clause 2.3 is basically a simplified version of JCT 80, clause 25, but the provisions for the contractor to notify the architect of delays affecting progress are less detailed, and there are other important differences.

Flowchart 10.4 illustrates the contractor's duties in claiming an extension of time under clause 2.3.

Flowchart 10.5 sets out the duties of the architect in relation to such a claim. The procedure under clause 2.3 is as follows:

As soon as progress is, or is likely to be, delayed – the contract says "upon it becoming reasonably apparent" – the contractor must give the architect written notice of the cause of the delay *forthwith*. The wording of clause 2.3 is such that we think that it imposes a duty on the contractor to notify the architect of any delay (or likely delay) to progress and that it is not confined to notifying him of the events listed later.

No particular form of notice is prescribed, but if the notification does not give sufficient detail, the architect can require the contractor to provide him with such further information as is reasonably necessary to enable him to discharge his functions under the clause. **Figure 10.6** is a suitable letter from the contractor to the architect notifying a delay giving grounds for extension of time, and **Figure 10.7** is an example of a letter providing further information.

On receipt of the notice and any necessary supporting information, if the architect thinks that the completion of the works is being, or is likely to be, delayed by one or more of the events specified in clause 2.4, he must grant the contractor in writing a "fair and reasonable" extension of time for completion. He must do this "so soon as (he is) able to estimate the length of the delay". In making this estimate, the architect should take into account the overall proviso to the clause. This proviso is in two parts: the contractor is required constantly to use his best endeavours to prevent (not to reduce) delay (eg, by re-programming); and he must do all that may be reasonably required to the satisfaction of the architect to proceed with the works. What steps he must take depends on the circumstance of the case, but the architect cannot require him to accelerate progress, and his obligation stops short of expending substantial sums of money.

There is no specific time limit, but the architect must grant a fair and reasonable extension of time for completion "so soon as (he is) able to estimate the delay" beyond

Figure 10.2
Certificate of non-completion under clause 2.6

To the employer

CERTIFICATE OF NON-COMPLETION

[*Heading*]

In accordance with clause 2.6 of the above contract, I/we hereby certify that the contractor [*insert name*] has failed to complete the works by the date for completion stated in the appendix [*or*] within the extended time fixed by me/us under clause 2.3, namely [*insert date*].

Dated this   day of   19

[*Signed*]   Architect

Copy: Contractor

Figure 10.3
Cancellation of certificate of non-completion under clause 2.6 where time subsequently extended

To the employer

CANCELLATION OF CERTIFICATE OF NON-COMPLETION

[Heading]

In accordance with clause 2.6 of the above contract, I/we hereby cancel my/our certificate of non-completion dated [insert date], having made a further extension of time of [insert number] weeks for completion, under clause 2.3 of the contract.

Dated this   day of   19

[Signed]   Architect

Copy: Contractor

the currently fixed completion date. The various decided cases suggest that he must do so as soon as reasonably possible, although where there are multiple causes of delay, he may have no alternative but to leave the decision until a later stage. **Figure 10.8** is a suggested letter from an architect to a contractor awarding an extension.

Indeed, because the architect has a 12-week period from practical completion in which to grant further extensions of time if the circumstances warrant it, it may be argued that parsimony is the order of the day – though that is not the view of contractors! Failure properly to grant an extension of time may result in the contract completion date becoming at large, so the architect must be careful, although he has some room to manoeuvre.

The contractor's written notice is not in fact a preconditon (or "condition precedent" in lawyer's language) to the grant of an extension of time, because the clause goes on to empower the architect to grant an extension of time up to 12 weeks after the date of practical completion "whether upon reviewing a previous decision or otherwise and whether or not the contractor has given notice". The architect must, therefore, consider the contract as a whole and decide whether any extension of time is justified even if the contractor has failed to notify him of delays to progress. Unless he does this within the time limit laid down, the architect will jeopardize the employer's right to liquidated damages.

When considering extensions of time after practical completion, the architect cannot reduce any extension of time previously granted. The only effect of the contractor's failing to notify the architect of delays as the clause requires is that he loses the benefit of an extension of time during the currency of the contract, but he is still entitled to it after practical completion if the circumstances warrant it. This is especially important if delay has been caused by one of the specified events which are the employer's responsibility in law (eg, late instructions or details). So we suggest that as a matter of practice the architect should review every contract, and write to the contractor accordingly, even though the contract does not require him to do so.

Figure 10.9 is a suitable letter for the architect to send to the contractor.

IFC 84 expressly empowers the granting of an extension of time in respect of specified events which occur after the original extended completion date has passed but before practical completion is achieved thus the events in question are the following:

- compliance by the contractor with architect's instructions about inconsistencies (clause 1.4), variations (clause 3.6), provisional sum expenditure (clause 3.8), postponement of work (clause 3.15), and named sub-contractors (clause 3.3, as specified in that clause);
- compliance with architect's instructions requiring opening up for inspection or testing where the results are in the contractor's favour (clauses 3.12, 3.13.1);
- late instructions or drawings (eg clause 1.7);
- execution of work not forming part of the contract by, or on behalf of, the employer, or failure to supply goods or materials which he has undertaken to supply;
- failure by the employer to give any agreed access to or from the site.

Figure 10.4
Contractor's duties in claiming an extension of time
   (clause 2.3)

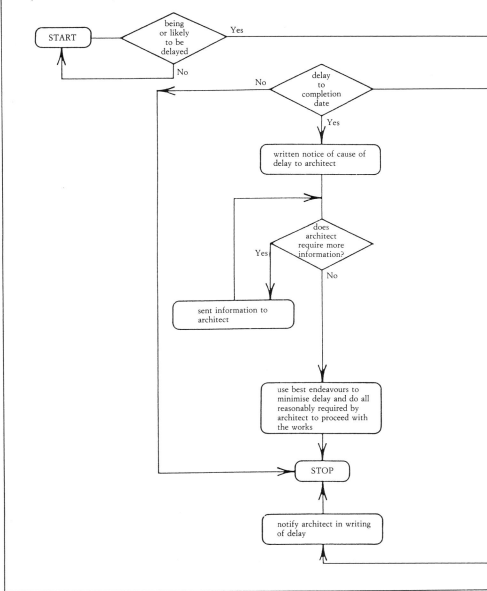

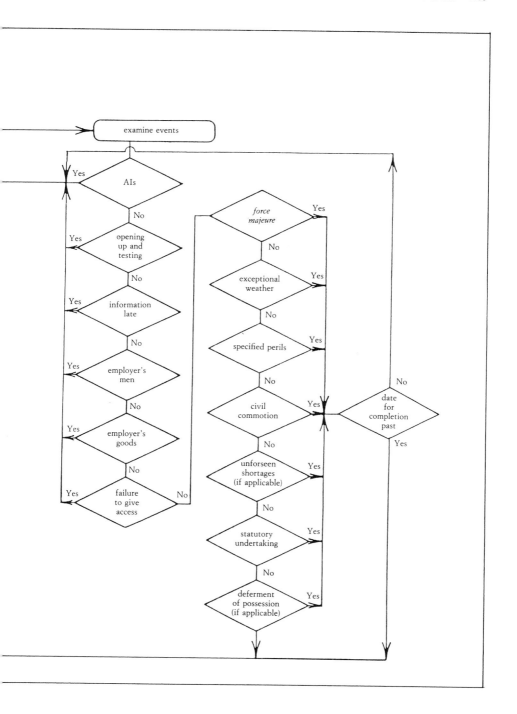

Figure 10.5
Architect's duties in relation to claim for extension of time (clause 2.3)

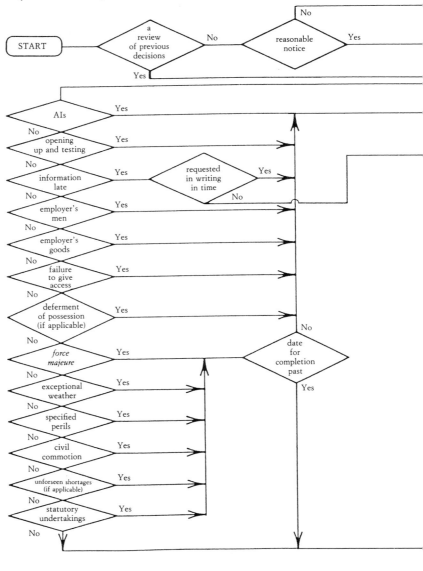

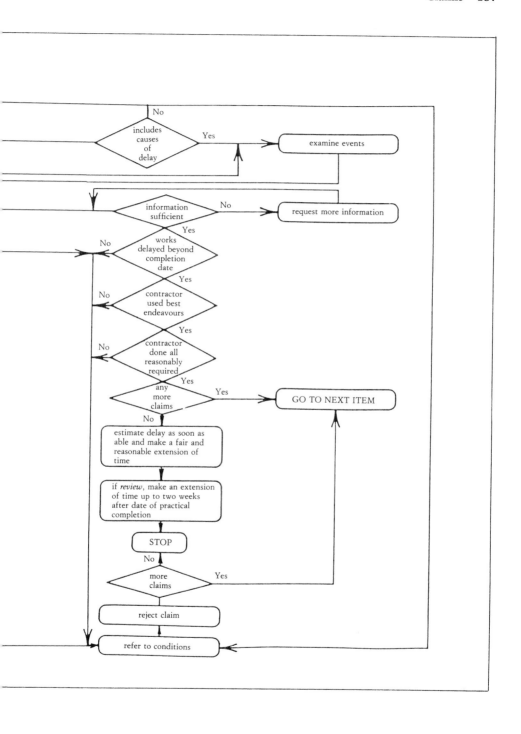

Where such an event occurs after the completion date but before practical completion, the architect must grant a fair and reasonable extension of the contract period for any resultant delay.

Although the provisions for the granting of extensions of time are explicit, considerable problems arise in practice. It cannot be over-emphasised that clause 2.3 is for the benefit of the employer as well as of the contractor. The proper exercise by the architect of clause 2.3 prevents the contract becoming "at large" and so preserves the employer's right to liquidated damages. The granting of an extension of time relieves the contractor of his liability to pay liquidated damages from the specified date and allows him extra time in which to complete the works where delay has been caused by events which the contract draughtsman has put at the employer's risk.

Many of the problems arise because the architect and the contractor are imperfectly aware of their obligations. Failure by the contractor to give notice of delay at the right time and to provide supporting information often results in extensions being granted later rather than sooner. It has to be admitted, however, that the fault is sometimes on the architect's side and we have known of cases where (unwisely) the architect has made unreasonable requests for further information in order to postpone the granting of an extension of time. **Figure 10.10** is a letter which may be useful in such circumstances. If the architect delays unreasonably in granting an extension of time, the contractor should write a letter along the lines of **Figure 10.11**.

10.2.4 Grounds

Fourteen events which may give rise to an extension of time are specified in clause 2.4, and the architect can extend the time for completion only if one or more of these events occurs and causes, or is likely to cause, delay to progress. The events listed are traditional and they largely parallel those in JCT 80, although there are differences.

The events divide into two distinct and separate groups: namely, those which merely entitle the contractor to an extension of time, and those which may also, quite independently, found a claim for loss and/or expense under clause 4.11.

Events giving rise to time only are as follows:

Force majeure

Although wider in its meaning than the English term "Act of God", this has a restricted meaning here, because many matters which would otherwise constitute *force majeure* are dealt with expressly. For an event to amount to *force majeure*, it must be catastrophic and outside the control or contemplation of either contracting party (clause 2.4.1).

Exceptionally adverse weather conditions

The key word is "exceptionally", since the contractor is expected to programme to take account of the sort of weather normally to be expected in the area at the relevant time of year. Moreover, the mere occurrence of exceptionally adverse weather – such as a fall of snow in the Midlands in mid-June – is not sufficient. It must actually delay progress (clause 2.4.2).

Figure 10.6
Contractor to architect notifying delay

Dear Sir

[Heading]

In accordance with clause 2.3. of the Contract we give you formal notice that the progress of the works is being delayed by [specify event] which is a ground for the grant of an extension of time under clause 2.3.

In order to assist you in reaching a decision, we provide the following information [specify]. This, as you will see, is likely to cause further delay to [specify activity]. We are, of course, using our best endeavours to minimize the delay, but we must ask you to exercise the power of granting an extension of time for completion in accordance with clause 2.3.

Yours faithfully

Figure 10.7
  Contractor to architect, providing further information

Dear Sir

[*Heading*]

Thank your for your letter of [*insert date*] requesting further information in respect of [*state what architect requires*].

As you request, we enclose [*specify enclosures*]. We trust that this information is sufficient for your purposes.

[*if architect is not specific in his request*]:

However, we believe that we gave you all the information which you require in our letter of [*insert date*] and it is not clear from your letter what further information you now require. If you will be good enough to be specific, we shall be pleased to provide you with any further information in our possession.

Yours faithfully

Clause 6.3 perils

These are the usual insurance risks – fire, tempest, and so on (clause 2.4.3).

Strikes and similar events

For the most part, the list of events is self-evident, and the breadth of the strike clause should be noted. It covers strikes, etc, affecting any of the trades employed on the works and also those engaged in preparing or transporting materials, needed for the works (clause 2.4.4).

Shortage of labour and materials

These are optional grounds and will rank for extension of time only if stated in the appendix to apply. The limitation should be noted: the inability must be for reasons beyond the contractor's control; and the shortage, etc, must not have been reasonably forseeable at the date of tender – ie, the date 10 days before the date fixed for receipt of tenders by the employer (see clause 8.3). It is suggested that clauses 2.4.10 and 2.4.11 should be stated to apply in the appendix unless it is reasonable in all the circumstances to expect contractors tendering for the work to take the risk that labour or materials or both will not be available (clauses 2.4.10 and 2.4.11).

Local authority or statutory undertaker's work

This covers only work done "in pursuance of . . . statutory obligations in relation to the works" or failure to carry out such work. If a statutory undertaker (eg, a gas board) does work under contract with the employer, this would fall under clause 3.11 and be dealt with under clause 2.4.8 as regards extension of time (clause 2.4.13).

The important point about all the foregoing events is that delay from one of them does not give rise to any claim for extra cost but merely to a claim for extension of time. Their common characteristic is that they are outside the control of either contracting party, whereas the second group consists of events which are the responsibility of the employer, either personally or through those for whom he is vicariously responsible in law.

Events giving rise to time and independently, to direct loss and/or expense are as follows:

Architect's instructions

Those referred to are: clause 1.4, inconsistencies; clause 3.6, variations; clause 3.8, expenditure of provisional sums; clause 3.15, postponement of any work to be executed under the contract; clause 3.3, named sub-contractors to the extent specified in clause 3.3 itself (clause 2.4.5); clauses 3.12 and 3.13.1, opening up or testing and failure of work – to the extent that the contractor is not at fault (clause 2.4.6).

Late instructions and drawings

The instructions must be those empowered by the contract (see **Table 4.2**), and there are limitations. The contractor must have made a specific application at the right

Figure 10.8
Architect to contractor, granting extension of time under clause 2.3

Dear Sir

[*Heading*]

I/we refer to your notice of delay of [*insert date*]. [*If appropriate add*] and the further information provided in your letter of [*insert date*].

In accordance with clause 2.3 of the contract, I/we hereby grant you an extension of time of [*specify period*], the revised date for completion now being [*insert date*].

Yours faithfully

Figure 10.9
Architect to contractor after reviewing extensions of time

Dear Sirs

[Heading]

In accordance with clause 2.3 of the contract, I/we have now considered the contract progress as a whole and [either] I/we confirm the date of completion (as extended) as being [insert date] [or] I/we hereby grant you an extension of time of [specify period] to take account of [specify], thus giving a revised date for completion of [insert date].

Yours faithfully

Figure 10.10
Contractor to architect who unreasonably requests further information

Dear Sir

[*Heading*]

Thank you for your letter of [*insert date*] in which you request further information in respect of [*specify*] to enable you to grant an extension of time.

On [*insert date*] we notified you of delay to progress as required by the contract and with that notice we enclosed full details of the effects of the notified event upon progress by reference to our up-dated programme. This showed that the delay was on the critical path. In response to your letter of [*insert date*] we provided you with the further information you requested.

We believe that we have given you the fullest information to enable you to reach a decision and we regret that we consider your letter under reply to be an attempt to postpone the granting of an extension of time. This is in neither in the interests of the employer nor of ourselves and we must call upon you to exercise the duty imposed on you by clause 2.3 of the contract and to grant a fair and reasonable extension of time for completion.

Yours faithfully

time, and this is a matter where there is much room for argument. The wording is clear – the contractor must make a specific written application in each case, and what is a reasonable time does not depend solely on the contractor's convenience. He must have need of the information and be able to act on it, and the reasonableness of the timing is to be judged by the contract completion date.

Work not forming part of the contract

Clause 3.11 enables the employer to carry out such work either himself or through others, and, because of the breadth of the wording, this ground extends to cover a situation where, for example, such work is done badly by direct contractors and delay is caused by subsequent remedial work (clause 2.4.8).

Supply or non-supply of materials by employer

This applies only where the employer has so agreed (clause 2.4.9).

Employer's failure to give agreed access

This is not so extensive as might at first sight appear. The wording should be noted. An extension of time cannot be granted on this ground if, for example, the employer fails to obtain a wayleave over a third party's property and certainly will not extend to deal with the situation where site access is impeded by third parties for whom the employer has no responsibility in law (clause 2.4.12).

Deferment of possession

This will give rise to an extension of time when clause 2.2 is stated to apply and an extension of time is an almost necessary concomitant of deferment of possession.

10.3 Loss and Expense Claims

10.3.1 Definition

Clause 4.11 gives the contractor a right to be reimbursed "direct loss and/or expense" which he incurs as the result of the events specified and for which there is no other payment under the contract, provided he follows the procedure laid down. Claims for loss and expenses are a regulated provision for the payment of sums equivalent to damages.

"Direct loss and/or expense" is to be equated with the damages recoverable for breach of contract at common law. The purpose of the clause is to set out the contractor's rights in anticipation of the specified events and is the means of putting the contractor back into the position in which he would have been but for the delay or disruption.

Since the settlement amounts to damages at common law, an exact establishment of the contractor's additional costs must be made. Many contractors hold a fallacious

Figure 10.11
Contractor to tardy architect

Dear Sir

[*Heading*]

On [*insert date*] we gave you formal notice of delay under clause 2.3 of the contract and requested you to grant us a fair and reasonable extension of time for completion. At your request, on [*insert date*] we provided you with further information to enable you to reach a decision, namely [*specify information provided*]. We enclose copies of both the notice of delay and the supporting information referred to.

It is now [*insert number*] weeks since the date of our notice and we consider that you have had more than sufficient time in which to reach your decision, particularly as you are aware that because of the delay, the [*specify activity*] work has had to be postponed. We shall be very grateful if you will proceed at once to grant the necessary extension of time in the interests of both the employer and ourselves.

Yours faithfully

view about claims generally, and the following three important points are often overlooked:

- the contractor must "mitigate his loss" ie, take reasonable steps to diminish his loss, for example by redeploying his resources;
- since damages are subject to the common-law "forseeability test", the contractor can recover only that part of the resultant loss and/or expense that was reasonably forseeable to result. This is to be judged at the time the contract was made and not in the light of the events which have occurred;
- the loss and/or expense must be direct. It must have been caused by the event relied on without any intervening cause.

10.3.2 Procedure

The contract requires the contractor to make a written application to the architect within a reasonable time of its becoming apparent that he has incurred, or is likely to incur, loss or expense resulting from specified causes. These are that the employer defers giving possession of the site under clause 2.2 (if applicable); *or* that the regular progress of the works is "materially" affected by one or more of the seven matters set out in clause 4.12. "Materially" means to a substantial extent.

The contractor's written application need not be in any particular set form, but the architect may require him to provide further information to enable the architect (or the quantity surveyor) to assess the claim. The sort of information that may be required will depend on the circumstances, and it is the contractor's duty to provide the architect (or the quantity surveyor) with sufficient documentary evidence to enable the claim to be dealt with. **Figures 10.12** and **10.13** may be used by the contractor as pro-formas. When the contractor has made a written application, the architect must decide whether he has incurred, or is likely to incur, loss and/or expense resulting from one or more of the specified matters, and he must also be satisfied that the contractor is not receiving payment in respect of it under some other contract provision (eg, under clause 3.7 in respect of variations).

If the architect is so satisfied, then he must ascertain the amount of the loss or expense, or instruct the quantity surveyor to do so on his behalf. Figures cannot be plucked out of the air: "ascertain" means to establish definitely and is not the same as "estimate" or "guess". The amount so ascertained is to be included in the next payment certificate.

The contract allows additional or alternative claims for breach of contract based on the same facts, as is made clear by the last sentence of clause 4.11, which preserves contractor's normal rights at common law. Because of this provision, the contractor may also bring common law claims, which are often based on implied terms relating to non-interference with his progress. The architect has no power or authority to deal with common law claims: the only claims which he can deal with are those arising under clause 4.11. From the contractor's point of view, the fact that his common law rights are preserved is a very real benefit, because if he has failed to make the written application required by clause 4.11, and so has lost his right to reimbursement under the contract terms, he can bring a claim at common law based on the same facts, given

Figure 10.12
  Written application for reimbursement of direct loss and/or expense

To the Architect

Dear Sir

[*Heading*]

In accordance with clause 4.11 of the contract we hereby make written application to you for reimbursement of direct loss and/or expense in the execution of this contract for which we will not be reimbursed by payment under any other contractual provision, because regular progress of the works has been affected by [*specify, eg, compliance with your Instruction No 3 or as appropriate*], this being a matter specified in clause [*insert number*].

Yours faithfully

Figure 10.13
Contractor's response to architect's request for information

Dear Sir

[*Heading*]

Thank you for your letter of [*date*] in which you request us to provide further information in support of our application for reimbursement of direct loss and/or expense dated [*date*].

[Specify information, eg As you will see from the enclosed updated programme showing the current situation on site, your variation instruction No [*insert number*] requiring us to [*specify nature of varied work*] will require an additional three weeks and the carrying out of this work means that the following activities will inevitably be disrupted and delayed].

We trust that this information is sufficient for your purposes.

Yours faithfully

---

that the event relied on is also a breach of contract (eg, late instructions from the architect). Such claims, however, must be pursued in arbitration or litigation.

Flowchart 10.14 sets out the contractor's duties under clause 4.11. **Flowchart 10.15** sets out the architect's duties under the provision.

10.3.3 Matters grounding a claim

Seven "matters" are listed in clause 4.12, and it is the occurrence of one of these – or the employer's deferment of giving possession of the site – which triggers off a claim.

The clause 4.12 matters are as follows:

- late instructions: the paragraph refers to the contractor's not having received necessary instructions, etc, from the architect in due time. Two conditions must be met before a claim can be allowed under this head: the contractor must have specifically applied to the architect in writing for the information; and his application must have been made in due time;
- opening up for inspection: the inspection or test must have shown that the work, materials, or goods were in accordance with the contract if a claim is to be made;
- execution of work by those engaged by the employer: see clause 3.11;
- supply or non-supply of materials by employer: the employer must have agreed with the contractor to so supply;
- postponement of work: see clause 3.15;
- failure to give ingress or egress: see clause 4.12.6;
- architect's instructions: (clause 4.12.7) those referred to are issued under clause
  .. nsistencies), 3.6 (variations), 3.8 (provisional sums), and 3.3 (named sub-
       ors: as specified in that clause).

ımmary

or time and money are distinct; there is no necessary connection between

nages

ıges are:
       -estimate of likely loss or a lesser sum;
       .thout proof of loss;
       ..ɔle by deduction under the contract only if the architect issued a cer-
       ..cate of delay *and* the employer has notified the contractor in writing of his
intention to require liquidated damages.

Extension of time

The architect is bound to grant a fair and reasonable extension of time for completion on the happening of certain events. Failure to do so may result in the contract date becoming "at large" and liquidated damages being irrecoverable.

The contractor must observe the contract notice procedure and, if he does so the architect must:

- grant in writing a fair and reasonable extension of time for completion as soon as practicable;
- review contract progress within 12 weeks of practical completion and adjust the contract time accordingly, even if the contractor has not notified him of an event giving rise to an extension of time;
- grant an extension of time only on grounds specified in the contract.

Loss and expense claims

The contractor has a right to be reimbursed "direct loss and/or expense" under the contract on the happening of certain disruptive events provided he invokes the contract procedures.

The contractor must:

- make written application to the architect at the right time;
- provide you with the necessary supporting evidence.

The architect must:

- be satisfied that the notified event is a valid ground of claim;
- ascertain (or instruct the quantity surveyor so to do) the amount of loss or expense directly incurred;
- include the sum so ascertained in the next certificate of payment.

The architect has no power under the contract to deal with common law or *ex gratia* claims.

Figure 10.14
Contractor's duties in claiming loss and/or expense (clause 4.11)

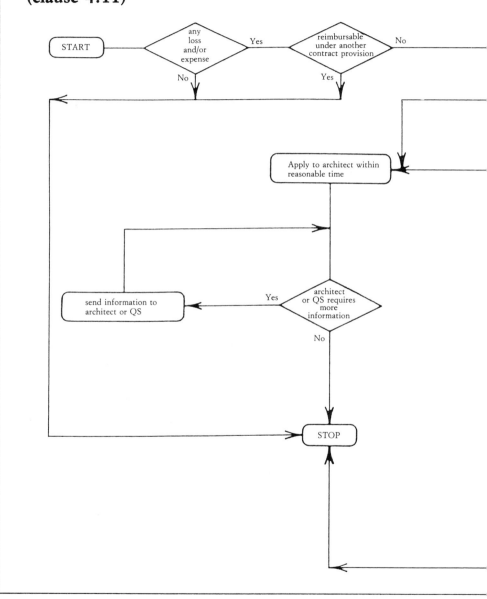

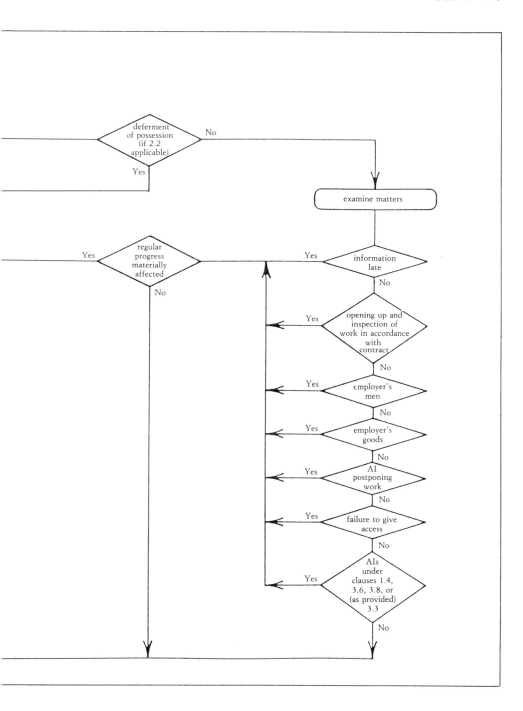

Figure 10.15
Architect's duties in relation to a claim for loss and/or expense (clause 4.11)

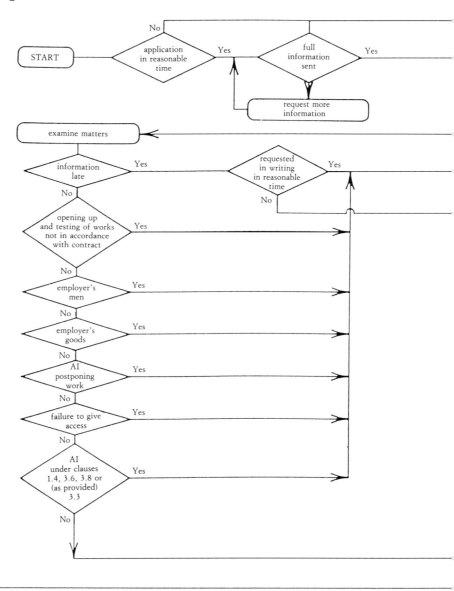

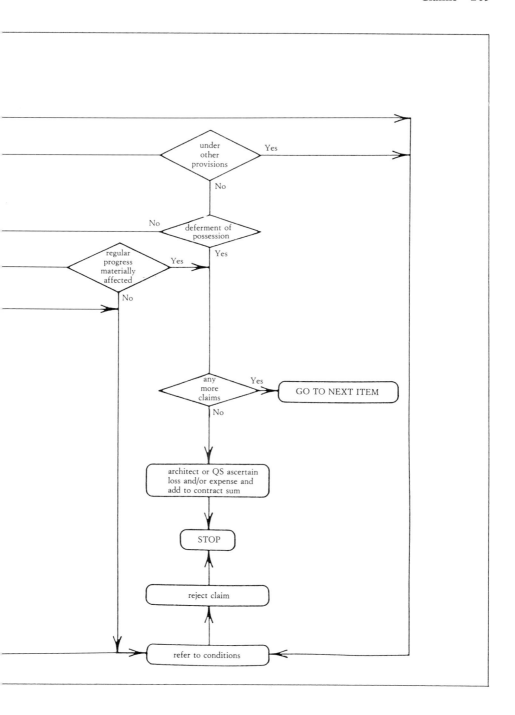

11–Payment

11.1 The Contract Sum

The figure shown in article 2 of the agreement is of great importance. It is the amount for which the contractor has agreed to carry out the whole of the work. In contracts such as IFC 84, which are known as "lump sum contracts", the contractor is entitled to payment provided he substantially completes the whole of the work. The fact that the contract provides the interim payments does not alter the position. If he abandons the work before it is finished, the employer is entitled to pay nothing more. The principle of interim payments is to provide sufficient money to allow the contractor to carry out the work. It is purely a business arrangement. It matters not that the contractor has imparted considerable benefit to the employer. If he does not substantially complete the work, he is not entitled to payment (*Hoenig* v *Isaacs* [1952] 2 All ER 176). In practice, this severe view is somewhat modified if the employer determines the contractor's employment (see **section 12.1.7**).

The contract sum may be adjusted only in accordance with the provisions of the contract (see **Table 11.1**). Errors or omissions of any kind in the computation of the contract sum are deemed to have been accepted by employer and contractor (clause 4.1). The only exceptions to that are those instances specifically provided for (see **section 3.1.3**). They are inconsistencies in or between documents; errors or omissions in description or quantity; errors or omissions in the particulars relating to named persons; and departures from the Standard Method of Measurement. The contractor may make all kinds of errors in pricing the contract documents. He may under- or over-price items, overlook items, or simply make a mistake in adding up totals. Once his price is accepted, however, it may not be altered. The quantity surveyor will have checked the contractor's calculations before the tender was accepted, but he may not have noticed the error. It is always bad, from the point of view of both contractor and employer, if the contractor finds, after the contract is in being, that he has made

Table 11.1
Contractual provisions which allow adjustment of the contract sum

Clause	Provision
2.10	Deduction for defects not to be made good
3.3.4(a)	Adjustments after determination of named person's employment
3.7	Additions or deductions in respect of instructions requiring a variation
3.9	Deduction for setting out errors not to be amended
3.12	Additions to cover the cost of opening up or testing if the works is in accordance with the contract
4.5	Final adjustment of the contract sum
4.9	Adjustment to take account of fluctuations
4.10	Adjustments to take account of fluctuations in respect of named persons
4.11	Additions for loss and/or expense
5.1	Additions for statutory fees and charges
6.2.4	Additions for insurance for the liability, etc, of the employer
6.3B.2	Additions for employer's failure to insure
6.3C.3	Additions for employer's failure to insure

an error which will result in his losing money. He will naturally attempt to recoup his losses by taking every opportunity to submit claims. So particular care must be exercised, before a tender is recommended for acceptance, that the checks made by the architect or the quantity surveyor have been thorough and that the final figure does not appear suspiciously low in comparison with other tenders.

11.2 Payment before Practical Completion

11.2.1 Method and timing

The parties may make whatever arrangements they wish for interim payments. Where the contract is of relatively high value, it is customary to pay at monthly intervals, but if the value is low or the priced documents make it convenient, it may suit both parties to agree that payment will be made on the completion of certain defined stages. The parties may have the agreement set out in the specification, schedules of work, or bills of quantities before entering into the contract, or they may agree the mode of payment before commencing work. If a particular system of payment is desired, it is best to have it set out in the contract documents at tender stage because

- the method and regularity of payment will significantly influence the contractor's tender, and because;
- if no agreement to the contrary is concluded after the parties have entered into a contract, the provisions of clause 4.2 will apply.

The contractual provisions are straightforward, but certain points will need careful study.

Payment is to be made after the architect issues his certificate. The interval between certificates is to be one month (ie, one calendar month) unless a different interval is stated in the appendix. The intervals are calculated from the date of possession. In the case of deferment, it is suggested that, to avoid absurdity, the intervals are to be calculated from the new or deferred date of possession. The architect's first certificate is due one month from the date of possession. It must include the total of the amounts as specified in clauses 4.2.1 and 4.2.2 at a date not more than seven days before the date of the certificate. The employer has 14 days from the date of the certificate to make payment.

If a calendar month is some four weeks, the contractor could wait six weeks from the date of possession before receiving his first payment for three weeks' work. The importance of prompt payment cannot be over-emphasised. It is a means of assisting the contractor's cash flow, reducing his overdraft requirements and hence the interest he has to pay, and so increasing his chance of making a reasonable profit, thus making him less likely to resort to the submission of claims.

11.2.2 Valuation

Whenever the architect feels that it is necessary to do so, he is empowered to request the quantity surveyor to carry out a valuation before he issues his certificate.

The clause says "necessary for the purpose of ascertaining the amount to be stated as due". To ascertain is to find out for certain, so the architect will take this step when he feels unable to know for certain without the aid of the quantity surveyor. Because the process of valuation is specialised, there will be few instances, in practice, when he will not require the quantity surveyor's assistance if he is wise.

The amount to be included on the architect's certificate is to be the total of amounts in clauses 4.2.1 and 4.2.2, less only any amounts included on previous certificates – note, not any amounts previously paid, but any amounts previously certified. Therefore, the architect need not concern himself, when certifying, whether the employer has paid or paid in full. The amounts to be included are divided into two categories: those items of which only 95% of their value are to be included (ie, the employer will keep 5% as retention); and those whose full value must be included (ie, no retention).

The items are discussed in **section 11.2.3.** The question of value requires more consideration. There is a very large difference of opinion about the meaning of the word "value" in this context. It is of great importance because, in the event of the contractor's insolvency, it is essential that the architect has not overcertified (*Sutcliffe* v *Thackrah* [1974] 1 All ER 319). Certification is his responsibility whether or not he has worked from the quantity surveyor's valuation. If the architect disagrees with the quantity surveyor's valuation, his duty is to change it. The architect must ensure that the quantity surveyor puts no value on defective work. He cannot be expected to know what the architect considers to be defective unless he is told this should be done in writing, every month before the valuation is carried out.

So what is the value of the contractor's work? One school of thought, generally accepted throughout the industry, is that the value of the contractor's work is to be ascertained by reference to the priced contract document. His entitlement is to be payment for the work he has properly done at the rates he has inserted in the document. It seems reasonable. Defective work is not included, and a sum of money is retained against problems arising. The biggest problem which could arise is that the contractor goes into liquidation immediately following a payment.

The second school of thought derives from this pessimistic outlook. The value of the contractor's work, from the employer's point of view, is the value of the whole contract less the cost of completing with the aid of another contractor and with additional professional fees. The additional cost to the employer in such circumstances is considerable.

The retention fund, even at a late stage, would not cover it. In operating the latter system, certificates in the early stages of a contract might be very low or even for minus figures. The chief difficulty is in deciding how much it would cost to complete the contract at the time of each valuation. (Here, the quantity surveyor, in his role as building economist, bears a heavy responsibility.) There are, therefore, two possible interpretations to put on the word "value": the value to the builder, or the value to the employer. The second system may seem harsh to the contractor, but it has the merit of ensuring an adequate supply of funds if the contractor has to abandon the work. Contractors obviously do not like this approach, moreover, that the first view is the better one is supported by *Townsend* v *Stone Toms & Partners* (1984) 27 BLR 26.

11.2.3 Amounts included

It is logical to consider the amounts separately in the two categories. Amounts on which the employer is allowed a 5% retention are the following:

- The total value of the work properly executed by the contractor, including items classed as variations (clause 3.7), and formulae adjustment (clause 4.9(b)). The interpretation put on "value" has already been discussed (**section 11.2.2**).
- The total value of materials which have been reasonably and not prematurely delivered to, or adjacent to, the works for incorporation, provided that they are adequately protected against weather and damage. The certificate need not include any materials which the contractor has clearly delivered to site for the express purpose of obtaining payment. Clause 1.10, unfixed materials, and clause 3.2.2, sub-contracting, are intended to ensure that materials paid for in this way by the employer become his property in law (clause 4.2.1(b)). Whether they are successful will very much depend on whether they are the sub-contractor's property in the first instance.
- The value of any off-site materials, at the architect's discretion. The inclusion of off-site materials in his certificate has the potential to raise serious problems. Clause 1.11 is intended to ensure that, once the employer has paid for them, the materials become his property. The contractor is not permitted to remove the materials, or to allow anyone else to do so, except for use on the works. All the while, the contractor is to remain responsible to the employer for any loss or damage. There are two dangers. First, that the supplier may have incorporated a retention-of-title clause in the contract of sale to the contractor. That means that, despite anything which might be written into this contract, the materials remain the property of the supplier until he receives payment from the contractor. Compare these provisions with the provisions for sub-contractor's materials in clause 3.2.2 (see **section 8.2.1**). The architect would be prudent to insist on inspecting the supplier's conditions of sale before considering including the value of off-site materials. Second, it is difficult to be sure that the materials inspected at the contractor's yard are not really intended for some other job. Unlike JCT 80 clause 30.3, IFC 84 contains no provisions which adequately protect the employer's interest. It is suggested that a wise architect would adopt JCT 80 clause 30.3 provisions. Even then, the situation is not absolutely safe. It has been known for a contractor to label and set aside, say, sink units for a particular contract until after inspection by the architect, then relabel them for the benefit of another architect and a different contract. That is sharp practice, but, if the contractor goes into liquidation, there is no consolation for the employer. In practice, the prudent architect should not include off-site materials unless he decides that it would be quite unfair not to do so, and he has satisfied himself, as far as it is possible to do so, that the employer's interests are fully protected. If something goes wrong, the employer's position will be that he paid only on the architect's advice. The architect might be liable.

Amounts on which the employer is allowed no retention are the following:
- in accordance with clause 2.1, where the employer requires use or occupation and an additional premium is required by the insurers;
- in accordance with clause 3.12, where the contractor has carried out opening up and/or testing and the work is found to be in accordance with the contract. The contractor is entitled to be paid the cost of the work and the cost of making good;
- in accordance with clause 4.9(a), contribution, levy, and tax fluctuations;
- in accordance with clause 4.10, named-person fluctuations;
- in accordance with clause 4.11, where the contractor is entitled to payment of direct loss and/or expense due to disturbance of regular progress;
- in accordance with clause 5.1, where the contractor has paid statutory fees or charges which were not provided for in the contract documents;
- in accordance with clause 6.2.4, where the contractor has taken out and maintained special insurance which is the liability of the employer;
- in accordance with clause 6.3A.4.4, where the contractor has insured the works and an insurance claim has been accepted;
- in accordance with clause 6.3B.2, where the employer, not being a local authority, has failed to insure and the contractor can produce evidence that he has taken out the appropriate insurance himself;
- in accordance with clause 6.3B.3.5 where the contractor has restored loss or damage;
- in accordance with clause 6.3C.1, where the employer has failed to insure and the contractor can produce evidence that he has taken out the appropriate insurance himself;
- in accordance with clause 6.3C.4.4 where the contractor has restored loss or damage and the employer has insured.

The amounts payable will depend on the amounts ascertained at the time of the valuation. Deductions are to be made in this category as follows:
- in accordance with clause 3.9, where the architect has instructed that errors in setting out should not be amended and an appropriate deduction should be made;
- in accordance with clause 4.9(a), contribution, levy, and tax fluctuations as appropriate;
- in accordance with clause 4.10, named-person fluctuations as appropriate.

Not included in this clause, probably by oversight, is the provision in clause 2.10 that if the architect instructs that defects, shrinkages, and other faults are not to be made good, an appropriate deduction is to be made.

11.3 Payment at Practical Completion

Although it is nowhere expressly stated, regular interim certificates and payments will cease at practical completion, simply because there will be no further work to certify. It may be that a particularly difficult claim will not be settled until a month or two after practical completion. The architect should make certain that, in such a case, money is released to the contractor whenever he is confident that any part of the claim is valid. There is no contractual liability upon him to do so, however, and he may, if he wishes, wait until the whole claim has been quantified before certifying. It is not permissible to wait until the issue of the final certificate. It is probable that, if practical completion has passed by more than 14 days, the contractor can invoke clause 4.2 to compel the architect to issue a certificate once the claim has been ascertained. The difficulty for the contractor lies in knowing precisely when ascertainment has taken place.

The contract provides for a special payment to be made at practical completion (clause 4.3). The architect must issue a certificate within 14 days of the date of practical completion. The employer must pay, as before, within 14 days of the date of the certificate. The amounts to be included fall into the same categories (see **section 11.2.3**) as for interim certificates. There is an important difference, however. The architect must include 97½% of the value of amounts in the first category, compared with 95% included in that category before practical completion. This has the effect that the employer releases half the retention he has been holding. The remaining retention is held by the employer until the final certificate.

11.4 Retention

Retention is dealt with specifically by clause 4.4. The object of the clause is to safeguard the contractor's interest in the retention, but there are other implications. So it is curious that the initial provision excludes local authorities from its operation. This must be because the draughtsman, while following accepted practice in assuming that a local authority will not become insolvent, overlooked the clause's broader application.

The employer is stated to be a trustee and his interest in the retention to be fiduciary (which amounts to much the same). He is a trustee for the contractor. That means that the contractor has the right to insist that the retention fund be kept in a separate bank account clearly designated as held in trust for the contractor. This safeguards the money if the employer becomes insolvent. Some contracts now have a special provision requiring the separate account.

Although the employer holds the retention in trust for the contractor, the clause states that he has no obligation to invest – that is, no obligation to make the best use of the money on behalf of the contractor and to return him interest on it. Since this provision is contrary to statute, it is probable that it is a position the employer could not defend if a contractor decided to take action on it. However, the point has yet to be decided by the courts.

The contractor's interest in the retention is said to be subject only to the employer's right to take money from it from time to time to pay amounts which the contract provides for him to deduct from sums due or to become due to the contractor. So this clause, which is not applicable to local authorities, is the only express term allowing the employer to use retention monies for other than the contractor's purposes. No doubt, in the complete absence of this clause, a term would be implied to allow the employer to deduct from the retention to make good the contractor's defaults. In the case of a local authority, the clause is not absent, but it is stated to apply only "where the employer is not a local authority". We suggest that local authorities should amend this clause with the aid of their expert advisors.

A list of the contract provisions referred to in this clause is given in **Table 11.2**.

11.5 Final Payment

The contract lays down a strict time sequence for the events leading up to, and the issue of, the final certificate (see **Figure 11.1**). The contractor has a duty to provide the architect, or the quantity surveyor if the architect so instructs, with all the documents which are reasonably required for the final adjustment of the contract sum (clause 4.5). **Figure 11.2** is a suitable letter. He may send them either before practical completion but no later than 6 months afterwards. The architect is entitled to request the kind of documents he requires or to request particular documents, provided that the requests are reasonable in the circumstances.

Armed with this information, the quantity surveyor must prepare a statement of all the final valuations under clause 3.7. A copy of all the computations to arrive at the finally adjusted contract sum together with the statement must be sent to the contractor within 3 months of receipt. But if the contractor is unreasonably late in sending his documents, he cannot expect the architect to adhere to this timetable.

The contract does not state that the contractor must agree the finally adjusted contract sum before the final certificate is issued. In practice it is customary to try to obtain agreement, and the contractor is usually sent two copies of the computations, one for him to sign as agreed and return. This is, no doubt, why the contract allows 28 days from sending the computations or issuing a certificate of making good defects under clause 2.10, whichever is the later, for the architect to issue his final certificate (clause 4.6). The contract unaccountably allows 28 days for the employer or the contractor, as the case may be, to pay.

The final certificate must include the following:
- the total value referred to in clause 4.2.1(a) – ie, release of all the retention;
- the amounts referred to in clause 4.2.2 finally ascertained, less any amount which is to be deducted under clause 2.10, defects liability; clause 3.9, levels; clause 4.9(a), contribution, levy and tax fluctuations; or clause 4.10, named-person fluctuations;
- less any sums previously certified.

If the result is in favour of the contractor, the employer will be liable to pay; if the result is in favour of the employer, the contractor will be liable to pay. The latter is a somewhat unusual situation.

If the architect fails to issue the final certificate in accordance with this timescale, the contractor should tell him immediately (**Figure 11.3**).

Table 11.2
Contract provisions which entitle the employer to deduct from any sum due or to become due to the contractor

Clause	Provisions
2.7	Liquidated damages
3.5.1	Costs of employing other persons to carry out instructions
6.2.3	Contractor's failure to insure
6.3A.2	Contractor's failure to insure

11.6 The Effect of Certificates

Clause 4.8 provides that no certificate, other than the final certificate, is conclusive evidence that any work, materials, or goods to which it relates are in accordance with the contract. All certificates, except the final certificate, are included, whether financial or not. For example the issue of the certificate of practical completion does not prevent the architect from requiring the contractor to make good work not in accordance with the contract. The issue of an interim certificate is not evidence that all the work included is in accordance with the contract. The architect is entitled to omit defective work from one certificate if it has been included on a previous certificate.

The final certificate is not conclusive (clause 4.7) as was once understood. There appears to be no good reason why it should be. The final certificate does have a conclusive effect in four respects:

- where, and to the extent that, approval of the quality of materials or of the standards of workmanship is a matter for the architect's opinion. The final certificate is conclusive that the quality and standards are to his reasonable satisfaction. The important nature of this clause, in conjunction with clause 1.1, has been discussed fully in **section 4.2.1**;
- the final certificate is conclusive evidence that the terms of the contract which require additions, deductions, or adjustments to the contract sum has been correctly operated;
- all due extensions of time have been given;
- reimbursement of loss and/or expense is in final settlement of all contractor's claims in respect of clause 4.12 matters.

There are two exceptions:

- if there have been any accidental inclusions or exclusions of any items, or any arithmetical errors in any computation, they may be corrected;
- if any matter is the subject of proceedings commenced before, or within 28 days after, the issue of the final certificate, the certificate is not conclusive regarding that matter. Thus, either party has 28 days after the date of issue to refer to arbitration or to commence legal action through the courts. If the matter is not one about which the certificate is stated to be conclusive, the parties have the normal limitation periods of either six or 12 years in which to bring an action, depending on whether the contract is under hand or under seal respectively.

The conclusion is that, provided that the architect has left nothing or very little to be to his satisfaction or approval, and provided that the quantity surveyor has done his adjustment of the contract sum correctly, the issue of the final certificate is very much in the employer's interest.

11.7 Variations

Unless the contract is extremely simple, the valuation of variations is best left in the hands of the quantity surveyor. This attitude is adopted in IFC 84, and clause

Figure 11.1
IFC 84 – Time Chart

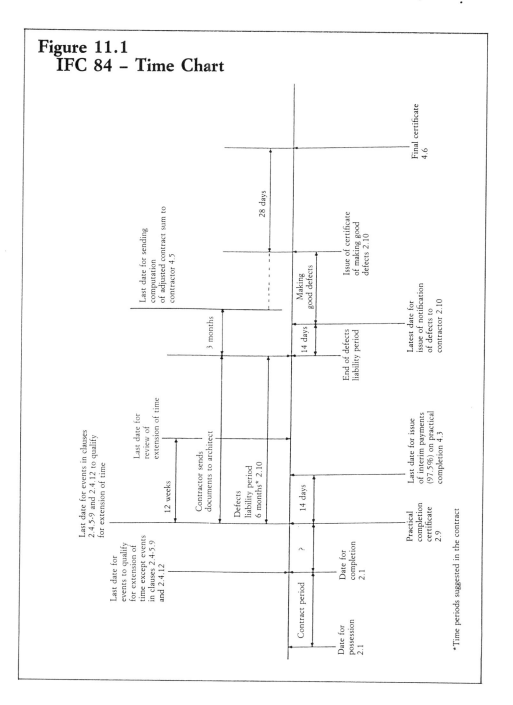

*Time periods suggested in the contract

Figure 11.2
Contractor to architect, enclosing all documentation for the preparation of final certificate

Dear Sir

In accordance with clause 4.5 of the contract we enclose full details of the final account for this contract together with all supporting documentation.

We should be pleased if you would proceed with the necessary calculations and verifications to enable the final certificate to be issued in accordance with the contract.

Yours faithfully

3.7 requires that the quantity surveyor shall make all valuations of variations. There is just one exception to this rule. The contractor and the employer may agree on the amount to be added to, or deducted from, the contract sum before the contractor carries out the work. This simply states the general position, because two parties to a contract can vary its terms in any way they both agree. The inclusion of the term merely makes it clear that if the contractor is asked to quote for carrying out some work which would normally be the subject of a valuation by the quantity surveyor, the employer may simply accept the quotation. The amount of the quotation is then added to, or deducted from, the contract sum as appropriate. Note that the contract expressly reserves the right of agreement to the employer, not to the architect.

The quantity surveyor's principal tool in carrying out valuations is what this contract refers to as the "priced document" (clause 3.7.1). The wide range of possible documents has been discussed in **section 3.1.1.** The priced documents may be any one of the following: the priced specification, or the priced schedule of work, or the priced bills of quantities, or the contract sum analysis, or the schedule of rates.

Omissions are to be valued in accordance with the relevant prices in the priced document. That is crystal clear and should cause no problems (clause 3.7.2).

Additional work may be valued in one of three ways:

- Work of similar character to that set out in the priced document: the valuation must be consistent with the values in the priced document, with due allowances for any change in the conditions or quantity. In this clause, it is probable that "similar" can be given its ordinary meaning of "almost identical", because the valuation is to be "consistent" – ie, following the sample principles – with the values in the priced document. Thus, if there is no change in the conditions under which the work is to be carried out and the quantity is unchanged, the prices in the document are to form the starting point for the valuation. Insofar as the "similar" character is different, the values, to be consistent, must be different also. Where the conditions and quantity are also changed, the valuation will depart even further from the values in the priced document. There will clearly come a point at which the relationship with the priced document will be very tenuous indeed and, in effect, a fair valuation will result.

- If there is no work of similar character in the priced document, or to the extent that the execution of additional or substituted work or execution of work for which an approximate quantity is included in the contract documents or the omission of work is not concerned, or to the extent that work or liabilities directly associated with the instruction cannot be valued in the same way as work of a similar character, then a fair valuation must be made.

- Where the priced document is the contract sum analysis or the schedule of rates, if the prices set out are not relevant, a fair valuation must be made (clauses 3.7.4 and 3.7.9).

The procedure is set out in a flowchart (**Figure 11.4**). In practice, the quantity surveyor will look at the architect's instruction requiring a variation and see whether or not it is of similar character to work included in the priced document. If it is, he will use those prices as a basis for his valuation. If not, he will make a fair valuation. The wording of the clauses probably gives the quantity surveyor considerable freedom.

Figure 11.3
Contractor to architect, if final certificate not issued on time

REGISTERED POST/RECORDED DELIVERY

Dear Sir

Clause 4.6 of the conditions of contract requires you to issue the final certificate within 28 days of the latest of the following events:

1. The sending to us of the computations of the adjusted contract sum, which we received on the [*insert date*].

2. Your certificate under clause 2.10, which was issued on [*insert date*].

Therefore, the final certificate should have been issued on the [*insert date*]. Some [*insert number*] weeks have passed since that date and we have received no such certificate. You are in breach of contract. A breach for which, we are advised, the employer is liable. If the final certificate is in our hands by [*insert date*], we will take no further action on such breach.

Yours faithfully

If it is decided that the proper basis of any fair valuation should be daywork, the valuation must comprise the prime cost of the work together with percentage additions on the prime costs at the rates set out by the contractor in the priced documents.

Definitions of prime costs are many and varied. The contract sets out those which are acceptable:

Generally: prime cost is to be calculated in accordance with the Definition of Prime Cost of Daywork carried out under a Building Contract, issued by the Royal Institution of Chartered Surveyors and the Building Employers' Confederation.

- If the work is within the province of any specialist trade and there is a published agreement between the RICS and the appropriate employers' body: prime cost is to be calculated in accordance with the definition in such an agreement. A footnote to clause 3.7.5 states that this sub-paragraph refers to three definitions, namely those agreed between the RICS and the Electrical Contractors' Association; between the RICS and the Electrical Contractors' Association of Scotland; and between the RICS and the Heating & Ventilating Contractors' Association. Since the footnotes are not part of the contract, there is nothing to prevent other definitions of prime cost from being used, provided that they fall within the meaning of the sub-paragraph.

The definitions to be used are those which were current at the date of tender.

There is no express requirement for the contractor to submit vouchers for verification, and it is for the architect and the quantity surveyor to decide what is required and to let the contractor know. Contractors generally prefer the valuation to be done by means of daywork, so there should be no difficulty. It is for the quantity surveyor, not the architect, to decide, in the light of the contract provisions, which method of valuation is most appropriate.

Additions or reductions to appropriate preliminary items must be included in the valuations except where compliance with an architect's instruction for the expenditure of a provisional sum for defined work in accordance with SMM 7 is involved (clause 3.7.6).

If the conditions under which any other work is carried out are substantially changed by reason of the contractor's carrying out of work in accordance with the architect's instructions, the other work must be treated as if it too had been varied. Two points should be noted:

- If an appointment quantity is included in the contract documents, this rule will apply to the extent that the actual quantity differs from the approximate quantity.
- If bills of quantity are used, this rule will apply to the expenditure of a provisional sum for defined work to the extent that the instruction differs from the bill description (clause 3.7.8).

For example, the architect's instruction to divide a large warehouse with brick walls may make it more difficult to lay floor screeds in some areas. In such a case, the quantity surveyor must value not only the cost of building the brick walls but also the cost of laying the floor screeds under different conditions. The change must be substantial – ie, it must not be trivial. It is for the quantity surveyor to decide where to draw the line.

Figure 11.4
Valuation of variations (clause 3.7)

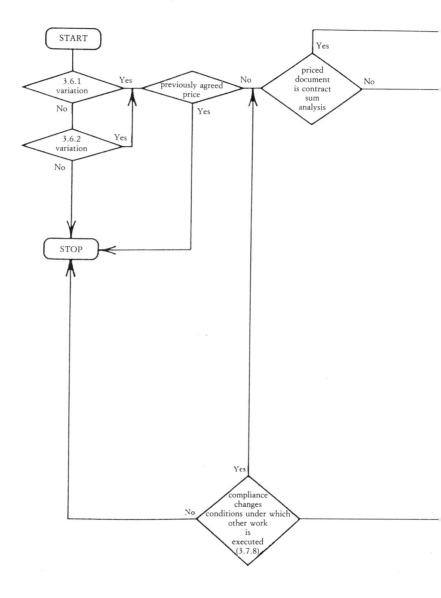

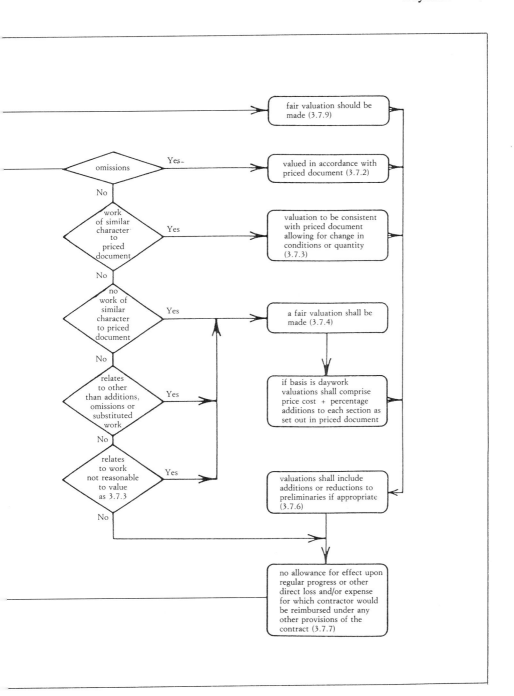

The quantity surveyor is not to make any allowance in his valuation for the effect of the architect's instruction on the regular progress of the works or for any other direct loss and/or expense for which the contractor would be reimbursed by any other provision of the contract (clause 3.7.7). This is clearly intended to avoid confusion between this clause and clause 4.11 and to prevent the contractor from claiming, and being paid, twice for the same matter. It is still open, of course, for the contractor to satisfy the quantity surveyor that the effect on progress and loss and/or expense are not covered by other contract provisions. If he can, he is entitled to be paid under this clause.

11.8 Fluctuations

There are two clauses which deal with fluctuations, clauses 4.9 and 4.10. The first deals with fluctuations allowable to the contractor's work; the second with fluctuations in respect of named persons. The fluctuations referred to in clause 4.9 are contained in supplemental conditions C and D. They are published as a separate booklet entitled JCT Fluctuations Clauses for use with the JCT Intermediate Form of Building Contract IFC 84.

Supplemental condition C will always apply unless supplemental condition D is stated in the appendix to apply. It is the contract sum, less amounts included for work by named persons, which is to be adjusted.

Supplemental condition C, contribution, levy, and tax fluctuations, provides for the bare minimum of fluctuations to cover changes in statutory payments such as National Insurance contributions.

Supplemental condition D, use of price adjustment formulae, is applicable only if bills of quantities are included in the contract documents. It allows for fluctuations in accordance with formula rules published by the Joint Contracts Tribunal. In effect, this provides full fluctuations.

The amounts included in the contract sum in respect of named persons are to be adjusted by the net amounts which the named person is due to receive or allow in accordance with the applicable sub-contract (NAM/SC) fluctuation provisions 33 or 34. There is a proviso. It applies if the period for completion of the sub-contract works has been extended by reason of an act, omission, or default of the contractor (NAM/SC clause 12.2.1). In that case, any sum which would have been excluded were it not for the extension of time, is to be excluded from the net amount mentioned above. This is because NAM/SC clause 33.4.7 or 34.7.1 (as applicable) "freezes" the application of the fluctuations clause if the sub-contractor fails to complete on time. Therefore, if it is the contractor's fault that the sub-contractor failed to complete, he is still liable to pay the fluctuations to the sub-contractor, but the employer need not pay those amounts to the contractor. The sub-contract provisions are complex. For example, if the NAM/SC provisions for extension of time are amended in any way, or if the contractor does not respond to claims for extension of time within the prescribed period, the right to freeze fluctuations is lost (NAM/SC clauses 33.4.8, and 34.7.2 and 3). This is identical to the provisions to be found in the Standard Form of Building Contract JCT 80. It is thought that in such circumstances, the proviso to clause 4.10 would be robbed of all effect, whether the amendment was carried out by the employer or by the contractor.

11.9 Summary

Contract sum

- the contract sum is the amount for which the contractor agrees to carry out the whole of the work;
- IFC 84 is a "lump-sum" contract;
- if the contractor abandons the work, he is entitled to nothing;
- the contract sum can be adjusted only in accordance with the provisions of the contract;
- once the contractor's price has been accepted, it is fixed.

Payment before practical completion

- the parties may make their own arrangements;
- if there is no agreement to the contrary, clause 4.2 applies;
- the usual interval is one month between certificates;
- the employer has 14 days in which to pay;
- a valuation may be carried out by the quantity surveyor not more than seven days before the certificate;
- the employer is not allowed a retention on all amounts.

Payment at practical completion

- the certificate must be issued within 14 days of the date of practical completion;
- half the retention must be released;
- unless the employer is a local authority, he acts as trustee for the retention fund;
- the contractor has the right to require the retention fund to be kept in a separate bank account;
- the employer, if not a local authority, has the right to take out money to pay amounts which the contract provides for him to deduct;
- the position of a local authority is unclear.

Final payment

- the contractor must send all documents for computing the final adjusted contract sum;
- they must be received no later than 6 months after practical completion;
- a copy of the quantity surveyor's final computations must be sent to the contractor before the end of the period of final measurement and valuation;
- the final certificate must be issued 28 days from either the date the computations are sent, or the date of the certificate of making good defects, whichever is the later.

Effect of certificates

- no certificate is conclusive evidence that work or materials are in accordance with the contract;
- the final certificate is conclusive that, if you are to be satisfied, you are satisfied; that terms of the contract requiring additions, deductions, or adjustments to the contract sum have been correctly operated; that extensions of time have been given; and that loss and/or expense has been reimbursed;
- the final certificate is not conclusive if items have been accidentally included or omitted or there are arithmetical errors, or if either party commences proceedings before 27 days after the date of issue.

Variations

- the amount may be agreed between the employer and the contractor before compliance;
- otherwise, the quantity surveyor must value in accordance with clause 3.7;
- valuation may be based on the priced document or be a fair valuation;
- the basis for a fair valuation may be daywork;
- acceptable definitions of "prime cost" are indicated in clause 3.7.5;
- adjustment to preliminary items must be included;
- work changed by a variation to other work must be treated as a variation;
- there is no allowance for loss and/or expense unless the contractor cannot otherwise recover.

Fluctuations

- supplemental condition C applies unless D is stated in the appendix to apply;
- C covers bare minimum statutory changes;
- D covers full fluctuations;
- named person fluctuations are to be paid net;
- if sub-contract works are extended through the contractor's fault, no fluctuations are paid for that period.

12-Determination

12.1 Determination by the Employer

12.1.1 General

Determination is one of those things which is best avoided. If it is impossible to avoid, it must be done properly, or the consequences will be unpleasant for the employer. The whole procedure is surrounded by difficulties and pitfalls for the unwary. Among them are the following.

If determination is properly carried out, the employer will be faced with a project to finish with the aid of another contractor. In theory, he can recover all his costs from the first contractor, but he cannot recover the time lost. Even the recovery of costs is likely to be uncertain unless the amount of retention is greater than the amount to be recovered when a simple deduction can be made. If determination is not properly carried out, the contractor may be able to bring an action for damages for unlawful repudiation of the contract. Many of the grounds for determination may give rise to dispute.

The employer will look to the architect for advice on whether or not to determine the contractor's employment. Indeed, it will probably be the architect who brings the matter to the attention of the employer. This will usually be because the situation on site has deteriorated to such a stage that the architect is pessimistic about the chances of ever achieving completion. Ideally, determination should be set in motion before that stage is reached, but in practice it is difficult to decide just when there is no hope of recovering the situation.

The procedure for determination is set out in a flowchart (**Figure 12.1**). The grounds for determination are set out in the contract in clauses 7.1, 7.2, 7.3, 7.8.1, and 6.3C.2. The consequences of determination are set out in clauses 7.4, 7.9, and 6.3C.2.

Figure 12.1
Determination by employer (clauses 7.1, 7.8, 6.3C.2)

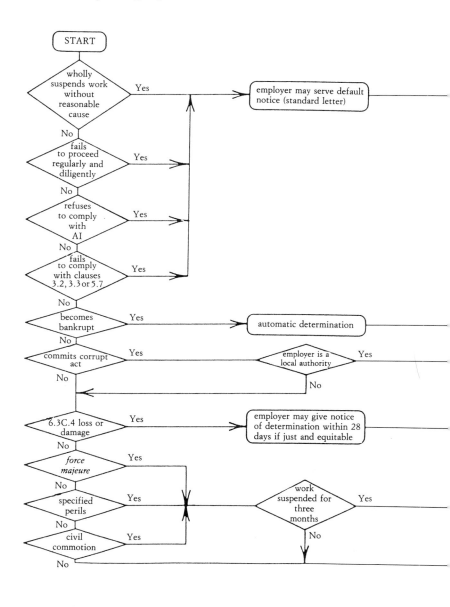

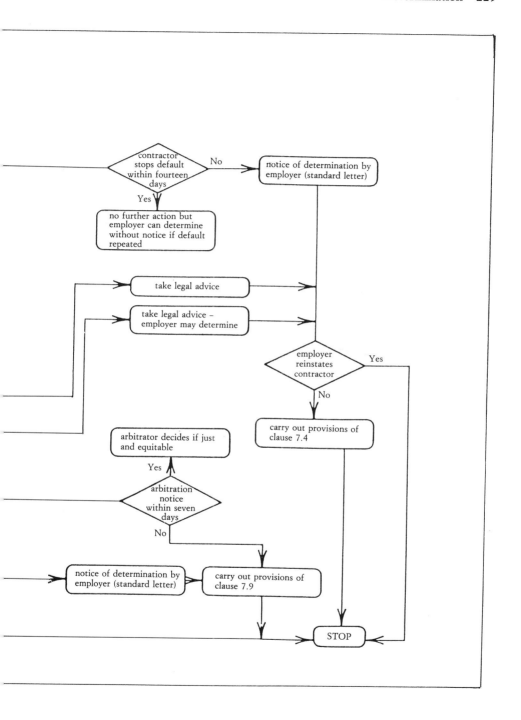

12.1.2 Grounds (clause 7.1): Contractor's defaults

There are four separate grounds for determination in clause 7.1. They are that the contractor:

- wholly suspends the carrying out of the work, before completion, without reasonable cause; or
- fails to proceed regularly and diligently with the works; or
- refuses or neglects to comply with a written notice from the architect requiring him to remove defective work or improper materials or goods, and thereby the works are materially affected; or
- fails to comply with clauses 3.2 (sub-contracting), or 3.3 (named persons).

If the employer decides to determine the contractor's employment, the procedure must be followed precisely. The contractor must be served with a notice of default (letter, **Figure 12.2**), which must clearly specify the default. The contract is silent on who is to send the letter, so it is prudent for the architect to draft a letter for the employer to sign. The letter must be sent by registered post or recorded delivery. It may be the thought that delivering by hand and obtaining a receipt would be just as good or even more certain, but it is wise to follow the contract provisions (*J M Hill and Sons Ltd* v *London Borough of Camden* (1980) 18 BLR 31). If the contractor continues the default for 14 days after receipt of the notice, the employer may determine the contractor's employment by a further notice by registered post or recorded delivery. It is usual for the architect to draft the letter for the employer's signature (**Figure 12.3**).

A point sometimes arises concerning the date on which the first notice was received and thus from which the 14 days begin to run. An assumption can be made about the date on which the notice would arrive in the ordinary course of the post, but if the assumption is wrong and the contractor can prove that the notice of determination was premature, the employer may be taken to have repudiated the contract unlawfully. The wise course is for the architect to arrange for the Post Office to confirm the delivery date.

There are two important provisos. First, if the contractor ceases his default within the 14 days, the employer can take no immediate action. But if the contractor repeats the *same default* at any time thereafter, the employer may determine forthwith without the necessity for a further 14 days' notice. this is a very powerful remedy in the hands of the employer. Second, the notice of determination must not be given unreasonably or vexatiously. There must be no malice or intention to annoy. This is particularly applicable to the case where the contractor has stopped a default for some weeks or months but commits the same default again. Special care must be taken that a change of unreasonableness cannot successfully be levelled at the employer. Despite the provisions of the contract, it would be prudent for the architect to send a warning letter (**Figure 12.4**), being careful to state that it is not a notice of default, or the 14 day period will begin again. This lets the contractor know that the employer intends to exercise his rights to determine. Usually, that will be sufficient to stop the default immediately. If it does not, the employer would certainly not be acting unreasonably if he then determined the contractor's employment. Great care must

Figure 12.2
Employer to contractor, giving notice of default

REGISTERED POST/RECORDED DELIVERY

Dear Sir

I hereby give you notice under clause 7.1 of the conditions of contract that you are in default in the following respect: [*insert details of the default, with dates if appropriate*].

If you continue the default for 14 days after receipt of this notice, or if you at any time repeat such default (whether previously repeated or not), the employer may thereupon determine your employment under this contract without further notice.

Yours faithfully

Copy: Architect
        Quantity surveyor

Figure 12.3
Employer to contractor, determining employment

REGISTERED POST/RECORDED DELIVERY

Dear Sir

I refer to the notice dated [*insert date of original notice*].

In accordance with clause 7.1 of the conditions of contract, take this as notice that I hereby determine your employment under this contract without prejudice to any other rights or remedies which I may possess.

The rights and duties of the parties are governed by clause 7.4. The architect will write to you within the next seven days with instructions regarding the temporary buildings, plant, tools, equipment, goods and materials on site. Subject only to your compliance with the architect's instructions you must give up possession of the site forthwith.

Yours faithfully

Copy: Architect
        Quantity surveyor

be taken that the latest default is the same as the original default. There is certainly scope for a contractor to challenge a determination on those grounds (**Figure 12.5**). If there is any doubt, the determination procedure should be set in train again.

Before the architect advises the employer to give notice, he must consider the four grounds carefully.

"Wholly suspends the carrying out of the works", etc (clause 7.1(a)):

The contractor must have completely ceased work, which probably means that he will have left the site. If a contractor, half way through a five million pound contract, has only one or two men on site doing token work, he would probably be regarded as having wholly suspended the work, but it is by no means certain. This ground appears to be intended to cover the situation where the contractor has, in effect, abandoned the work. Note that the suspension must be without reasonable cause. Before advising the employer to send the initial notice of default, the architect would have to ask the contractor why he had stopped. The course of action would depend on his reply. He might, for example, have suspended work for some reason which ranked for an extension of time.

"Fails to proceed regularly and diligently with the works" (clause 7.1(b)):

This ground implies more than simply failing to keep to his programme. The contractor's programme is not a contract document, although it may be a good indication of the contractor's intentions. "Regularly and diligently" means that the contractor must work constantly, systematically and industriously. In deciding whether the contractor is working as required, regard must be had to such things as – the number of men on site, compared to the number of men required; the amount of plant and equipment in use; the work to be done; the time available for completion of the work; the actual progress being made; and factors outside the contractor's control (which may not all be clause 2.3 "events") which hinder progress. It is clear that it is no easy matter to prove lack of regular and diligent progress. In *Greater London Council* v *Cleveland Bridge and Engineering Ltd* (1986) 8 ConLR 30, a similar expression was considered and the court was of the view that provided the contractor carried out his work so as to meet any key dates and the completion date in the contract, he was not failing to exercise due diligence and expedition. It has been suggested that a contractor will be able to argue his way out of any determination on this ground if he is making any progress at all.

"Refuses or neglects to comply", etc (clause 7.1(c)):

Refusal to comply with the architect's instructions to remove defective work can be dealt with under clause 3.5.1, the employer engaging others to do the work. It should be noted that JCT Amendment 3, issued in 1988, removed the word "persistently" from before "neglects". The JCT Guidance Notes suggest that the provision "notice must not be given unreasonably or vexatiously would prevent the use of trivial or 'one-off' instances of neglect by the Contractor . . . being used improperly as a ground for determination . . . the deletion of 'persistently' would not therefore change the meaning of clause 7.1''. We do not share this view. The change clearly means that "one-off" instances of neglect are covered in appropriate circumstances. In such circumstances, there would be no question of the instance being used improperly because it would be used in accordance with the contract provisions. This ground is probably intended to cover the situation when the contractor ignores instructions to such an extent that the work is in danger of grinding to a halt. It would also refer to the case where so much work is defective work that further work cannot be done without "building in" the defective work and necessitating any future satisfactory work being taken down to make good the defective parts. The work on site would have to be in a very sorry state before determination should be attempted under this ground.

Fails to comply with clause 3.2 or 3.3 (clause 7.1(d)):

Clause 3.2 refers to sub-contracting without consent. The object is to prevent the contractor from arranging vicarious performance of part of the contract by another. Because sub-contracting is traditional in the building industry, the contract makes provision for it provided that the architect consents. If the contractor does sub-let without consent, it is for the architect to decide whether the sub-contractor is suitable. If he is, there would seem to be no point and little chance of success, in trying to determine the contract. Even if the sub-contractor is clearly unsuitable, a less draconian method of dealing with the situation, probably by a letter (**Figure 12.6**), would probably be appropriate. Determination is best reserved for the occasions when the contractor sub-lets the whole or large portions of the work without the architect's approval.

Clause 3.3 refers to named persons. The provisions of this clause are complex, but briefly, this ground is aimed at giving the employer a remedy if the contractor fails to sub-contract with a named person under any of the procedures or is otherwise in breach of his obligations under that clause.

12.1.3 Grounds (clause 7.2): Insolvency

Under this clause, termination is automatic for any of the following reasons:
- the contractor becomes bankrupt; *or*
- he makes a composition or arrangement with his creditors; *or*
- he has a proposal for composition of debts, etc approved in accordance with the Insolvency Act 1986; *or*
- he has an application made under the Insolvency Act 1986 in respect of his company to the court for appointment of an administrator; *or*
- he has a winding-up order made (except for the purposes of amalgamation or reconstruction); *or*
- a resolution for voluntary winding up is passed; *or*
- a provisional liquidator, receiver, or manager of the contractor's business is duly appointed; *or*
- he has an administrative receiver, as defined in the Insolvency Act 1986, appointed; *or*

Figure 12.4
   Architect to contractor, giving warning of repeated default

Dear Sir

This is not a notice of default under clause 7.1 of the conditions of contract.

A notice of default dated [*insert date*] was sent to you in respect of the following: [*insert details of default*].

It has come to my attention that the above default is being repeated. Under clause 7.1, the employer has the right to determine your employment under this contract without further warning. The employer intends to exercise his right unless the default ceases immediately. I will visit the site on [*insert date*], and if you are still in default, I will advise the employer accordingly.

Yours faithfully

Copy: Employer
        Quantity surveyor

Figure 12.5
Contractor to employer, if employer determines on the basis of repeated default

REGISTERED POST/RECORDED DELIVERY

Dear Sir

We have today received your purported notice of determination dated [*insert date*] citing clause 7.1 and our alleged previous default which you specified in your default notice dated [*insert date*]. In our view this determination is invalid and you are not entitled to so determine our employment under the contract.

We deny that we are in default as suggested or at all. Without prejudice to that contention our default, if demonstrated, is certainly not a repetition of any previously notified default such as you specify.

Your attempted determination, therefore, amounts to a repudiation of the contract. As reasonable people we are proceeding with the works and if we receive your formal withdrawal of notice of determination within three working days of the date of this letter, we are prepared to carry on working normally. If we do not receive your withdrawal as aforesaid, we will pursue appropriate remedies which will include substantial damages.

Yours faithfully

Copy: Architect

- possession is taken by or on behalf of the holders of any debentures secured by a floating charge, of any property comprised in, or subject to, the floating charge.

In general terms – if the contractor becomes insolvent.

Neither the architect nor the employer is required to do any further if the determination is to stand. However, even when a receiver or manager is appointed, it may be in the best interests of the employer to continue the contract. This can be decided only after a thorough discussion between all parties concerned. The employer would also be prudent to obtain legal advice regarding the implications in a particular case. The contractor's employment may be reinstated if agreement can be reached between the employer and the contractor, his trustee in bankruptcy, liquidator, provisional liquidator, receiver, or administrative receiver (whichever is appropriate).

12.1.4 Grounds (clause 7.3): Corruption

This clause applies only if the employer is a local authority. The employer may determine the contractor's employment if the contractor has given or received bribes in connection with this or any other contract with the employer, or if the contractor commits any other offence in relation to the contract or any other contract with the employer under the Prevention of Corruption Acts 1889 to 1916 or under subsection (2) of s117 of the Local Government Act 1972. A most onerous part of the provisions of this clause, so far as the contractor is concerned, is the fact that his employment may be determined because of the corrupt actions of one of his employees or of some person acting on his behalf. It matters not that the contractor may have no knowledge of the affair.

In any case, corruption is a criminal offence for which there are strict penalties, and the employer is entitled at common law to rescind the contract and/or recover any secret commissions.

Legal advice is indicated, followed by a simple notice of determination, if that is the decision.

12.1.5 Grounds (clause 7.8.1): Vis major

The employer (or the contractor) may determine the contractor's employment if the carrying out of the whole or substantially the whole of the uncompleted works is suspended for three months because of *force majeure,* or loss or damage to the works caused by specified perils or civil commotion.

For either party to operate this clause, the works must be totally lacking in any significant progress for the entire three-month period as a result of the same cause. One week of frenzied activity on the part of the contractor, after one month of the period has elapsed, may be sufficient to prejudice any attempt at determination, even if the site relapses into inactivity for two months thereafter. It is probable, however, that the period must be viewed as a whole.

No period of notice is required. At the end of the three months suspension of work, either party may forthwith determine the contractor's employment by written notice

Figure 12.6
Architect to contractor if contractor sub-lets without consent

Dear Sir

It has been brought to my attention that you have purported to sub-let [*insert the portion of the works sub-let*] to [*insert name of purported sub-contractor*].

You have taken this course of action after I have refused consent/without asking my consent [*delete as appropriate*] to sub-letting. Since I have no intention of giving my consent, you are not permitted to use the above-mentioned purported sub-contractor on the works.

I send this letter because I trust the incident is an oversight on your part and I am reluctant to advise the employer to use his rights under clause 7.1 if you will confirm to me, by return, that you will comply with this letter.

Yours faithfully

Copy: Employer
       Quantity surveyor
       Clerk of works

sent by registered post or recorded delivery (**Figure 12.7**). The clause contains a proviso that the notice must not be given unreasonably or vexatiously.

All the causes of suspension are events beyond the control of the parties. *Force majeure* (discussed earlier) could embrace a war, a major strike, and any violent disturbance down to a civil commotion (the third of the causes). A civil commotion is more serious than a riot but not as serious as a civil war. Clause 6.3 perils are the insurance risks noted earlier. It is likely that both parties will be relieved to bring the contractor's employment to an end in such circumstances.

12.1.6 Grounds (clause 6.3C.4): Insurance risks

This clause provides for the employer (or the contractor) to determine the contractor's employment within 28 days of the occurrence of loss or damage to the works or to any unfixed materials or goods caused by any risks covered by the Joint Names Policy in clauses 6.3C.2 or 6.3C.3. The clause refers to existing structures to which work is being done by way of alteration or extension or both. The contractor must give notice in writing to the architect and to the employer as soon as he discovers the damage. His notice must state the extent, nature, and location of the damage. Although the 28 days begin to run from the occurrence and not from the notification, in practice, if the damage is likely to be such as to form the basis for determination, it will be discovered and notified immediately it occurs.

A very important proviso says, "if it is just and equitable to do so". This proviso goes to the heart of the matter and points to the difference between this ground for determination and the ground in clause 7.8.1(b), which requires a three-month period of suspension. What is just and equitable is dependent on the particular circumstances. Despite the words at the beginning of the clause, "If any loss or damage", the sort of situation in which determination would clearly be just and equitable involves such catastrophic damage that it is uncertain not only when work could recommence but whether work could recommence at all.

Take the case of a large factory, worth several million pounds. It may be that a small alteration and extension contract is let, worth £150,000. If, during the course of the work, the whole building is totally destroyed by fire, it will be just and equitable to determine the contractor's employment. (In that case, the contract may also be considered to be frustrated.) Even much less than total destruction in such circumstances would give grounds for determination under this clause. The right of either party to seek arbitration is limited in two ways. Written request to concur in the appointment of an arbitrator under article 5 must be given within seven days of receipt of a notice of determination, and the arbitrator is to decide whether determination will be just and equitable.

12.1.7 Consequences (clauses 7.4)

This clause lays down the prodedure to be followed after determination under clauses 7.1, 7.2, and 7.3. The procedure is stated to be "without prejudice to any arbitration or proceedings in which the validity of the determination is in issue". In

Figure 12.7
Employer to contractor, determining employment under clause 7.8.1

REGISTERED POST/RECORDED DELIVERY

Dear Sir

The whole or substantially the whole of the uncompleted works has been suspended since [insert date], a period of three months, by reason of: [insert reason for suspension].

In accordance with clause 7.8.1 of the conditions of contract, take this as notice that I forthwith determine your employment under this contract without prejudice to any other rights or remedies which I may possess.

The rights and duties of the parties are governed by clause 7.9. The architect will draw up a statement of account as soon as reasonably practicable.

Yours faithfully

Copy: Architect
      Quantity surveyor

other words, the procedure cannot affect the arbitration and the determination itself cannot become a *fait accompli*. In the event that the contractor seeks arbitration, the employer may deem it prudent to await the outcome in any case, because, if it is not possible to reinstate the original contractor, he will be entitled to substantial damages (including loss of profit) if he wins.

Assuming that the contractor does not seek arbitration or that the employer decides, nevertheless, to proceed, the consequences of the determination are as follows:

- The contractor must give up possession of the site of the works. If he does not do so within a reasonable time after receiving the notice of determination, he will become, in law, a trespasser, and the architect should send him a further notice to that effect (**Figure 12.8**). The contractor's liability for insurance ceases, and the employer must take out appropriate insurance cover without delay. This is best done at the time the notice of determination is sent and the architect should remind him (**Figure 12.9**). This clause makes no provision for the contractor to ensure that the works are left in a safe condition, but the contractor (like anyone else) has a duty of care to those he can reasonably foresee could suffer injury. He must not, therefore, leave walls or beams in a precarious condition.
- Clause 7.4(c) allows the employer to use any temporary buildings, etc, for the benefit of a subsequent contractor and to purchase any other materials necessary for completing the works. The architect must advise the employer whether use of the contractor's plant is desirable and may constitute a saving. If it is decided not to use it, the architect has the power to instruct the original contractor to remove it from the works and in what order (clause 7.4(b)). The contractor has a reasonable time in which to comply, and then the employer may remove and sell it. All proceeds, less costs, must be held to the credit of the contractor.
- The employer may employ another contractor to complete the works. The completion of a partly finished building by another contractor is always an expensive procedure. In order to avoid a potential dispute, it is wise to have bills of quantities prepared for the completion work and to go out to tender in the normal way. This will prevent the original contractor from contending that the employer has not obtained a reasonable price.

Until the works are complete, the employer is not bound, and would not be wise, to make any further payment to the original contractor. When the contract is completed and the subsequent contractor paid in full, the employer must draw up a set of accounts which must show:

- all the expenses and direct loss and/or damage caused to the employer by the determination. It will include the cost of completing the contract, including all professional fees consequent on the determination, and the cost of engaging another contractor;
- the amount paid to the original contractor before determination. If the total of the two amounts is greater or less than what would have been paid had the contract been completed in the normal way, the difference is a debt payable by the original contractor to the employer, or vice versa.

Invariably, the contractor owes a debt to the employer. The architect must carefully calculate, with the assistance of the quantity surveyor, the final amounts. It is

Figure 12.8
Architect to contractor if contractor refuses to give up possession of site

REGISTERED POST/RECORDED DELIVERY

Dear Sir

[*Either*]
The employer determined your employment under this contract under clause [*insert clause 7.1 or 7.3*] on [*insert date*].

[*Or*]
Your employment was automatically determined under this contract under clause 7.2 on [*insert date*].

[*Then*]
The consequences of determination are laid down in clause 7.4. Subsection (a) of that clause requires you to give up possession of the site. It is now [*insert number*] days since notice of determination was served on you and you have not given up possession. In law, you are a trespasser, and if you have not given up possession of the site by [*insert date*], the employer intends to take whatever action he deems necessary to secure your removal.

Yours faithfully

Copy: Employer

essential that he makes sure that, on paper at least, the employer has been put in the same position as he would have been had the contract not been determined but had continued in an orderly way to its conclusion. Obtaining payment from a contractor who may be insovent is another matter (clause 7.4(d)).

12.1.8 Consequences (clauses 7.9 and 6.3C.4)

The consequences of determination covered by these clauses are covered in **section 12.2.7**.

12.2 Determination by the Contractor

12.2.1 General

If the contractor is successful in determining his employment under the contract, the results for the employer will be catastrophic. Among the consequences are these:
- the employer will be left with the project to complete with another contractor, completion bills must be prepared, and a great deal of additional expense will be incurred in the form of increased cost of completion and additional professional fees. The employer will be looking around to blame, and possibly sue, someone, possibly one or all of the professional team;
- the completion date will be considerably exceeded;
- under some of the grounds for determination, the contractor is entitled to receive loss of the profit he expected to make on the whole contract: *Wraight Ltd* v *P H & T (Holdings) Ltd* (1968) 8 BLR 22.

The procedure for determination by the contractor is set out in a flowchart (**Figure 12.10**). The grounds for determination are set out in clauses 7.5, 7.6, 7.8.1, and 6.3C.2. The consequences of determination are set out in clauses 7.7, 7.9, and 6.3C.2.

12.2.2 Grounds (clause 7.5): Employer's faults

There are three separate grounds for determination in clause 7.5, and they subdivide as follows:
- the employer does not pay the contractor under clauses 4.2, interim payments; or 4.3, interim payments on practical completion; or 4.6, final certificate;
- the employer interferes with, or obstructs, the issue of any certificates;
- the carrying out of the whole or substantially the whole of the works is suspended for a continuous period of one month due to one of the following reasons:
  - architect's instructions under clauses 1.4, inconsistencies; or 3.6, variations; or 3.15, postponement, unless caused by contractor's default;
  - the contractor not having received, at the proper time, instructions, etc, for which he specifically applied at a time reasonable in relation to the date on which they were required;

Figure 12.9
Architect to employer, regarding insurance if contractor's employment determined

Dear Sir

Your notice of determination is being sent to the contractor today. The contractor no longer has any liability to insure the works. You should consult your own broker without delay to obtain cover similar to that which the contractor was required to have under clauses 6.2 and 6.3A of the conditions of contract. Your insurance cover should be maintained at least until suitable arrangements have been made to complete the contract with another contractor.

Yours faithfully

– failure or delay in executing work not forming part of this contract by the employer or his men, or failure or delay in supplying materials which the employer has agreed to supply;

– failure of the employer to give, at the appropriate time, ingress to, or egress from the site or any part; this includes the necessary passage over adjoining land in the possession and control of the employer after the contractor has given any notice required by the contract documents; or failure of the employer to give ingress or egress as agreed between the architect and the contractor.

If the contractor decides to determine on any of the above grounds, he must follow the procedure precisely, otherwise he may be simply attempting unlawful repudiation of the contract. He must send a notice to the employer (not to the architect) by registered post or recorded delivery (**Figure 12.11**), specifying one of the matters referred to in this clause. If the employer continues to make default in respect of the matter for 14 days after receipt of the notice or at any time thereafter repeats that default, the contractor may thereupon serve notice by registered post or recorded delivery to determine his employment under the contract. There is a proviso that the notice of determination must not be given unreasonably or vexatiously.

The remarks regarding postage of notices in **section 12.1.2** are applicable.

The contractor has the same important power to determine his employment if the employer repeats his default or is given to the employer in clause 7.1. This means, in theory, that if the employer, after having defaulted once and been given notice, defaults a second time in payment by only one day, the contractor can serve notice of determination (**Figure 12.12**). In practice, such a step might be held to be unreasonable or vexatious. But there would be nothing unreasonable in the contractor's giving notice of determination if the payment on a second occasion was a week late. Most contractors are reluctant to determine because it gives them a bad reputation, whatever the reason. So in all likelihood, the contractor will send a warning letter in the event of a second default.

Before determining his employment the contractor should consider the three grounds carefully.

The employer does not pay the contractor, etc (clause 7.5.1)

This is the employer's responsibility. The architect must make him aware, at the beginning of the contract, that prompt payment is vital. The architect's only responsibility is to ensure that the employer receives the certificate. It is perhaps needful to stress this. We still encounter both architects and contractors who think the payment period does not begin to run until the contractor presents his copy of the certificate to the employer. Where possible, financial certificates should always be delivered by hand and a receipt obtained. If that is not practical, they should be sent by recorded delivery or registered post. The period of time allotted for payment begins to run from the date of issue of the certificate, not from the date of receipt. The periods are: 14 days for interim payments and the interim payment on practical completion, and 28 days for the final certificate. Determination for failure to pay the amount shown on the final certificate would be a singularly pointless gesture; the contractor is more likely to issue a writ for summary judgment.

Figure 12.10
Determination by contractor (clauses 7.5, 7.8, 6.3C.2)

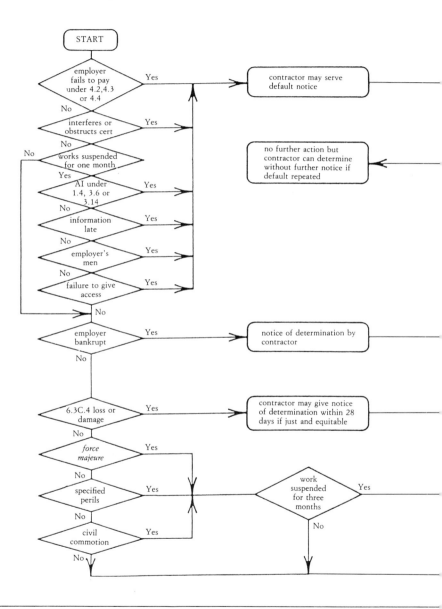

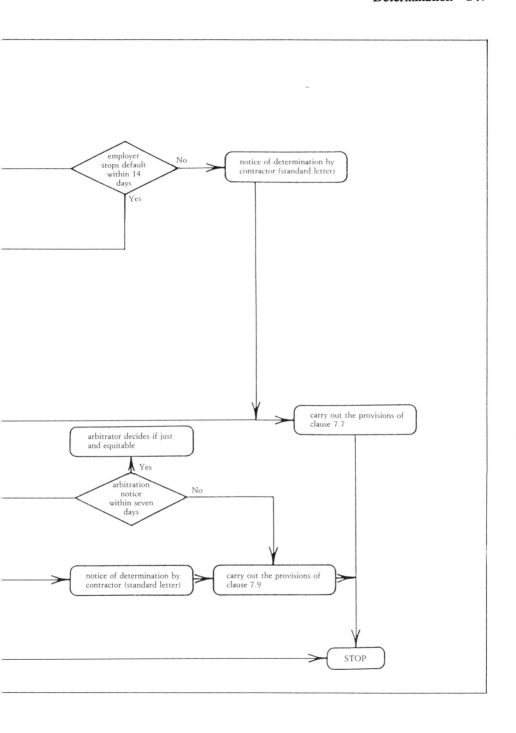

Figure 12.11
Contractor to employer, giving notice of default before determination

REGISTERED POST/RECORDED DELIVERY

Dear Sir

We hereby give you notice under clause 7.5 of the conditions of contract that you are in default in the following respect:

[*Insert details of the default, with dates if appropriate*].

If you continue to make default for 14 days after receipt of this notice or if at any time thereafter you repeat such default (whether previously repeated or not), we may thereupon determine our employment under this contract.

Yours faithfully

Copy: Architect

Figure 12.12
Contractor to employer, determining employment after repetition of default

REGISTERED POST/RECORDED DELIVERY

Dear Sir

We refer to the notice of default sent to you on the [*insert date*]. You repeated that default on the [*specify date or dates*] in that you [*describe circumstances briefly*].

Take this as notice that, in accordance with clause 7.5 of the conditions of contract we hereby determine our employment under this contract without prejudice to any other rights or remedies which we may possess.

We are making arrangements to remove all our temporary buildings, plant, etc and materials from the works and we will write to you again within the next week regarding financial matters.

Yours faithfully

Copy: Architect

The employer interferes with or obstructs the issue of any certificate (clause 7.5.2)

It is important to note that this ground refers to any certificate, not merely financial certificates. There are other certificates (**Table 4.3**) the architect is required to issue which the employer conceivably may try to prevent. It will, of course, be difficult for the contractor to prove that the employer is obstructing the issue of a certificate unless the architect tells him so. The architect has a clear duty under the contract to issue certificates. He must make it plain to the employer that the employer is in breach if he tries to interfere with that duty. If, despite the warning, he absolutely forbids the architect to issue a certificate, the architect is in a difficult position. His duty is then to write and confirm the instructions received, by setting out the consequences to the employer (**Figure 12.13**). The architect has no duty to deliberately inform the contractor, but if the contractor suspects and determines anyway, the architect will be obliged to reveal the facts in any proceedings which may follow.

The carrying out of the whole or substantially the whole is suspended for a continuous period of one month, etc (clause 7.5.3)

If the carrying out of virtually the whole of the work is suspended for a month for any of the reasons set out, the contractor may determine as described. The first of the reasons is very clear. If the architect issues instructions regarding the correction of inconsistencies, errors in bills, etc, instructions requiring a variation, or instructions postponing the carrying out of the work, and the contractor is delayed one month thereby, he will be in very serious trouble. For any period up to one month, he would be entitled to put together a claim for loss and/or expense under clause 4.11. For any contractor handling this value of work, a one-month delay could be disastrous. This clause quite reasonably gives him the option of determination if he foresees no quick end to the suspension and he feels unable to afford to keep the site open. The clause unnecessarily emphasises that the delay must not be due to the contractor's own default. Amendment 3 (1988) applies the "contractor" to include his servants or agents or any person employed or engaged upon or in connection with the works or any part thereof, his servants or agents other than the employer or any person employed, engaged or authorised by the employer or by any local authority or statutory undertaker executing work solely in pursuance of its statutory obligations.

The second reason relates to the contractor's not having received the necessary drawings and other information when required. For the delay to last a month implies a major fault on the architects's part or a major change of mind on the part of the employer. The information must have been applied for by the contractor in writing. He must have applied for it at a reasonable time, having regard to when it would be required. The architect's responsibilities under clause 1.7 do not absolve the contractor from this requirement as far as the contract is concerned, although he might have a claim at common law. A reasonable time to apply is a matter which depends on the circumstances of each individual case. The contractor has to take into account his own ordering timetable and also the length of time the architect will require to produce the information. It is a subject which often causes dispute and to which there is no

Figure 12.13
Architect to employer if employer obstructs issue of a certificate

Dear Sir

I confirm that a certificate under clause [*insert clause number*] of the conditions of contract is/was [*delete as appropriate*] due on [*insert date*].

I further confirm that you have instructed that I am not to issue this certificate. I am obliged to take your instructions in this matter, but you place me in a very difficult position. The contractor is certain to enquire about the certificate, and if he suspects that you have obstructed its issue, he may exercise his right to determine his employment under clause 7.5.2 of the conditions of contract. There will be serious financial repercussions for you.

In the light of the above, I look forward to hearing that you have reconsidered your position.

Yours faithfully

easy answer unless the architect removes any necessity for requests for further information by having everything prepared at the very beginning of the contract. That is easier said than done, of course.

The third reason relates to failure or delay in work or materials which is the responsibility of the employer under clause 3.11. This clause is straightforward except for one point which could be overlooked. The contractor may determine only if there is one month's delay caused by *failure or delay* in the carrying out of the work or in the supply of the goods. If, for example, the work is carried out properly without any delay and the works are suspended as a consequence, the contractor has no power to determine. The contractor may, in such circumstances, claim an extension of time under clause 2.4.8 or 2.4.9 and loss and/or expense under clause 4.12.3 or 4.12.4.

The fourth reason is concerned with the employer's failure to give ingress or egress to the site in due time – ie, at the date for possession – and continuously thereafter until the works are completed. This is a pretty fundamental point which is the responsibility of the employer. For the clause to bite, the employer must be in possession and control of the land over which access is required. Obstructions outside the employer's land (eg, in the public highway) do not give grounds for determination under this clause, no matter how long they last. If the contract requires notice to be given by the contractor before access is granted, the period of delay will not begin to run until after the architect has received the notice. There is an overriding proviso, however, which could be very dangerous for the employer. The architect has the power to agree other arrangements for access with the contractor, and the employer will be bound by the agreement. Needless to say, the architect would be foolhardy to agree with the contractor anything in respect of access without the express written agreement of the employer. If the architect binds him to do something which proves to be impossible or expensive, he could face an action for negligence.

12.2.3 Grounds (clause 7.6): Insolvency

The grounds for determination under this clause are almost exactly the same as for the contractor's insolvency under clause 7.2 (see section 12.1.3). There are two points to note. The first is that determination is not automatic, and notice must be served by registered post or recorded delivery. It is highly unlikely that the contractor would wish to continue and take his chance of being paid. The second point is that in JCT 80, there is no provision for the contractor to determine on these grounds if the employer is a local authority. There is no such proviso presumably because none of the events referred to is applicable to local authorities as as matter of law, though some may think that the omission is a sign of the times!

12.2.4 Grounds (clause 7.8.1): Vis major

The grounds for determination under this clause have already been covered in **section 11.1.5.** If the contractor wishes to determine, however, there is a proviso (clause 7.8.2) to the effect that he is not entitled to give notice if the loss or damage due to specified perils is caused by his own negligence, the negligence of his sub-contractors,

Figure 12.14
Contractor to employer if determining under clause 7.8.1

REGISTERED POST/RECORDED DELIVERY

Dear Sir

In accordance with clause 7.8 of the conditions of contract, we hereby forthwith determine our employment under the contract because [*insert appropriate details*].

We are making arrangements to remove all our temporary buildings, plant, etc, and materials from the works and we will write to you again within the next week regarding financial matters. This notice is without prejudice to any other rights and remedies which we may possess.

Yours faithfully

Copy: Architect

or that of their respective servants or agents. This proviso is only expressly stating what must be implied – that the contractor must not be able to profit by his own default. (**Figure 12.14** is a suitable letter)

12.2.5 Grounds (clause 6.3C.4): Insurance risks

The grounds and procedure for determination under this clause are exactly the same as for the employer (see **section 12.1.6**).

12.2.6 Consequences (clause 7.7)

This clause lays down the procedure to be followed after determination under clauses 7.5 and 7.6. The proviso which heads this clause is somewhat different from that heading clause 7.4. The procedure is said to be "without prejudice to the accrued rights or remedies of either party or to any liability of the classes mentioned in clause 6.1 (Injury)" arising before or during removal of temporary buildings, etc. Thus, while emphasising that accrued rights and remedies are not affected by the procedure (the employer's right to have defective work made good, for example), the contractor's liability to indemnify the employer against injury before or during the removal of temporary buildings, etc, is preserved. The procedure is as follows:

- The contractor must remove from site all his temporary buildings, plant, equipment, etc. He has a reasonable time in which to do this, but he must carry out the removal as quickly as practicable. From the time of determination until all temporary plant is removed, he must carry out his activities on site in such a way as to prevent injury, death, or damage for which he carried liability under clause 6.1. He must give his sub-contractors facilities to remove their plant also. If his sub-contractors default, the contractor has no duty to remove their plant, but if, after a reasonable time, some plant still remains on site, the employer would be entitled to give notice to the contractor that any plant remaining on site after, say, seven days from the date of the notice would be sold and the proceeds, after all costs have been deducted, put to the contractor's credit (**Figure 12.15**).
- There is no express provision for the contractor to give up possession of the site, which is a pity, but the point must be academic, since if the contractor has removed all his plant, etc, he can hardly claim to be in possession.
- The contractor's liability to insure the works ends on determination, and the architect must immediately remind the employer to insure.
- The amount to be paid to the contractor is clearly set out. The architect will require the assistance of the quantity surveyor to ascertain the amounts.
  The contractor must be paid:
- the total value of the work done at the date of determination, less only amounts previously paid;
- any sum ascertained in respect of direct loss and/or expense under clause 4.10;
- the cost of materials properly ordered for the works for which the contractor has paid or is legally bound to pay (ie, because a contract has been entered into). Materials "properly" ordered are those which it is reasonable that the contractor

Figure 12.15
Employer to contractor if plant left on site

Dear Sir

Clause 7.7 of the conditions of contract lays down that you must remove all temporary buildings, plant, tools, equipment, goods or materials from site with reasonable dispatch. It is now [*insert number*] days since I received your notice of determination.

Take this as notice that any of the above items remaining on site seven days after the date of this notice will be sold and the proceeds of the sale held to your credit, pending the statement of account being prepared by the architect.

Yours faithfully

has ordered at the time of determination. Regard must be had to the suitability of the materials and also to the delivery period. Materials paid for become the property of the employer;

- the reasonable costs incurred by the contractor in removing his plant, etc, from site;
- any direct loss and/or damage caused to the contractor by the determination. This is potentially the most damaging clause to the employer, depending on the value of the contract remaining incomplete. Quite rightly, and in accordance with normal contract principles, the contractor is to be paid the profit he would have expected to have made if the contract had run its course.

The contractor has a right to be paid, but there is no requirement for the architect to issue a certificate. Presumably he will simply send a statement of account to be agreed by the employer and contractor.

12.2.7 Consequences (clauses 7.9 and 6.3C.4)

After either party has determined the employment of the contractor under clauses 7.8.1 or 6.3C.4, all the provisions of clause 7.7 (**see section 12.2.6**) apply, except that the contractor is not entititled to any direct loss and/or damage caused by the determination. This is to reflect the fact that these consequences refer to determination for causes beyond the control of the parties.

Effect of determination on other rights

The right of either party to determine is expressly stated to be without prejudice to any other rights or remedies which either party may possess. This means that all their ordinary rights at common law are preserved. Neither employer nor contractor is limited to the grounds for determination set out in the contract. If either considers that he has sufficient grounds to determine, he can rely on his common law rights.

12.3 Summary

Grounds for determination by the employer

- the contractor stops work without good reason;
- the contractor fails to proceed diligently;
- the contractor fails to comply with the architect's notice and serious consequences follow;
- the contractor fails to comply with certain clauses;
- the contractor becomes insolvent;
- the contractor is corrupt and the employer is a local authority.

Grounds for determination by the contractor

- the employer does not pay on time;
- the employer obstructs a certificate;

- the work is stopped for one month because of certain instructions, late information, delay in employer's work, or failure to give access;
- the employer becomes insolvent.

Grounds for determination by either party

- damage is caused to work to an existing building by clause 6.3 perils and it is fair to determine;
- the work is stopped for three months because of *force majeure*, loss of damage by specified perils or civil commotion.

13–Arbitration

13.1 General

Arbitration is the traditional method of settling building contract disputes and is ideally suited to that purpose. Arbitration is the chosen method of disputes settlement under IFC 84 which provides for it to be conducted in accordance with the JCT Arbitration Rules which were issued in July 1988. These provide a choice of procedures for the conduct of the arbitration including strict time-scales and sanctions for failure to comply.

Under article 5 of IFC 84, all disputes between the employer (or the architect on his behalf) and the contractor have to be submitted to arbitration in accordance with the provisions in Section 9. There are two exceptions:

- Disputes about Value Added Tax (Supplemental Condition A7).
- Disputes under the statutory tax deduction scheme where statute provides for some other method of resolving the dispute (Supplemental Condition B8).

The scope of the arbitration agreement is wide. It covers "any dispute or difference" about the interpretation of the contract as well as "any matter or thing of whatsoever nature arising thereunder or in connection therewith", and can take place before practical completion.

Arbitration, like marriage, should not be entered into lightly or inadvisedly. It is the last resort. Despite the advantages brought about by the incorporation of the JCT Arbitration Rules it can be costly and time-consuming and those involved in the contract should do everything possible to avoid it. Some contractors will threaten arbitration over trivial matters in an attempt to persuade the architect to alter a decision which they dislike.

Wise contract administrators deal with such tactics firmly, and a letter to the contractor along the lines of **Figure 13.1** may be useful if the amount involved is paltry in financial terms and the architect is sure of his ground. This often has the desired effect. A different approach will have to be adopted if the architect believes that the

Figure 13.1
Architect to contractor when arbitration threatened over a small matter

Dear Sir

[*Heading*]

I have received your letter of [*insert date*] in which you say that you intend to go to arbitration unless I [*specify what contractor has required you to do. If contractor's letter was addressed to the employer, adapt appropriately*].

As I am sure you appreciate, arbitration is both costly and time-consuming, whatever the eventual outcome. In the present case, the legal and related costs are likely to outweigh any financial advantage many times over.

While I am, of course, confident that my decision would be upheld by an arbitrator, I am sure that on reflection you will consider that such a drastic course should be avoided if at all possible. In the circumstances, I hope you will agree that it would be best for us to meet as soon as possible in an attempt to solve this problem. Perhaps you will be good enough to telephone me tomorrow.

Yours faithfully

Copy: Employer

contractor is likely to proceed to arbitration: **Figure 13.2.** Of course, the architect must be sure of the position and it may be necessary to obtain specialist legal advice.

With the advent of the JCT Arbitration Rules, a full-scale conventional arbitration with a hearing is seldom necessary since the rules provide three procedures:

- Procedure without a hearing under Rule 5. This is a documents-only arbitration and is the norm unless the parties otherwise agree, or the arbitrator directs that the full procedure with a hearing shall apply if the parties are in disagreement.
- The full conventional procedure (Rule 6) is only suitable where there is disagreement as to facts so that oral evidence subject to cross-examination is required.
- The short procedure with a hearing under Rule 7 is ideally suited to many common disputes and provides for a quick decision "on site" and an award with the minimum of delay. The parties must agree between themselves that this procedure be used, and the wise architect or contractor should suggest this procedure where appropriate: **Figure 13.3.**

Although article 5 provides for the settlement of contractual disputes by arbitration, either party may sue in the courts. If that happens, and the defendant wishes the matter to be settled by arbitration, he must apply to the court for an order staying the proceedings. Usually this is granted, unless there is no real dispute, eg where a contractor sues for money due on a certificate. In practice the courts are reluctant to intervene and replace their own process with the contractual machinery agreed by the parties.

Arbitration has both advantages and disadvantages. Its main advantages are:

- Privacy.
- Technical expertise of the arbitrator.
- The arbitrator is employed by the parties as a kind of private judge. He must act as they require, subject to law. This means that matters such as the timetable and venue are fixed by agreement to suit the convenience of the parties and their witnesses and, under IFC 84, there is a choice of procedures.
- Arbitration is often quicker than litigation – especially where the shortened JCT procedures are used.

13.2 Appointing an Arbitrator

Under IFC 84, intermediate arbitration is available in every case. There is no need to wait until completion or alleged completion of the work, or the determination or alleged determination of the contractor's employment under the contract, provided that there is a "dispute or difference as to the construction of this Contract or any matter or thing of whatsoever nature arising thereunder or in connection therewith" between the parties, either the contractor or the employer can set the machinery in motion. The first step in the procedure is for one party to write to the other requesting him to concur in the appointment of an arbitrator (clause 9.1). In most cases, it will be the contractor who does this (**Figure 13.4**) but there is no reason why the employer should not be the initiator and then the architect may draft a suitable letter on his behalf.

Figure 13.2
Architect to contractor when threat to seek arbitration is serious

Dear Sir

[*Heading*]

Thank you for your letter of [*insert date*] informing me of your intention to go to arbitration under clause 9.1. [*Adapt suitably if letter is addressed to the employer*].

The step you propose is a most serious one with severe cost implications for both parties. I firmly hold that my decision, which you are seeking to question, is correct.

Obviously, neither I nor the employer can prevent you from invoking the arbitration agreement, nor would we wish to do so. No doubt, however, as a reasonable person, you will wish to avoid unnecessary time and expense, and I suggest that we meet to discuss the problem as soon as possible. If you wish to have a meeting, perhaps you will telephone me to arrange a mutually convenient appointment.

Yours faithfully

Copy: Employer

Figure 13.3
Letter suggesting short procedure

Dear Sir

[*Heading*]

It is our view that this dispute would be suited to resolution under the provisions of Rule 7 of the JCT Arbitration Rules which will apply to this arbitration. We hope you will agree so that costs will be kept to a minimum and a saving in time achieved.

Therefore, in accordance with Rule 4.2.2, we enclose a copy of our case formulated in writing in sufficient detail to identify the matters in dispute. At the preliminary meeting, we will request you to agree that Rule 7 shall apply to the conduct of this arbitration.

Yours faithfully

Copy: Arbitrator

Figure 13.4
Letter requesting concurrence in appointment of arbitrator

REGISTERED POST/RECORDED DELIVERY

Dear Sir

[*Heading*]

I/we hereby give you notice that we require the undermentioned dispute(s) or difference(s) between us to be referred to arbitration in accordance with article 5 and clause 9.1 of the contract between us dated [*insert date*]. Please treat this as a request to concur in the appointment of an arbitrator under clause 9.1.

The dispute(s) or difference(s) (is)are: [*specify*].

I/we propose the following three persons for your consideration and require your concurrence in the appointment within 14 days of the date of service of this letter, failing which I/we shall apply to the President of the Royal Institute of British Architects/Royal Institution of Chartered Surveyors/Chartered Institute of Arbitrators for the appointment of an arbitrator under clause 9.1.

The names and addresses of those we propose are: [*insert names and addresses*].

Yours faithfully

It is usual and desirable to suggest the names of three people, any of whom would be acceptable as arbitrator, leaving the choice to the other party.

The Chartered Institute of Arbitrators, 75 Cannon Street, London EC4N 5BH will supply the names of suitably qualified arbitrators on request. Arbitrators listed on the Institute's Panels will have the necessary specialist knowledge and expertise. If the Institute's advice is sought, it is necessary to provide broad details of the nature of the dispute, the type of project, and so on, so that suitable people may be recommended.

The arbitrator must, of course, be independent and impartial. He must not have an existing connection with the employer or the contractor or any other person involved in the dispute.

If possible, it is sensible for the employer and the contractor to agree on an arbitrator, but in the nature of things, since they are in dispute, they are often unwilling or unable to do this. Requests to concur in the appointment of an arbitrator are often ignored. To avoid deadlock, clause 9.1 provides that if the parties cannot agree on an arbitrator within 14 days after the date of the notice to concur, the arbitrator will be appointed by a third party – the president or a vice-president of either the Royal Institute of British Architects, the Royal Institution of Chartered Surveyors or the Chartered Institute of Arbitrators. The appointer will be specified in the Appendix.

The three bodies all maintain panels of suitably qualified people from whom the appointment is made. All of them charge substantial fees which, currently, range from £350 to £1,000 a day, depending on the complexity of the dispute and the standing and expertise of the arbitrator. The consensual nature of arbitration really requires that the arbitrator should be appointed by agreement.

As noted, there is a time limit of 14 days before the employer or the contractor can apply to the appointing body. This runs from the date of the notice to concur in the appointment of an arbitrator. **Figure 13.5** is a suitable letter to the appointing body, but all of them have special forms which must be completed and there are fees to be paid on the application.

At this stage, it is desirable that legal advice should have been obtained, although in some cases the services of a lawyer will not be necessary, eg where the dispute is of a technical nature and the JCT short procedure will be used. The flowchart at **Figure 13.6** illustrates the arbitration procedure.

13.3 An Arbitrator's Powers

Arbitrators have very wide powers under the Arbitration Acts 1950–1979 and this is the meaning of the reference to "the generality of his powers" in clause 9.3.

Clause 9.3 confers additional powers on the arbitrator. These are:

- To rectify the contract so that it accurately reflects the true agreement made between the parties, ie to order the correction of errors where the contract fails to represent what the parties actually agreed. It must be shown that the parties

Figure 13.5
Letter to body appointing arbitrators

The Legal Secretary
Royal Institute of British Architects
66 Portland Place
London W1N 4AD

[*or*]

The Appointments Secretary (Arbitrations)
Royal Institution of Chartered Surveyors
12 Great George Street
London SW1P 3AD

[*or*]

The Secretary
Chartered Institute of Arbitrators
75 Cannon Street
London EC4N 5BH

Dear Sir

[I am acting as architect for [*insert name of employer*]] or [We are contractors] under a contract in IFC 84 form, clause 9.1 of which makes provision for your President to appoint an arbitrator in default of agreement.

Please will you send me/us the appropriate form of application and supporting documentation, with a note of the current fee payable on application.

Yours faithfully

were in complete agreement on the terms of the contract, but by an error wrote them down wrongly.

- To direct such measurements and/or valuations as may be desirable to determine the rights of the parties and to ascertain and award any sum which ought to have been certified.
- To open up, review, and revise any certificate, opinion, decision, requirement, or notice.
- To determine all matters in dispute submitted to him as if no such certificate, opinion, decision, requirement or notice had been given.

The last two powers are very important. The arbitrator can review the exercise of the architect's discretion and in effect substitute his own opinion. This is especially important as regards such matters as extensions of time and claims for direct loss and/or expense. Oddly, the courts do not have the power to open up, review and revise certificates or opinions as they think fit, because for them to do so would be to modify the contractual obligations of the parties. Where the parties have agreed on arbitration, the courts cannot and will not substitute their own process for the machinery agreed between the two parties.

Four matters are excluded from this wide power. They are:

- Clause 3.5.2: Where the contractor has asked the architect for his contractual authority for issuing an instruction and the architect has responded (see **section 4.1.3**). Unless the matter is submitted to immediate arbitration, the architect's answer is "deemed for all the purposes of this contract to have been empowered" by the provision specified.
- Clause 4.7: The provision in clause 4.7 about the conclusive effect of the final certificate "except on any matter which is the subject of proceedings commenced within 21 days after" its date.
- Supplemental Conditions C4.3 and D.8: Agreement between the parties as to the amount of fluctuations.

The arbitrator's powers are also enhanced by the JCT Arbitration Rules. **Table 13.1** summarises the arbitrator's powers.

13.4 Appeals to the High Court

The Arbitration Act 1979, ss1 and 2, makes provision for:

- appeals to the High Court on questions of law arising out of an arbitrator's award; and for
- the determination by the High Court of questions of law which arise during the arbitration proceedings. These powers are subject to certain requirements, one precondition being that the parties have given their consent.

Clause 9.5 gives the necessary consent, and its inclusion means that disputed matters can be referred to the courts.

Figure 13.6
Arbitration (Article 5 and Clause 9)

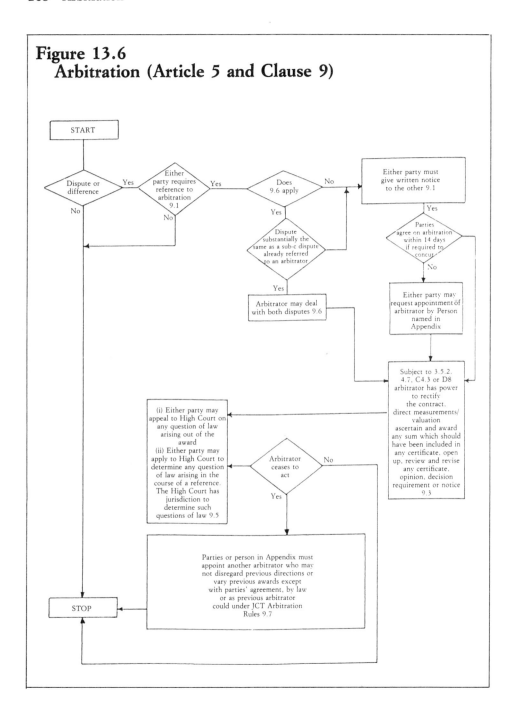

13.5 Third-Party Procedure

Clause 9.6 is an attempt to introduce a third-party procedure into the arbitration and to give the arbitrator the same powers that the High Court has for joining parties in legal proceedings. Its legal effect is doubtful. Arbitration is a voluntary process, based on agreement, and there is no way that people can be compelled to take part in an arbitration without their consent.

There is an obvious need to join sub-contractors in main-contract arbitration proceedings, and this is achieved by inserting a corresponding provision in clause 35.4 of Sub-contract Conditions NAM/SC, with its reference to "issues which are substantially the same as or connected with issues raised in a related dispute under the main contract". A similar provision would need to be inserted in any ordinary sub-contract, and clause 9.6 cannot be used if that is not done, nor could it be used to bring in the architect or other consultants, such as structural engineers, without their consent. Clause 9.6 applies, in any case, only where the appendix entry so states, except in the event of arbitration under clause 3.13.2 (arbitration on instructions following failure of work, etc – see **section 4.1.4**).

The effect of clause 9.6 is to try to make provision that all the parties will join in the arbitration if the dispute referred to arbitration raises issues which are "substantially the same as or connected with" the issues raised in a related sub-contract dispute whose arbitration has already been commenced. The same arbitrator is to determine all the disputes and the clause attempts to confer on him powers which he would not otherwise have.

13.6 Summary

- Article 5 states that arbitration is to be used to settle disputes under the contract.
- Arbitration can be commenced by either party at any time.
- Failing agreement between employer and contractor on an arbitrator, the appointment is made by the president or a vice-president of the RIBA or the RICS or CIARB.
- The arbitrator has the widest powers, including power to revise any decision of the architect.
- There is provision for legal points to be decided by the High Court.
- Arbitration or litigation should be avoided if possible.

Table 13.1
Arbitrator's powers

Power	Authority
To rectify the contract so that it accurately reflects the true agreement made by the parties	Clause 9.3 These are the express powers conferred on the arbitrator by the parties
To direct measurements and valuations to determine the rights of the parties	
To ascertain and award any sum which ought to have been the subject of, or included in, any certificate	
To open up, review, and revise any certificate, opinion, decision, requirement, or notice	
To determine all matters in dispute which shall be submitted to him de novo	
To take evidence on oath	Arbitration Act 1950, s12(1)
To order disclosure and inspection of documents	1950 Act, s12(1)
To do all other things required for determining facts or law, including the power to make procedural orders	1950 Act, s12(1)
To apply to the High Court for additional and default powers if a party fails to comply with his orders	1950, s12(6) and 1979 Act, s5
To make interim and final awards	1950 Act, ss13, 14
To order specific performance where appropriate	1950 Act, s15
To award costs and to tax and settle their amount	1950 Act, s18
To award interest	1950 Act, s20 as amended
To take legal or technical advice on any matter arising out of or in connection with the arbitration [After consulting the parties]	JCT Arbitration Rules
Give directions for protecting, securing or disposing of property the subject of the dispute	
Order security for costs	
Proceed ex parte after reasonable notice	
Tax costs if not agreed	

Table 13.1 (continued)	
Power	Authority
Direct affidavit evidence	
Order production, inspection and copies of relevant documents	
Direct that some other Rule applies if he thinks it necessary for the just and expeditious determination of the dispute [After considering parties' representations]	

Appendix A–Form of Tender and Agreement NAM/T

The provisions for named sub-contractors discussed in **Chapter 8** depend for their operation on the correct and full completion of the JCT Form of Tender and Agreement NAM/T, the use of which is mandatory, whichever of the two procedures for naming sub-contractors is used. The administrative burden on the architect, sub-contractor and the contractor is a heavy one.

The printed form opens with a warning printed in italic type: "Should there be a separate agreement between the employer and the sub-contractor relating to such matters as are referred to in clause 3.3.7 of the main contract conditions [design, etc], it should *not* be attached to the Form of Tender and Agreement, either where the form is included in the main contract documents or where it is included in an instruction of the architect . . . for the expenditure of a provisional sum".

That separate agreement is the RIBA/CASEC Form of Employer/Specialist Agreement ESA/1, which creates a collateral contract between the employer and the named person in respect of design liabilities and associated matters. ESA/1 is summarised in Appendix C. The guidance given in Practice Note IN/1 about the use of NAM/T is not especially helpful and the form is much more complicated than appears at first sight. It is divided into the following three parts.

Section 1 – Invitation to tender

The whole of this part is to be completed by the architect. It gives the proposed sub-contractor the necessary basic information on which to base his tender. Great care must be taken in its completion because, in this section (and section II, below) are to be found those "particulars" which may prevent the contractor from actually entering into a sub-contract with the proposed named sub-contractor and are also referred to in the recitals of the main contract.

Section I sets out the following information:

- the name and address of the tenderer, and an invitation to him to submit a tender by completing and returning the whole form to the architect;
- the "priced documents" which the sub-contractor will be required to provide if it is decided to name him;
- any other contractual documents (called "the numbered documents") which form part of the basis of tender. Page 1 must then be signed and dated by the architect;
- details of the main contract works and location, taken from the first recital of the main contract, together with any job reference;
- details of the sub-contract works;
- details of employer, architect, quantity surveyor, and main contractor (if appointed);
- relevant main-contract information, including any changes in the printed conditions, whether the main contract is to be entered into by hand or under seal, and where the contract documentation can be inspected (if the main contractor is already appointed);
- a copy of the main-contract appendix. This is especially important as, among other things, it will fix the proposed named sub-contractor with notice of any liquidated damages provision in the main contract and give him vital information;
- access, order of works, and obligations and restrictions imposed by the employer and not covered by the main-contract conditions;
- there are three alternatives, respectively where the work is to be included in the main-contract documents for pricing by the main contractor, or is to be included in a provisional-sum instruction, or in an architect's instruction naming the tenderer as a replacement sub-contractor;
- any deviations from the main-contract appendix entries (for example, if the named person's work is of a small amount compared with the contract value as a whole, it may be necessary to limit his liability for liquidated damages in the event of delay);
- the sub-contract commencement and completion dates (at this stage, an estimate only, as the adjacent note makes clear) and period of time the architect will require to approve shop and other drawings after submission;
- the statement that the sub-contractor designate will be required to tender in accordance with the Sub-contract Conditions NAM/SC form of sub-contract, and indication of whether the main contractor will have a right of reasonable objection to the person named (ie, if 12(b) or 12(c) applies);
- sub-contract fluctuations;
- contractor's special and general attendances.

Section II – Tender by sub-contractor

This takes the form of an offer addressed to the employer and the contractor, although of course any resulting sub-contract will not involve the employer. It is expressed in the alternative – and the alternatives are mutually exclusive: *either*

- "to conclude a sub-contract with the contractor by completing section III within 21 days of the contractor's entering into the main contract with the employer" (where the work is to be priced by the main contractor); *or*
- to the same effect but subject to the main contractor's right of reasonable objection. Interestingly, the reference here is only to "item 12(b) of section 1 and there is no reference to item 12(c)", which refers to replacement named sub-contractors.

There are various options which must be deleted, as advised in the notes on completion. One of the more interesting features is the following statement: "This Tender, subject to any extension of the period for its acceptance, is withdrawn if not accepted by the contractor within . . . (weeks) of the date of this Tender".

Despite this statement – which indicates an intention to hold the offer open for a stated period – under the general law, the proposed sub-contractor is entitled to revoke or withdraw his tender at any time before it has been accepted by the contractor. So problems are likely to arise if in fact a proposed sub-contractor withdraws or if, as is possible, the offer comes to an end through the passage of time. Lapse of time would in any event kill the sub-contractor's tender; the guidance note on page 12 puts you on guard as to the position and advises you to seek an extension of the period of validity if necessary.

In section II, the sub-contractor can specify any special requirements which he has and also give programme information.

When this section is signed by or on behalf of the sub-contractor, it is capable of being a firm offer in law. It can be accepted only by the contractor, and the architect is advised to study carefully the note (dd) on page 12 which requires him to counter-sign the tender before passing it on to the main contractor, having deleted one of the alternatives. Note that the sub-contractor is not bound to accept any changes in the information and may decide to withdraw his tender if there are changes.

Section III – Articles of agreement

The architect will not be concerned with the completion of section III, which is in standard legal form. Contractors and named sub-contractors are referred to the discussion of clause 3.3.1 for the sort of difficulties that are likely to arise and for what is to happen if a sub-contract does not eventuate.

The Articles of Agreement are themselves straightforward; the appropriate deletions should be made to recital 4 dependent on the tax status of the parties. Articles 1 to 3 and the Attestation Clause should be completed appropriately. On completion by the contractor and sub-contractor, there will be a binding sub-contract between them on Conditions NAM/SC. The articles can be entered into under seal or merely by signature.

Provision is made for the names of both an adjudicator and a trustee-stakeholder under Conditions NAM/SC, and it is essential that those names and addresses be inserted if the relevant sub-contract provisions are to be operable.

Appendix B–
NAM/SC
Sub-contract conditions

These conditions are deemed to be incorporated in article 1.2 of the articles of agreement in section III of the JCT Standard Form of Tender and Agreement NAM/T. The following amendments have been issued:
1: November 1986
2: August 1987
3: July 1988
4: July 1988
5: April 1989
The provisions are briefly set out below.

1 Interpretation, definitions, etc

This clause states that the contract is to be read as a whole. The contents of Tender and Agreement NAM/T are subject to the sub-contract conditions unless otherwise specifically stated. The major part of the clause is taken up by a useful set of definitions.

2 Sub-contract documents

The documents are to be those referred to in article 1.1. Nothing contained in any document issued in connection with the works imposes greater obligations than those in the sub-contract documents. In the event of conflict, NAM/T prevails over NAM/SC, and these documents together prevail over any other sub-contract documents. The sub-contract documents prevail over the main contract provisions. The contractor must provide two copies of any further information required, and he is to issue directions to correct inconsistencies.

3 Quality and quantity of work

Where bills of quantities are included, they are to be in accordance with SMM7, and the quality and quantity of work are to be as set out therein. If there are no bills of quantities but quantities are contained in the numbered documents, they will control the quality and quantity of work. Otherwise, the sub-contract documents taken together will determine the quality and quantity of the work, the contract drawings prevailing. Inconsistencies are to be corrected by the contractor's directions.

4 Sub-contract sum – additions or deductions

Provisions for additions or deductions in the conditions are to be taken into account in the next interim payment following ascertainment.

5 Execution of the sub-contract works – directions of the contractor

The sub-contractor's obligations to complete in accordance with the sub-contract documents are set out. Where approval of workmanship or materials is to be to the satisfaction of the architect, they are to be so. The contractor may issue reasonable directions in writing. The architect's written instructions affecting the sub-contract works are to be taken as from the contractor. Variations will not vitiate the sub-contract. The sub-contractor must comply forthwith unless the variation relates to "obligations or restrictions" in regard to access, etc, when he may make reasonable objection. The contractor may issue a seven-day notice of compliance and, if this is ignored, can employ others, pay them, and deduct the money from monies due to the sub-contractor. The contractor may issue directions for opening up and testing, but if the work is in accordance with the sub-contract, the cost must be added to the sub-contract sum. If any work or materials fail, the contractor has the power to ask that similar work be opened up and tested, provided that he uses the power reasonably. Reasonableness may be tested by arbitration.

6 Sub-contractor's liability under incorporated provisions of the main contract

The sub-contractor is to observe and comply with all main contract provisions as far as they relate to the sub-contract, and he is to indemnify the contractor against breach, act, or omission of the main contract provisions insofar as they relate to the sub-contract and against any claim resulting from the sub-contractor's negligence. But the sub-contractor has no liability in respect of negligence by the employer, contractor, his other sub-contractors, or their servants or agents.

7 Injury to persons and property – indemnity to contractor

The sub-contractor is liable for, and must indemnify the contractor against, loss, etc, arising from personal injury or death in connection with the sub-contract works unless and to the extent caused by the negligence of the contractor or of the employer. The sub-contractor must generally indemnify the contractor against loss etc, arising from damage to property caused by the carrying out of the sub-contract works unless and to the extent it is caused by the negligence of the contractor or employer.

8 Insurance – sub-contractor

The sub-contractor must maintain insurances to cover the liabilities in clause 7. Where appropriate, the insurance must comply with any applicable legislation. Otherwise, the insurance cover must be the sum stated in NAM/T, section II, item 2.

9 Loss or damage by clause 6.3 perils to the works and materials and goods property on site

Prior to the commencement of the sub-contract works the contractor must ensure that either the sub-contractor is recognised as an insured or the insurers waive rights of subrogation. The sub-contractor is not responsible for the cost of restoration of the sub-contract works if the loss or damage is due to a Specified Peril or negligence by the contractor or if the employer of the contractor does not make a claim. The sub-contractor is responsible insofar as the loss is due to perils other than Specified Perils. The sub-contractor must give notice on discovering the loss or damage and commence restoration and repair work as directed by the contractor. Where the sub-contractor is not responsible, compliance with the contractor's directions is to be treated as a variation. The occurrence of loss or damage is to be ignored in computing the amounts payable to the sub-contractor under the sub-contract.

10 Policies of insurance

When reasonably required to do so, the sub-contractor must produce documentary evidence (policies and premium receipts) that he has taken out the appropriate insurance. If the sub-contractor fails to insure, the contractor may himself insure and deduct the premium money from monies due to the sub-contractor.

11 Sub-contractor's responsibility for his own plant

Property of the sub-contractor on site and not for incorporation is at his sole risk as regards loss or damage not caused by the negligence of the contractor.

12 Sub-contractor's obligations – carrying out and completion of sub-contract works, extension of sub-contract period

The sub-contractor must carry out and complete the works in accordance with the dates and periods stipulated in NAM/T and reasonably in accordance with progress of the works. If it is reasonably apparent that progress is or will be delayed, the sub-contractor must give notice of the delay, specifying the cause. If, for certain causes, the works are likely to be delayed beyond the period fixed for completion, the contractor must make in writing a fair and reasonable extension of time as soon as he is able. The causes are contractor's default; force majeure; exceptionally adverse weather conditions; loss or damage by perils; civil commotion, strike, etc; compliance with certain contractor's directions; late receipt of information; employer's workmen; employer's materials; inability to obtain labour or materials if the provision applies; inability to obtain access; statutory undertakers' work; deferment of posession; valid suspension by the sub-contractor under clause 19.6; or inaccurate approximate quantities. There is provision for extension of time if certain defaults or events occur after the expiry of the periods for completion. At any time, the contractor may make an extension of time as a result of a review of previous decisions or otherwise, provided that previous extensions are not reduced. The sub-contractor must use his best endeavours to prevent delay and do all reasonably required by the contractor to proceed with the works. He must also provide such further information as the contractor requires.

13 Failure of sub-contractor to complete on time

If the sub-contractor fails to complete on time, the contractor must give him a notice to that effect within a reasonable time. If the contractor subsequently grants a further extension, the notice is deemed to be cancelled.

14 Disturbance of regular progress

The agreed amount must be added to the sub-contract sum if the sub-contractor makes a written application to the contractor within a reasonable time of its becoming apparent that he is likely to incur direct loss and/or expense because the sub-contract works are being affected by any of the following: late receipt of information, opening up or testing of work found to be in accordance with the main or sub-contracts, employer's workmen, employer's materials, inability to obtain access, certain architect's instructions and certain contractor's directions, deferment of possession, valid suspension by the sub-contractor under clause 19.6, or inaccurate approximate quantities.

If regular progress is materially affected by the sub-contractor's own default and the contractor makes a written application within a reasonable time thereafter, the agreed amount of direct loss and/or expense may be deducted from monies due from the contractor to the sub-contractor or it may be recoverable by the contractor as a debt. The contractor must provide such information as the sub-contractor requires. These provisions are without prejudice to the other rights and remedies possessed by the parties.

15 Practical completion of sub-contract works – liability for defects

The sub-contractor must notify the contractor in writing when he considers that practical completion of the sub-contract works has been achieved and if the contractor does not dissent within 14 days, practical completion is deemed to have taken place on the date notified. The contractor must give reasons if he dissents, and the date will be as agreed or the arbitrator must decide when practical completion has occurred. If there is no agreement or decision of the arbitrator, practical completion will be when the architect certifies practical completion of the main-contract works. The sub-contractor is liable to make good at no cost to the contractor, defects, shrinkages, and other faults not caused by frost, occurring after practical completion, and to accept any similar liability of the contractor under the main contract in respect of sub-contract works. If the architect instructs that certain defects are not to be made good but a deduction is to be made from the contract sum, the contractor will pass on the instruction and deduction to the sub-contractor insofar as it affects the sub-contract works.

16 Valuation of variations and provisional-sum work

The contractor and sub-contractor may agree the amount to be added to, or deducted from, the sub-contract sum in connection with a variation before the variation is carried out. Otherwise, omissions must be valued at the relevant prices in the priced document (as identified in NAM/T, section I), while work similar in character to that in the priced document is to be consistently valued, making due allowance for any changes. If the priced document is a contract sum analysis or schedule of rates without appropriate prices, or if there is no work of similar character, if the work to be valued is not added, omitted, or substituted, or if it is not reasonable to do otherwise, a fair valuation must be made. The clause states how prime cost is to be defined in relation to daywork, deals with preliminary items, and excludes claims for loss and/or expense which can be dealt with elsewhere.

17A Value Added Tax

This is the normal VAT clause providing for recovery of tax and clarifying the application of the Finance Act 1972 or amendment or re-enactment. It also provides that the sub-contract sum is to be exclusive of tax.

17B Value Added Tax – special arrangement

This is an alternative VAT clause for use where, under VAT (General) Regulations 1985, regulations 12(3) and 26(5B), the contractor has been allowed to prepare the tax documents in substitution for the sub-contractor's authenticated receipt and where the sub-contractor consents to this system.

18 Tax deduction scheme

This extensive clause deals with the provisions of the Finance (No 2) Act in 1975 in regard to the deduction of income tax.

19 Payment of sub-contractor

Interim payments must be made at not greater than monthly intervals, the first payment becoming due one month at latest from commencement of sub-contract works on site or off site as agreed. The contractor has 17 days in which to pay from the due date. The clause details which amounts are to be included and which amounts are to be subject to retention of 5% (2½% after practical completion). Unfixed materials for incorporation must not be removed without the contractor's consent. Provisions are included which are intended to ensure that, if the value of any materials has been included in an architect's certificate, the goods become the property of the employer or, if the contractor has paid for them, of the contractor. An important provision allows the sub-contractor to suspend his work if the main contractor fails to pay as provided seven days after receipt of the sub-contractor's notice.

Final payment is due not later than seven days after the architect's final certificate under the main contract. The contractor must notify the sub-contractor of the amount before the due date. Payment must be made within 14 days of the due date; the contractor's entitlement to cash discount depends on prompt payment. All documents reasonably required must be sent to the contractor before or not later than 5 months after practical completion of the sub-contract works. The final certificate is conclusive that, where quality and standards are to be to the satisfaction of the architect, they are to his reasonable satisfaction, and that effect has been given to sub-contract provisions requiring adjustment of the sub-contract sum, that extensions of time have been given and that reimbursement has been made of loss and/or expense. It is not conclusive if proceedings commenced before or within 10 days of the contractor's notice to the sub-contractor of the amount or the date the final payment is made, whichever is first, or in case of accidental inclusion or deduction of items or of arithmetical errors.

20 Benefits under main contract

The contractor must obtain any lawful benefits of the main contract for the sub-contractor, provided that the sub-contractor requests and is prepared to pay any costs involved.

21 Contractor's right to set off

This clause specifies the only rights to set off under the sub-contract. The contractor may deduct from amounts due to the sub-contractor any amounts agreed between them as owing and any amounts awarded in litigation or arbitration in connection with the sub-contract. The contractor may set off against money due to the sub-contractor under the sub-contract only properly quantified amounts relating to loss and/or expense actually incurred by the contractor, provided that the contractor gives notice in writing not less than 3 days before the payment becomes due. No amounts set off prejudice the respective rights of the parties in subsequent negotiations or proceedings.

22 Contractor's claims not agreed by the sub-contractor – appointment of adjudicator

If the sub-contractor objects to the contractor's setting off sums due, he may seek arbitration and adjudication, giving his reasons in writing to the contractor and the adjudicator, provided that he does so within 14 days of receipt by him of the contractor's notice of intending set off. The adjudicator has power to request further written information; to order that the contractor retains the amount, or that the sub-contractor be paid the amount, or that the amount be deposited with a trustee-stakeholder pending arbitration; or to order any combination of the above.

The adjudicator's decision is binding, pending the results of arbitration or litigation, and he must notify the parties in writing. The trustee-stakeholder must pay any interest on the sums deposited, but he is entitled to deduct his costs. The sub-contractor must pay the adjudicator's fees, but the arbitrator may make such interim orders regarding the sums as he thinks fit.

23 Right of access for contractor and the architect

The contractor and the architect and their representatives must be given access to sub-contract work in preparation.

24 Assignment – sub-letting

The sub-contractor is not allowed to assign the sub-contract or sub-let any portion of the works without the consent of the contractor.

25 Attendance

This clause sets out the specific items of attendance which the sub-contractor may expect free of charge from the contractor, including those items set out in NAM/T I and II. The sub-contractor's responsibilities are detailed, together with his rights in regard to erected scaffolding.

26 Contractor and sub-contractor not to make wrongful use of, or interfere with, the property of the other

There are prohibitions against wrongful use of the other's equipment and against infringement of Acts of Parliament, regulations, etc. This clause is without prejudice to the parties' rights to carry out their respective statutory or contractual duties.

27 Determination of the employment of the sub-contractor by the contractor

This clause is stated to be without prejudice to any rights or remedies which the contractor may possess. The contractor may determine if:
- the sub-contractor suspends the whole of the work without reasonable cause;
- the sub-contractor does not proceed with the sub-contract works properly, without reasonable cause;
- the sub-contractor neglets to comply with the contractor's notice to remove defective works and the works are materially affected thereby, or fails his obligations in respect of remedial work to defect; or
- the sub-contractor contravenes the provisions for assignment and sub-letting.

This is provided that the sub-contractor has failed to rectify his default 10 days after the contractor's written notice. If the sub-contractor becomes insolvent, the contractor can determine forthwith.

Detailed provisions are included regarding the procedure following determination. Items covered are the removal of equipment from the works, employment of others to carry out the sub-contract works, and payment.

28 Determination of employment under the sub-contract by the sub-contractor

This clause is stated to be without prejudice to any other rights or remedies which the sub-contractor may possess. The sub-contractor may determine if the contractor suspends the whole of the works without reasonable cause, or seriously affects the sub-contractor's work by failing to proceed with his own work without reasonable cause, or fails to pay as required by the sub-contract.

This is provided that the contractor has failed to rectify his default 10 days after receipt of the sub-contractor's written notice. If the contractor subsequently repeats the same default, the sub-contractor may determine forthwith. If the sub-contractor has suspended the work in accordance with the provisions in clause 19, he cannot determine until 10 days after the commencement of the suspension.

Detailed provisions are included regarding the procedure to be followed after determination. Removal of equipment from site and payment are covered. The subcontractor is entitled to recover direct loss and/or expense.

29 Determination of the contractor's employment under the main contract

This clause provides for the automatic determination of the sub-contractor's employment under the sub-contract if the main contractor's employment is determined under the main contract. The consequences are to be as in clause 28, except that if the contractor's employment is determined under main-contract clause 7.8, the sub-contract will not be entitled to direct loss and/or expense.

30

This clause is left blank since the Fair Wages provisions were discontinued.

31 Strikes – loss or expense

If the works are affected by strikes or lockouts, neither party may make any claim on the other therefor; the contractor must try to keep the works available for the subcontractor and the sub-contractor must try to proceed with his own work. This clause does not affect any other rights of either party under the sub-contract.

32 Choice of fluctuation provisions

Fluctuations are to be dealt with in accordance with clause 33 or 34 (as noted in NAM/T, section I, item 16).

33 Contribution, levy, and tax fluctuations

Under this clause, minimum fluctuations are allowed, relating to changes in the amounts of rates or taxes payable at the date of tender. The provisions are "frozen" after the date on which the sub-contractor fails to complete, provided that the extension-of-time clause is not amended and that the contractor carries out his duty to give a decision each time the sub-contractor makes application. The clause itself is long and complex.

34 Formula adjustment

This clause allows what amounts to full fluctuations based on NAM/SC Formula Rules. Provision for "freezing" is made subject to the same conditions as in clause 33. This clause also is long and complex, detailing provisions for notices, payment, and arbitration.

35 Settlement of disputes – arbitration

Disputes are to be settled by reference to arbitration. The provisions are in standard form and include provision for appeal to the High Court on questions of law arising out of an award or arising during the course of the reference. Provision is also made to allow joining of parties to dispute as between the employer, contractor, and sub-contractor, for the death of the arbitrator and for the use of the JCT Arbitration Rules.

Appendix C–The RIBA/CASEC Form of Employer/Specialist Agreement ESA/1

Under IFC 84, for certain defaults of a named sub-contractor, the employer can suffer loss or damage for which he has no contractual remedy against the main contractor. This is because of the terms of clause 3.3.7, which exempts the main contractor from liability to the employer in respect of a named sub-contractor's failure to exercise reasonable care and skill in any of the following:

- the design of the sub-contract works so far as the named sub-contractor has designed or will design them;
- the selection of the kinds of materials and goods for the sub-contract works so far as such goods etc, have been or will be selected by the named sub-contractor;
- the satisfaction of any performance specification or requirement relating to the sub-contract works.

Almost inevitably there will be a design or related element in a named sub-contractor's work. Clause 3.3.7 reverses the general rule of law, which is that the main contractor is responsible for sub-contractors' defaults of design, fabrication, or otherwise.

The specified areas are ones where the employer needs further protection, which is also necessary if the sub-contractor fails to provide information to the architect, so causing him to give late instructions to the contractor, and, as a result, the contractor has a valid claim for extension of time and extra cost.

These are the main areas which ESA/1 seeks to cover, the device adopted being a direct contract between the employer and the named person, which is intended to be completed contemporaneously with the submission of a tender in Form NAM/1.

ESA/1 in some respects is akin to Form NSC2 (or 2a) as used in connection with JCT 80 for nominated sub-contractors. It was prepared not by the Join Contracts Tribunal but by the Royal Institute of British Architects and the Committee of Associations of Specialist Engineering Contractors and is a fairly short form.

However, its simplicity is deceptive, and you will need to take care in its completion. It can be used in two ways – designated "procedure A" and "procedure B"– and it includes comprehensive guidance notes on its correct completion. One of those notes (no 3) suggests that the need for it "must be considered according to the circumstances of each project and the degree of involvement of the specialist", but we feel that its use is essential in the employer's interests in all but the simplest cases.

Procedure A is to be used when sufficient information is available for the architect to invite a final tender from the named sub-contractor. In this case, the boxed paragraphs A and AA on pages 1 and 3 will be used. Procedure B is to be used in other cases, when paragraphs B and BB will apply. The essential difference between the two procedures, apart from matters of minor detail, is that in the first, the specialist is invited "to submit herewith a tender of the sub-contract works . . . and to satisfy the requirements described by or referred to in the schedule". This is to be used when sufficient information is available for a final tender to be requested. In the second, the invitation is to submit "an approximate estimate", where the information is insufficient for a final tender to be obtained at that stage. Procedure A is as follows:

● the architect must complete the relevant parts of ESA/1. The agreement can be entered into under seal, in which case no consideration is necessary, but if it is to be entered into under signature only, £10 is payable as consideration (the price for which the employer is buying the specialist's promises), and the appropriate alternative must be deleted;

● the partly completed ESA/1 is sent to the proposed named sub-contractor by the architect at the same time as he sends him NAM/T;

● the proposed sub-contractor will complete the remaining parts of ESA/1 by filling in part AA and signing and dating the offer when he completes NAM/T. He makes a copy of the latter form, attaches it to ESA/1, and returns both documents to the architect;

● if the architect decides to recommend acceptance of the specialist offer in ESA/1, the employer must sign and date the agreement, and the agreement is attested appropriately, thus bringing about a direct contract for the purpose specified in the form itself.

Procedure B is broadly similar, the sub-contractor filling part BB and signing and dating the offer, but in this case ESA/1 has some of the characteristics of a letter of intent. The intention is that the specialist will proceed with the development of his design so as to enable a final tender to be submitted, though it is likely that some of the legal tensions thrown up by letters of intent are likely to remain under ESA/1. For example, under procedure B, the proviso states that, should the sub-contract not be entered into by the specialist, the employer undertakes to pay to the specialist "the amount of any expenses reasonably and properly incurred". This is in contrast to the optional clause 7.2 (dealing with materials and goods), where the undertaking is merely to "pay . . . for any such materials and goods or the fabrication of components for the sub-contract works" in like circumstances. "Expenses" has a limited meaning, and the change in wording is presumably deliberate and not inadvertent, It is not clear exactly what is intended, save that under procedure B, a limited payment in respect of design costs must be intended.

The contents of ESA/1 are as follows:

- the preliminary part, which names the employer and the specialist, identifies the architect, and states that certain specified information is being made available to the specialist. This information is detailed in the appendix on the last page and consists of information provided by the employer with the form, further information to be provided at a later stage, and time requirements referred to in the form;
- in a box, the employer's invitation to the specialist to submit a tender on alternative bases as described above (A or B) – a firm offer in law, or "an approximate estimate". The alternatives are mutually exclusive;
- a schedule (described as the "offer and agreement") which consists of seven numbered paragraphs:

1 The employer's requirements described by, or referred to in, ESA/1 itself, and the qualifying statement that the specialist will satisfy the employer's time requirements "subject to the employer providing . . . [any] further information referred to in the appendix" at the correct time

2 The specialist's undertaking to provide any information which he is required to provide to the architect at a time which will enable the architect to co-ordinate and integrate the design of the sub-contract works into the design for the main contract works as a whole. This suggests early rather than later provision of such information

3 A further undertaking by the specialist to provide the architect with the necessary specified information either to enable him to obtain tenders for the main contract works and include details in the main contract documents, or to allow him to provide the main contractor with the appropriate information when issuing his provisional sum instruction creating a named sub-contractor. There is a further undertaking to provide information at such times that can instruct the main contractor as the contract progresses and thus avoid claims for late instructions

4 A statement that the employer is entitled to use the specialist's drawings and information for the purposes of the main contract works

5 A threefold undertaking by the sub-contractor as to the exercise of reasonable care and skill in design and related matters. This is a limited obligation and not as extensive as that which would be imposed on a sub-contractor undertaking design under the general law. It equates to the ordinary professional standard of reasonable care and skill and so, by implication, excludes the more stringent requirement of suitability for intended purpose

6 A definitions clause – the definitions are self-explanatory

7 An optional provision in two parts, whereby the employer may require the specialist to buy goods or materials or to fabricate components for the sub-contract works before the sub-contract is entered into. In that event, should a sub-contract not be entered into, the employer undertakes to pay the specialist for the

materials or goods so purchased or for properly fabricated components. This is said to be "subject to any agreement to the contrary". On payment, the goods, etc, become the employer's property. This statement will not, of course, override any retention-of-title clause in any contract of supply entered into by the specialist, nor can it in any way affect the rights of third parties;

- the specialist's formal offer to satisfy the requirements in the alternative forms AA and BB, both conditioned by the statement that the offer is withdrawn if not accepted within . . . weeks of its date;
- a statement of the consideration of £10 (plus VAT) which is payable to the specialist and to be deleted if ESA/1 is entered into under seal;
- space for the specialist's signature;
- the employer's acceptance. Since this is described as "(on behalf of)" the employer (sic), it may be assumed that the architect may sign on the employer's behalf, but it would be best to seek his express authority in writing;
- alternative attestation clauses.

Appendix D–
Clause Number Index

Appendix E–
Index of Cases